The Vision by the Tigris

Daniel's Greatest Prophecy Unsealed

Timothy John Hayden

TEACH Services, Inc.
P U B L I S H I N G
www.TEACHServices.com

World rights reserved. This book or any portion thereof may not be copied or reproduced in any form or manner whatever, except as provided by law, without the written permission of the publisher, except by a reviewer who may quote brief passages in a review.

This book was written to provide truthful information in regard to the subject matter covered. The author assumes full responsibility for the accuracy of all facts and quotations as cited in this book. The opinions expressed in this book are the author's personal views and interpretation of the Bible, Spirit of Prophecy, and/or contemporary authors and do not necessarily reflect those of TEACH Services, Inc.

This book is sold with the understanding that the publisher is not engaged in giving spiritual, legal, medical, or other professional advice. If authoritative advice is needed, the reader should seek the counsel of a competent professional

Copyright © 2006, 2011 Timothy John Hayden
Copyright © 2006, 2011 TEACH Services, Inc.
ISBN-13: 978-1-57258-446-4 (Paperback)
ISBN-13: 978-1-57258-951-3 (Ebook)
Library of Congress Control Number: 2006929620

Unless otherwise noted, all scripture quotations are taken from the King James Version.

Published by

www.TEACHServices.com

Acknowledgment and Dedication

I wish to acknowledge my brothers and sisters in Christ from Sault Ste. Marie, Michigan who have given their comments, criticism, time, and support to this work. Special thanks belong to my loving wife, Charmaine, for her endless patience, and for her encouragement and cooperation during the writing of this demanding project.

This book is dedicated to those who have selflessly given their lives for the proclamation of truth in every age of this earth's history.

Table of Contents

Introduction 9
Principles of Interpretation 13
Chapter 1: Lessons from Daniel 19
    A Great, Long Conflict 19
    Diet and Prophecy 21
    Beholding Jesus 23
    Walking with Jesus 24
    Acceptance with God 26
    Prayer and Faith 28
    Michael and the Unseen Struggle 30
    Daniel's Faithful People 31
    The Divine Connection 33
    The Power of God 35
    The Rise and Fall of Nations 36
    Summary of Chapter One 38
Chapter 2: From Persia to Rome 41
    The Medo-Persian Dominion 41
    The Rise of Alexander the Great 44
    The Dividing of the Greek Empire 47
    The Kings of the North and South 49
    The Kings Attempt Peace through Marriage 50
    Ptolemy Euergetes Stands Up 51
    Antiochus becomes King of the North 53
    The Battle of Raphia 54
    Rome Establishes the Vision 55
    Rome Overthrows Antiochus the Great 58
    Rome and the King of the North 60
    Summary of Chapter Two 61
Chapter 3: Rome and the Prince 63
    Julius Caesar Asserts his Authority 63
    Caesar Corrupts Cleopatra 66
    Caesar Takes the Isles 68
    Antony Speaks on Caesar's Behalf 69
    The Murder of Julius Caesar 71
    Augustus Caesar Stands Up 72
    Tiberius Caesar Stands Up 74
    The Prince of the Covenant 76
    The Time of the Prince 77
    The Purpose of the Covenant 78
    The Application of the Covenant 81

Summary of Chapter Three 83
Chapter 4: The Rise of the Papacy 85
    Types and Antitypes in the Scriptures 85
    Types and the Book of Revelation 87
    Types and the Vision by the Tigris 89
    Christian Philosophy 91
    Philosophy Corrupts the Church 93
    Constantine and Christian Warfare 96
    The Edict of Milan 99
    The Original Sunday Law 100
    The Overthrow of Licinius 103
    The Council of Nicaea 104
    The Establishment of the Papacy 107
    Summary of Chapter Four 111
Chapter 5: The Papal Dominion 113
    The Papal Church-State Union 113
    The Dark Ages 115
    The Long Ages of Persecution 117
    Help from the Comforter 119
    Purification by Trial 120
    The Popes Blaspheme God 122
    The Pope Enforces Celibacy 124
    Death and the Immortal Soul 126
    The Worship of Patron Saints 128
    Idolatry and Land Distribution 130
    America and Freedom 132
    Summary of Chapter Five 136
Chapter 6: The Final Conflict 137
    The Moslems in Bible Prophecy 137
    The Atheist Beast 145
    The Second Advent Movement 149
    The Judgment and the Woman 154
    The European Beast 157
    The American Beast 160
    The Final Powers Identified 165
    Babylon Attacks the Church 168
    Babylon Overthrows Egypt 171
    The Sealed Remnant 173
    The Loud Cry 177
    Summary of Chapter Six 181
Chapter 7: Babylon's Destruction 183
    The Time of Trouble 183

The Plagues Fall on Babylon	187
The Second Coming	190
The Millennium	194
The End of Sin and Sinners	197
New Heavens and a New Earth	200
Many Run To and Fro	203
The 1260 Years	204
The Wise Understand	206
The 1290 and 1335 Years	208
Daniel Rests	210
Summary of Chapter Seven	212
Conclusion	213
Appendix A	217

Introduction

In each age of this earth's history there has been a present truth for the people of God. (See 2 Peter 1:12.) Accordingly, there must be present truth today. Yet, it appears that the popular ministry is powerless to reveal it. Countless scandals have erupted and speculative theories, which read like theatrical productions, are forced upon the attention of all. Spiritual manifestations are sweeping the land and Satan is converted according to modern gospel standards. His teachers are even presenting themselves as "ministers of righteousness," but they are indoctrinating multitudes with his delusions. 2 Corinthians 11:15. The countless theories that he has produced have proven successful in diverting minds from present truth. The views of the reformers and the methods that they used to interpret the prophecies are today looked upon with contempt. Despite the fact that their interpretations were based upon sound principles, and are required to understand present truth, Satan has successfully replaced them with his counterfeit methods, which were introduced in the Counter Reformation. Hence, it seems impossible for men to find present truth through the fog of error that now clouds the religious landscape.

The answer to this dilemma is not difficult to detect, for the crisis in modern Christianity is no different now from that which confronted God's people in ancient times. Those who overcame the sophistries of Satan in the past searched earnestly for truth until the Bible became the guide of every thought and action in their lives. These people burrowed deep into the Word of God and unearthed the truth for their time. They did not just stumble haphazardly upon it. They yielded themselves to the Holy Spirit, searched the scriptures daily, and the love of truth was planted within their hearts. (See John 16:13; 17:17; Acts 17:11; 2 Thessalonians 2:9-12.) The acceptance of truth, however, is always accompanied by the rejection of popular theories, and the exposure of and opposition to these errors inevitably results in strife, separation, and persecution. It was obviously so in the days of Jesus and the Apostles and in the days of the Reformation. Consequently, we should expect similar conditions to exist as the final conflict unfolds. (See Revelation 12:17; 13:7, 15; 17:6.)

One thing becomes apparent when studying the works of godly men. They all accepted the leading of God in their lives, even if they did not have a perfect understanding of the outcome. They recognized His plan, and shared it with others. Noah built an ark and sounded the warning because he believed that God's promise to destroy the earth by a flood was true. (Genesis 6:13-22;

2 Peter 2:5.) Abraham believed that his descendants would become a great nation. (Genesis 12:1-5.) In faith "he went out, not knowing whither he went." Hebrews 11:8. Joseph cherished the dreams that guaranteed that he would become a great man, and he accepted the sufferings and imprisonment, which he was forced to endure. (Genesis 37:5-36.) He worked for his captors as if he was working for the God of the universe until the time came that the promise was fulfilled. (Genesis 39-46:7.) Moses yielded to the plan of God, stood against Pharaoh, and delivered his people from Egyptian captivity. (Exodus 2-12.) These examples demonstrate how the Lord related to people in ancient times. He revealed His plan directly to them and worked through them to fulfill His purposes.

In latter times God spoke through prophets. These people called men from sin, and they were used to establish Israel as a nation, to guide its kings, and to instruct and prepare it for war. In many instances they wrote their messages for future benefit; prophets such as Ezekiel, Daniel, and John were given messages for later generations. Jesus referred to Daniel specifically as a prophet and admonished His followers to "understand" his writings. Matthew 24:15. Jesus was also a prophet, and His warning about the destruction of Jerusalem prepared His followers so that none of them perished in the siege of the city. (Luke 21:20-22.) The Apostle Paul used the prophecies of the Old Testament to warn the Church in his day of the great apostasy that would arise. (See 2 Thessalonians 2:1-10.) And Jesus and the Apostles also gave prophecies of end time events. (Matthew 24; 1 Thessalonians 4:13-5:6; 1 Timothy 4:1-5; 2 Timothy 3:1-5; 2 Peter 3; Jude 17-19.)

The prophetic writings in the Bible also strengthened the resolve of martyrs and reformers in the Christian era. The great men of the Reformation diligently studied the prophecies of Daniel, Jesus, Paul, and John and drew energy from them. The reformer Martin Luther doubted and hesitated to oppose the Church of his day until he began to understand the prophecies. He declared, "... 'Twas so I fought with myself and with Satan, till Christ, by his own infallible word, fortified my heart against these doubts." *Martyn*, pp. 372-373. These men knew that they had discovered truth, and it kindled a fire in their souls to oppose ecclesiastical traditions and to warn others of the popular falsehoods.

The greatest revival of the 19th century is likewise traced to the prophecies of Daniel and the Revelation. William Miller studied the prophecy of Daniel chapter eight as it related to the other prophecies of the Bible until he was convinced that the Second Coming of Christ and the judgment of God upon the earth were at hand. He went forth to call tens of thousands from sin and to prepare them for the pending judgment and the fires of the last days. So great was the effect of his preaching of the prophecies that in a period of twelve years, without the aid of modern media or transportation, over 500,000 people flocked to hear him. (See Nichol, *The Midnight Cry*, p. 160.) Hundreds of other men throughout the entire earth also united in giving the proclamation, and a great revival was effected. In every instance where God chose to make a change in the established order, He used prophecy to drive the needed reformation. Hence, prophecy is the light that reveals God's plan; it is the guiding star illuminating the path to present truth. It gives men power and courage to live, to share, and if necessary to die for truth. Peter admonished:

> "We have also a more sure word of prophecy; whereunto ye do well that ye take heed, as unto a light that shineth in a dark place, until the day dawn, and the day star arise in your hearts." 2 Peter 1:19.

Christian churches spend hundreds of millions of dollars annually in support of gospel missions and other institutions with the intent of preparing people for the coming of Jesus Christ. Yet, without a clear interpretation of the prophecies, which is based upon sound biblical principles, such efforts will be counter productive. Few realize that the Lord in His mercy places His hand over certain prophecies until the time that He has chosen to reveal them. In this way they will have the effect that He wants upon His children — bringing revival and strengthening them for trial. The revelation of Daniel's greatest prophecy, the vision by the Tigris River, found in the final three chapters of his book, is the last of his prophecies to be revealed. This vision guarantees that it will be fully understood at "the time of the end" as God's children search the scriptures. Daniel 12:4. The world is waiting, and when this prophecy is finally unsealed it will clear the fog of error, challenge the popular ministry, and produce the greatest revival that men have ever witnessed.

Principles of Interpretation

It would be unfair to open a discussion on the vision that Daniel received beside the Tigris River without a clear knowledge of the principles of prophetic interpretation. Within this work is presented an accumulation of many ideas from various interpreters. Principles for understanding the prophecy have been developed and are strictly followed. Some of the principles used can be found in the Appendix, while still others are developed within the prophecy itself and are pointed out where needed. Five of the most important of these principles, which form the foundation of prophetic interpretation, are given here:

1. The central focus of prophecy is Jesus, His Church, and His work in salvation history. "To him give all the prophets witness…" Acts 10:43. The book of Daniel often refers to Jesus. He is seen protecting His servants from the fiery furnace, being crucified by Rome, and receiving the eternal kingdom. (Daniel 3:25; 8:11; 9:26; 7:13-14.) The vision by the Tigris is no exception. (See Daniel 11:22; 12:1.) Only as its connection to Jesus, who is the truth (see John 14:6), is realized can we "come to the knowledge of the truth." 2 Timothy 3:7. Thus we should expect to gain a closer connection to Jesus as we study.

The heavenly messenger also reveals to Daniel in the vision the troubles that would "befall thy people in the latter days." Daniel 10:14. We should not be quick to criticize or shun the prophecy if we do not like what it has to say. The Lord's purpose in giving prophecy is for our salvation. He is "not willing that any should perish, but that all should come to repentance." 2 Peter 3:9. All of the prophecies have warnings for God's children, and we should study and take heed of the events that they reveal. The "things which are revealed belong unto us and to our children for ever." Deuteronomy 29:29. All these things "are written for our admonition, upon whom the ends of the world are come." 1 Corinthians 10:11. Therefore we should expect the prophecies to concentrate on events of this earth that directly affect the Church.

Those who lightly pass over this principle will misrepresent the vision as the Jews misrepresented the prophecies about Jesus in their day. They searched the scriptures, but failed to realize that they testified of Him (see John 5:39-40), and because of their ignorance they sent the Lord to the cross, unconsciously fulfilled the prophecies, and lost eternal life. Similarly the Christians of our day, who hold to Futurism's literalistic theories that center on the Jews and the Middle East (see principle three below), will persecute God's children, fulfill the prophecies, and suffer a fate similar to the unbelieving Jews. Almost the entire Christian world is now given over to fanciful interpretations of prophecy because its religion focuses upon emotional songs, tear-jerking stories, and unedifying babble rather than fact and faith. The vast majority will be deceived simply because they are not watching and inquiring as to what is truth. (See Revelation 12:9; Matthew 24:42-44; 2 Thessalonians 2:9-12.) Therefore, since Daniel's greatest prophecy is now to be revealed, it follows that our reception of it will determine where we stand in the last conflict that this earth will endure. We would do well to "take heed" of the "sure word of prophecy" and Jesus' part in it. 2 Peter 1:19. (See also Luke 24:44; Matthew 5:17-18.)

2. Established truth cannot be ignored. Prophecies that have been clearly revealed in the past must be accepted and built upon, and cannot be discarded for personal, social, religious, or political reasons. (See Galatians 1:6-12.) An example of this principle is the teaching by the Reformers that the Papacy is the Antichrist. George Ladd, former Professor of Fuller Theological Seminary, reveals the correctness of this truth in the following statement:

> "Many of the great Christians of Reformation and post-Reformation times shared this view of prophetic truth and identified Antichrist with the Roman Papacy. This is a fact which should be well pondered by modern students..." *The Blessed Hope*, p. 33.

These believers, many of whom were at one time Catholic priests, were in agreement when they declared the Papacy to be the Antichrist. As they observed the loose moral standards of the Roman hierarchy, beheld religious superstitions forced upon the people, and witnessed the torture and persecution of dissenters, they were compelled to reexamine their religious beliefs by prayerful, meticulous study of the scriptures. Their experience and earnest study proved and solidified their position, and their basic interpretations of the prophecies as they related to Rome are correct and must still stand. Hence any further prophetic light must rest upon their foundation of prophetic truth.

Unfortunately, since the middle of the 19th century Protestants have been slowly reinterpreting the prophecies that were clearly understood by God's children throughout the ages. Nevertheless, while many where abandoning past light others during that century were building upon it and unlocked the prophecy found in Daniel chapter eight. (See chapter 6: The Second Advent Movement.) This principle must therefore be accepted before Daniel's greatest prophecy can likewise be unsealed.

3. The *Historicist* view is the only valid method of prophetic interpretation. The prophecies of Daniel and the Revelation are historical in nature, and have gradually unfolded as the foretold events occurred. This prophecy is unsealed or entirely understood at the end of time, but it describes the events of history beginning with Daniel's day, as do his other prophecies. (See Daniel 2:28-45.) A basic understanding of history is therefore necessary to have a clear perception of the prophecy, and especially to grasp those events of our own time. Moreover, the historical portions of the prophecy are meant to lead us step by step to the climax of this earth's history, so that we might know when the last crisis is imminent. We cannot start at the end of the prophecy and expect to come to a proper conclusion. It must be interpreted from the beginning, and revealed verse by verse until the end is reached. In this way it will unfold correctly, and give us opportunity to escape the snares of Satan. The vision by the Tigris must therefore be understood by the Historicist method.

The Historicist view of prophetic interpretation stands in direct contrast to the *Preterist* and *Futurist* methods, which were developed by papal Rome to counteract the Protestant Reformation. The Preterist view was advanced by the Jesuit Alcazar in A.D. 1614, and espouses the idea that the prophecies were all fulfilled in the past. It has a relatively modest following, mainly in the theological community. Similarly, the Jesuit Ribera initiated Futurism in A.D. 1591. This method maintains the theory that large portions of prophecy are still future, induces large gaps that skip the Christian era, and focuses entirely upon the Middle East. It is true that some of the prophecies are yet in the future, but Futurism places many of the purely historical portions, that have already been fulfilled, forward in time.

Both the Preterist and the Futurist methods effectively release Rome from any connection to the Antichrist, and they were both firmly resisted by Protestantism for 250 years. To accept either method is to deny the Reformation, for Professor Ladd concludes his statement above by declaring, "they all shared the historical view; none of them was a futurist..." *Ibid.*, p. 34. Despite this, Futurism is the method that most Protestants accept today, and few of them realize that they have almost nothing in common with their forefathers. In contrast, the Historicist method of interpretation was well accepted for centuries, "it has existed from the beginning, and includes the larger part of the greatest and best teachers of the Church for 1800 years." Guinness, *Romanism and the Reformation*, p. 100. It teaches that the prophecies span hundreds of years of time and focus upon Jesus Christ and the ultimate victory of His Church.

4. The prophecies are a collection of related events. The visions and dreams in the book of Daniel are not to be understood separately as disconnected revelations, but as united and simultaneous descriptions of history. They span the history of the great empires of antiquity, Babylon, Medo-Persia, Greece, Rome, and papal Rome, and they end with the establishment of the kingdom of God upon the earth. (See the image on the next page.) They are all understandable when properly united. Moreover, not only are the prophecies of Daniel related to one another, but the prophecies of the Revelation also contain many similarities to those of Daniel. Their relationship is close and decided because the same God who inspired Daniel also inspired the apostle John and the other prophets. Thus a full understanding of Daniel cannot be obtained without an equally clear knowledge of the book of Revelation. They are not separate or privately interpreted:

> "Knowing this first, that no prophecy of the scripture is of any private interpretation. For the prophecy came not in old time by the will of man: but holy men of God spake as they were moved by the Holy Ghost." 2 Peter 1:20-21.

The Greek word translated "private" in the passage above means: to be alone, to be separate, or to set apart by itself. Hence this passage shows us plainly that the prophecies are all related to one another. The Lord clearly tells us: "I have multiplied visions, and used similitudes, by the ministry of the prophets." Hosea 12:10. By using similar representations the Lord can clarify events so that the prophecies are plain to us. We are told of Pharaoh's two similar dreams that "the dream was doubled unto Pharaoh twice; it is because the thing is established by God, and God will shortly bring it to pass." Genesis 41:32.

Many of the prophecies in the Old Testament testified of the coming of the Messiah the first time to this earth, but only a few people recognized them for what they were. Even Jesus' disciples did not comprehend their meaning until after His resurrection when He opened their eyes to understand the things that were "written in the law of Moses, and in the prophets, and in the psalms." Luke 24:44-48. Jesus used the principles laid down by the prophet Isaiah: "For precept must be upon precept, precept upon precept; line upon line, line upon line; here a little, and there a little." Isaiah 28:9-13. Thus, if, through the leading of the Holy Spirit, we properly combine the various dreams and visions of the Bible, we will be able to understand the prophecy since we are living in the time of its unfolding or revelation.

Outline of Daniel

605 B.C. Babylon		331 B.C. Greece	✝		Kingdom of God Setup
Daniel 2 - The Great Image					
Gold	Silver	Brass		Iron	Iron and Clay
Daniel 7 - The Four Great Beasts					
Lion	Bear	Leopard		Horned Beast	Little Horn
Daniel 8-9 - The Vision of the 2300 Days					
	Ram	Goat		Horn - Daily	Horn - Transgression
Daniel 10-12 - The Vision by the Tigris					
	539 B.C. Medo-Persia			201 B.C. Rome	538 A.D. Papal Rome

5. Typology is the key to understanding prophecies of end time events. The historical events before the cross focus upon certain geographical areas of the earth. However, after the cross, when the Church is scattered throughout the nations (see Acts 8:1; James 1:1; 1 Peter 1:1), the same geographical language is again used by scripture, but then in type-antitype relationships. For example, the Church of the New Testament is referred to as "the Israel of God" and "mount Sion," and Christians are declared to be "Abraham's seed" and "Jews." Galatians 3:29; 6:16; Hebrews 12:22-23; Romans 2:28-29. (See also Galatians 3:7-9; Philippians 3:3; Revelation 2:9; 3:9.) Hence, typical language is common throughout the New Testament, but it is also used in the prophecies of the Old Testament. For instance, "the land of Egypt" is spoken of "at the time of the end" by Daniel, and this same power is designated "spiritually...Egypt" in the Revelation. Daniel 11:40, 42; Revelation 11:8. They are both the same power, and neither is to be understood geographically. This will become apparent as we proceed. Unfortunately, many in our day fail to see the spiritual significance of Babylon and Egypt. Some claim that the city of Babylon must be rebuilt at the end of time because it is spoken of in the prophecies, but the claim is unwarranted. The book of Isaiah tells us that it will never be rebuilt:

> "And Babylon, the glory of kingdoms, the beauty of the Chaldees' excellency, shall be as when God overthrew Sodom and Gomorrah. It shall never be inhabited, neither shall it be dwelt in from generation to generation: neither shall the Arabian pitch tent there; neither shall the shepherds make their fold there." *Isaiah 13:19-20*.

Babylon and Egypt are the two great powers in the Old Testament that opposed God's people, and made war with each other. (See 2 Kings 24:7; Ezekiel 29:19-20; 30:10-11, 25.) It was to ancient Babylon that the prophet Daniel was taken captive, and it was there that he received his visions and dreams. (See Daniel 1; 7:1; 8:1; 10:1-4.) Babylon in particular is brought to view in the book of Revelation, and is the great antitypical system that opposes God's people at the end of time. (See Revelation 17:1-6.) The destruction of ancient Babylon is typical of the destruction of spiritual Babylon. (See Revelation 16:19-21.) It is not, however, geographically located on the literal Euphrates River because the waters on which it sits are symbolic of people. (Revelation 17:15.) It is this system that is also at the center of opposition to God's people in the last conflict revealed in the vision that Daniel received by the Tigris River, and its identification is made clear as the prophecy unfolds.

These five principles cannot be pushed aside and forgotten, for they are the basis to understanding prophecy. Unfortunately, even those who understand typology almost never consider it when interpreting the Old Testament prophecies, and it has never been properly applied to Daniel's greatest prophecy. Typology was clearly used to expose the heavenly sanctuary that needed cleansing in Daniel chapter eight, and is the missing link, the key, that now unseals Daniel's greatest prophecy. Consequently, the major difference with this exposition of the vision by the Tigris River is the unique use of the types to reveal the spiritual powers that exist after the cross. Many will find freshness and strength in this approach and will be amazed at the clearness and obvious connection to the historical events as opposed to the fables of Futurism expounded by many of today's writers. With this background we now turn to examine the vision as Daniel received it as he was "moved by the Holy Ghost."

Chapter 1: Lessons from Daniel

The events of this chapter are a foundation to the prophetic narrative of the vision. Daniel prepared himself to receive the vision by three weeks of fasting and prayer, and the details of his experience should be studied and followed as we attempt to understand the things contained within the vision by the Tigris River.

A Great, Long Conflict

The city of Babylon was one of the architectural marvels of the ancient world. It was laid out in a square and the Euphrates River ran diagonally through the midst of it. Traversing the river was a large bridge, a number of smaller wooden drawbridges, and a tunnel. A large deep mote and a massive wall, which was about 85 feet thick and 350 feet high, surrounded the city, and chariots could race on the top of the wall. The fortifications of the palace were constructed of various shades of enameled brick and engraved with mammoth hunting scenes and animal forms, and the famous Hanging Gardens were considered by the Greeks to be one of the Seven Wonders of the World. King Nebuchadnezzar ruled the kingdom of Babylonia in the days of the prophet Daniel, and it was to the city of Babylon that Daniel and his companions were taken captive, in 605 B.C., when Nebuchadnezzar marched his armies into Jerusalem and overthrew it. (Daniel 1:1-7.)

During their stay in Babylon God blessed Daniel with visions and dreams to enlighten and encourage His people in their captivity from which they longed to be free. About the year 550 B.C. Daniel received the vision of chapter eight, which introduced a time period of 2300-days, and the angel Gabriel, who was sent to help Daniel "understand the vision," told him that it was for "many days." Daniel 8:16, 26. Daniel therefore, realizing that the vision must be longer than a mere six and a half years, believed that his people had been so sinful that God was extending their captivity. In his distress he declared: "I Daniel fainted, and was sick certain days…and I was astonished at the vision, but none understood it." Daniel 8:27.

Babylon was conquered in 539 B.C., "and Darius the Median took the kingdom, being about threescore and two years old." Daniel 5:31. Twenty-three hundred literal days had long since passed, and Daniel's people were still in captivity. It was at this time that Daniel tells us that he "understood" by the book of "Jeremiah the prophet, that he would accomplish seventy years in the desolations of Jerusalem." Daniel 9:1-3. The 70 years were soon to end, so he set himself to prayer that he might gain insight into the 2300-day vision and the return of his people from captivity. Daniel was in deep distress and agony over their sins, and prayed that the people, the temple, and the city of Jerusalem would soon be restored. (See Daniel 9:4-19.) In the midst of his prayer the angel Gabriel came to Daniel and again said, "I am now come forth to give thee skill and understanding" of the "vision." Daniel 9:20-23. The angel next gave him another prophecy describing 70 weeks of probationary time for the Jewish nation that was to commence with the decree "to restore and to build Jerusalem" and to conclude with the coming of the Messiah. Daniel then just ends the chapter without any fuller explanation from the angel. (See Daniel 9:24-27.)

When Cyrus came to the throne in Persia a year later he made a decree that the Jews could return and build the temple. (See Ezra 1:1-4.) However, as the work progressed Daniel's people received great resistance in their restoration effort. (See Ezra 4:1-5.) After 70 literal weeks had passed Daniel could see that the temple was a long way from being finished, the city walls were still broken down, and the Messiah had not yet come. Hence, Daniel realized that the 70 weeks were not literal. It was therefore in a solemn spirit that he came before God seeking understanding of the previous revelations, and it was through that solemn experience that the vision by the Tigris River was received:

"In the third year of Cyrus king of Persia a thing was revealed unto Daniel, whose name was called Belteshazzar; and the thing was true, but the time appointed was long: and he understood the thing, and had understanding of the vision." Daniel 10:1.

The year that Daniel receivevd this incredible vision, "the third year of Cyrus," must have been in 535 B.C., and was about three years after he received his vision recorded in chapter nine. Daniel was obviously known in the empire by his Babylonian name, "Belteshazzar," and he gives it here to clarify his identity. Imposters were not few in those days, and it could be that there were many false prophets peddling their predictions to the Jewish people to discourage them and to hinder their work in Jerusalem. After all, it was Satan's determined purpose to destroy these people through whom the Messiah would come, and the angel indicates that the conflict would be intense. The phrase translated "the time appointed was long" could also be rendered "the conflict was great," or it was "a great, long conflict." Thus the vision by the Tigris River describes a prolonged, intense struggle that Daniel's people would have to endure.

After Daniel received this prophecy he could finally say, "he understood the thing, and had understanding of the vision," and he had at last obtained what he was seeking. It should be just as obvious then that the vision here is connected with the previous visions in chapters eight and nine, since it is evidently the clarification of those visions for which Daniel was seeking understanding. However, we should not be led to think that Daniel understood every minute detail of the vision, for he tells us later, when the angel is giving specifics about it: "I heard, but I understood not." Thus the particulars of the vision are left for God's people to discover at "the time of the end." Daniel 12:8-9.

Diet and Prophecy

The great men of God knew how to restrain their appetite. The apostle Paul said, "I keep under my body, and bring it into subjection." 1 Corinthians 9:27. Peter claimed, "I have never eaten any thing that is common or unclean." Acts 10:14. John the Baptist also had a simple diet of "locusts and wild honey." Matthew 3:4. And Isaiah tells us that the coming Messiah was to eat "Butter and honey…that he may know to refuse the evil, and choose the good." Isaiah 7:14-15. (See also Matthew 1:22-23.) Daniel and his companions were no exception. When confronted with the dissipating food of the king of Babylon they refused to partake of it, and asked for a ten-day test in which they would have only "pulse to eat, and water to drink." Daniel 1:12. At the end "their countenances appeared fairer and fatter in flesh than all the children which did eat the portion of the king's meat." Because of their restraint "God gave them knowledge and skill in all learning and wisdom: and Daniel had understanding in all visions and dreams." Daniel 1:15-17. Daniel, at nearly 90 years of age, again follows this strict regimen as he comes before God seeking for greater insight into the visions that he had received:

> **"In those days I Daniel was mourning three full weeks. I ate no pleasant bread, neither came flesh nor wine in my mouth, neither did I anoint myself at all, till three whole weeks were fulfilled."** *Daniel 10:2-3.*

The Lord's choice of Daniel as a prophet was not by chance. (See Matthew 24:15.) Daniel surrendered himself to the Lord in every part of his life. The words that he spoke, the prayers that he prayed, the clothes that he wore, and even the food that he ate were entirely surrendered to the Lord of heaven. Daniel's diet was normally very healthful, but during times of spiritual need he restricted himself even more. His fast was not a complete abstinence of food, but he restrained himself from those things that are hurtful: "I ate no pleasant bread, neither came flesh nor wine in my mouth." Cookies, cakes, candies of every kind, flesh meat, and stimulating beverages were all absent from the table of Daniel during his fast. He ate to strengthen his body and mind, so that he could endure the long hours of prayer and to prepare himself for the divine revelation. Neither did Daniel make an outward show by anointing himself, as was the custom in those days. His was a selfless desire for understanding, and after "three whole weeks were fulfilled" he received a response to his supplications.

The simple diet that the Lord laid out for man in the book of Genesis should be examined carefully, for it has special benefit for the people of God as they go through the final conflict. The diet that God first provided for Adam and Eve has great power to clear the mind and strengthen the body. They were given "every herb bearing seed, which is upon the face of all the earth, and every tree, in the which is the fruit of a tree yielding seed." Genesis 1:29. Thus the diet given to man was clearly a vegetarian diet of fruits, nuts and seeds, and whole grains. Vegetables were wisely added to the diet of man after the entrance of sin and are healthful for our degenerate bodies. (See Genesis 3:18.) Such a diet is not well liked in today's world, and is often ridiculed, but it is the diet that was given by the Creator for the well being of His children. This is the simple, natural diet that Daniel chose to follow as he prepared for an encounter with the God of heaven.

As for the consumption of flesh, it was added after the flood as a temporary measure until the vegetation returned, however God later approved the use of clean meats for His people in the Levitical health laws, which remain until our day. (See Genesis 7:2; 9:3-4; Leviticus 11; Acts 15:28-29.) Many try to use passages in the New Testament to overthrow this restriction upon the use of flesh meat, but they do it by twisting the scriptures to support their appetites, and to the detriment of their health. These Christians see no need to obey God in the restraint of appetite, and are following Eve in eating the things that the Lord would have them refrain from. Today's false doctrines of righteousness and salvation allow for the indulgence of anything that the heart desires, for it is much easier to pamper the passions, and to accept a religion that supports them, then to deny the desires of the human heart. The truth of this is reflected in the many fables that are palmed off as prophetic truth. Those who give free run to their desires cannot hear the voice of Jesus, and Satan is leading them to interpret the prophecies according to his perversions. We must faithfully follow Daniel in the surrender of our appetites and passions to God if we are determined to understand the vision, for the Lord is faithful and will also give us "understanding in all visions and dreams."

Beholding Jesus

To behold Jesus intelligently as the scripture declares will change anyone into a perfect Christian, for by beholding Him we become "changed into the same image from glory to glory, even as by the Spirit of the Lord." 2 Corinthians 3:18. Beholding Him brings eternal life and satisfies man's greatest need. (See Isaiah 45:22; John 6:40.) This is first done, as the scripture declares, through the lessons taught in nature: "For the invisible things of him from the creation of the world are clearly seen, being understood by the things that are made, even his eternal power and Godhead." Romans 1:20. Thus all can know of His existence. Secondly, in the scripture itself we are invited to behold Him: "Looking unto Jesus," "Seeing then...Jesus," "Consider...Christ Jesus," and "Behold the Lamb of God." Hebrews 12:2; 4:14; 3:1; John 1:29. Thus through nature and the study of the Word we behold His character and love for man, and His mighty power to save us from the dominion of sin.

As men behold Jesus and are transformed they are blessed with greater and still greater manifestations of His presence and glory. Moses was enabled to speak unto the Lord "face to face, as a man speaketh unto his friend." Exodus 33:11. Elijah beheld the power of God and was finally translated and "went up by a whirlwind into heaven." 2 Kings 2:11. The apostle Paul had "visions and revelations of the Lord," and was caught up into the "third heaven." 2 Corinthians 12:1-2. The disciples Peter, James, and John saw Jesus transfigured (see Matthew 17:1-6), and later, along with other believers, beheld Jesus' trial and crucifixion, spoke with Him after His resurrection, and saw His ascension into the clouds of heaven. (See John 18:15-27; 19:25-27; 20:19-29; Acts 1:1-14.) Daniel was no exception; he often found a quiet place in nature along the banks of the rivers of Babylon where he might draw closer to God through prayer and study of the scriptures. In doing so he was blessed with the presence of God, and received visions and dreams. (See Daniel 8:1-2.) It was on one of these days that Daniel received this vision by the Tigris River:

> **"And in the four and twentieth day of the first month, as I was by the side of the great river, which is Hiddekel; Then I lifted up mine eyes, and looked, and behold a certain man clothed in linen, whose loins were girded with fine gold of Uphaz: His body also was like the beryl, and his face as the appearance of lightning, and his eyes as lamps of fire, and his arms and his feet like in colour to polished brass, and the voice of his words like the voice of a multitude."** Daniel 10:4-6.

The vision that Daniel received in chapter eight was by "the river of Ulai" (Daniel 8:2), which is the Euphrates River. The "great river, which is Hiddekel," is the Tigris River, and thus the name of this book. It was on the banks of this great river, in the quiet solitude of nature and free from the pressures of the court of Medo-Persia, that the elderly prophet fasted and received this incredible vision. The Euphrates and the Tigris rivers are in the land of ancient Babylon, our modern Iraq, and just as these two rivers join, so these prophecies of Daniel are connected and give greater force and urgency to their message as we approach the end of time.

The vision actually opens in verse five, and as Daniel looks up he sees Jesus, the Son of God, standing before him "clothed in linen, whose loins were girded with fine gold of Uphaz." He gives a description that is similar to that of John the Revelator where he sees "one like unto the Son of man, clothed with a garment down to the foot, and girt about the paps with a golden girdle…and his voice as the sound of many waters." Revelation 1:12-17. Both prophetic books call us to behold Jesus, and His work for the salvation of His people. He is the central figure, and any attempt to interpret or understand the prophecies without Jesus is futile. The scriptures in their entirety "testify" of Jesus (John 5:39), and the prophecies of the apostle John are declared to be: "The Revelation of Jesus Christ." Revelation 1:1. Thus this prophecy calls us to behold Jesus, His ministry, and His purpose for our lives.

The experience of Daniel cannot be learned in the crisis of the end times. A relationship must be developed with the Lord beforehand, so that we can know His voice when He speaks. Joseph spent many years in slavery and in prison. He had to learn to trust in the Lord before He could exalt him to the position of Prime Minister of Egypt. (See Acts 7:9-10.) Moses spent 40 years in the wilderness of Midian unlearning what he had learned in Egypt, and relearning the lessons that God wanted him to know before he could lead his people out of Egypt. (See Acts 7:20-36.) Consequently, now is the time to prepare for the events that are before us. We must spend time in nature and the study of the scriptures to behold Jesus and to learn of Him and His will for us. Only then shall we be prepared, as Daniel was, to receive visions of the glory of God, and to occupy the positions that the Lord would have us to fill in the last crisis.

Walking with Jesus

The admonition throughout scripture is to walk with the Lord: "Ye shall walk after the LORD your God, and fear him, and keep his commandments;" "Blessed are the undefiled in the way, who walk in the law of the LORD;" and "Walk while ye have the light, lest darkness come upon you." Deuteronomy

13:4; Psalms 119:1; John 12:35. These are all clear passages admonishing us to walk with God by keeping His law. The apostle Paul reveals to us that our walk with God determines our eternal destiny:

> "There is therefore now no condemnation to them which are in Christ Jesus, who walk not after the flesh, but after the Spirit." Romans 8:1.

To walk after the flesh is to disobey God, for "the minding of the flesh is enmity against God: for it is not subject to the law of God, neither indeed can be." Romans 8:7, margin. Those who walk or "live after the flesh, shall die: but if ye through the Spirit do mortify the deeds of the body, ye shall live." Romans 8:13. Thus our walk determines our destiny.

The Lord speaking through the prophet Ezekiel compares the righteousness of Daniel to that of Noah and Job. (See Ezekiel 14:20.) His righteousness was not something just written in a book in heaven, but it was a daily experience in his life — his walk with God. He was accustomed to beholding the glory of God through nature and study, and as he beheld his Lord he became changed into His image and learned to walk in His ways. Many times Daniel was lonely and singled out as the object of persecution because of his obedience to God. But the Lord accounted his obedience of great worth and He protected him and entrusted him with the words of life for a dying world while others were passed by:

> **"And I Daniel alone saw the vision: for the men that were with me saw not the vision; but a great quaking fell upon them, so that they fled to hide themselves. Therefore I was left alone, and saw this great vision, and there remained no strength in me: for my comeliness was turned in me into corruption, and I retained no strength. Yet heard I the voice of his words: and when I heard the voice of his words, then was I in a deep sleep on my face, and my face toward the ground."** *Daniel 10:7-9.*

Daniel tells us that he "alone saw the vision." His holy life allowed him to view the sight while the others, who saw no need to restrain themselves as he did, trembled and "fled to hide themselves." This unfortunately will be the experience of many when Jesus appears in glory at the end of time:

> "And the kings of the earth, and the great men, and the rich men, and the chief captains, and the mighty men, and every bondman, and every free man, hid themselves in the dens and in the rocks of the

mountains; And said to the mountains and rocks, fall on us, and hide us from the face of him that sitteth on the throne, and from the wrath of the Lamb: For the great day of his wrath is come; and who shall be able to stand?" *Revelation 6:15-17*.

Purity of life must characterize those who stand in the last great conflict. Daniel's example is given to us here and throughout the book so that we will realize the significance of preparation as the prophecies unfold. The last events will be incredibly intense, and unless we are willing to surrender all to the will of God and to walk with Him we will not stand. Even Daniel, when he saw the vision, perceived the holiness of the One standing before him, and, as he realized the sinfulness of his own nature, he lost all of his physical strength: "for my comeliness was turned in me into corruption, and I retained no strength." Then, as he heard Jesus speak he says that he was in a deep sleep on his face and that his face was "toward the ground." The vision must have been tremendous to cause such physical reactions, and, if it had such an incredible effect upon this holy man of God, what will happen to us if we fail to prepare and walk in the ways of the Lord? Listen to the prophet Micah:

"He hath shewed thee, O man, what is good; and what doth the LORD require of thee, but to do justly, and to love mercy, and to walk humbly with thy God?" *Micah 6:8*.

We must prepare and learn to walk with Jesus now in all that we do if we shall stand when He comes. The road that we walk may be lonely and long, but we can be assured that Jesus will be by our side, for He promised: "I will not leave you comfortless: I will come to you." John 14:18. Only in walking with Him and in His ways can we be assured of His continued presence and acceptance in our lives.

Acceptance with God

God does not accept men simply because they were born of a specific race, nationality, or religion. As Peter stood before the Gentile believers he declared: "Of a truth I perceive that God is no respecter of persons: But in every nation he that feareth him, and worketh righteousness, is accepted with him." Acts 10:34-35. Peter understood that God's acceptance was not connected to nationality, but he opens for us, in the passage just quoted, the truth that our works determine our acceptance with God. Peter says also in his first epistle that God "without respect of persons judgeth according to every man's work." 1 Peter 1:17. Thus it is easy to see why, when he offered his useless, disobedient sacrifice, God rebuked Cain and said: "If thou doest well, shalt thou not be accepted?" Genesis 4:5-7. The words of the Lord are clear. He expects obedience to His will before he accepts the worship of any man.

That God accepted Daniel's devotion is clear from the words of the angel Gabriel after his prayer in chapter nine. Gabriel left the throne of God as Daniel began his prayer and he appeared and spoke with him to let him know of his acceptance of heaven: "At the beginning of thy supplications the commandment came forth, and I am come to shew thee; for thou art greatly beloved." Daniel 9:23. His obedience brought the angel to his side, and the angel again repeats the words of heaven's acceptance to Daniel in the vision that he received by the Tigris River:

> **"And, behold, an hand touched me, which set me upon my knees and upon the palms of my hands. And he said unto me, O Daniel, a man greatly beloved, understand the words that I speak unto thee, and stand upright: for unto thee am I now sent. And when he had spoken this word unto me, I stood trembling."** *Daniel 10:10-11.*

Daniel was "greatly beloved" and accepted by heaven because of his willingness to obey no matter what the cost to himself, and therefore he was also blessed with the vision. The touch of the angel Gabriel set him upon his hands and knees, and his familiar voice gave Daniel the strength to rise to his feet and "stand upright." He was then equipped to listen to what Gabriel had to say. However, at the sight of the vision he was still much afraid and he "stood trembling."

None of us know exactly the trials that will befall us in the near future. At times we may be placed in dangerous situations, have to testify for our faith in courts of law, or at other times we may be given visions and dreams similar to what Daniel received. These experiences may lift us to great heights of emotion or drop us to the depths of despair, but if we are surrendered we can be assured that we are accepted of Heaven, as was Daniel. Thus the admonition of the apostle Paul should sink clearly into our minds:

> "I beseech you therefore, brethren, by the mercies of God, that ye present your bodies a living sacrifice, holy, acceptable unto God, which is your reasonable service." Romans 12:1.

Those who are obedient are accepted of heaven and will be blessed with the divine presence, for Jesus promised to reveal Himself to His people: "He that hath my commandments, and keepeth them, he it is that loveth me…and I will love him, and will manifest myself to him." John 14:21. Few know of this experience, for almost the entire Christian world has given itself to an emotional religion, but those that know God understand that the religion of the Bible requires a struggle against the sinful nature. Daniel understood man's duty, that only those who "Fear God, and keep his commandments" will be accepted by Him and thus be blessed with the divine presence. Ecclesiastes 12:13. His experience is to be ours, and it is recorded in the Bible as an example for us to imitate.

Prayer and Faith

One of the greatest prayers recorded in the scripture is found in the ninth chapter of Daniel. With deep contrition and fasting he came before the Lord confessing his sins and those of his people. He knew that prayer would move the arm of God, for he had experienced it many times. (See Daniel 2:17-23; 6:10-23.) Faith had driven him to his knees, and thus when Daniel began to pray the angel Gabriel was commanded to fly and speak with the prophet:

> "Yea, whiles I was speaking in prayer, even the man Gabriel, whom I had seen in the vision at the beginning, being caused to fly swiftly, touched me about the time of the evening oblation. And he informed me, and talked with me, and said, O Daniel, I am now come forth to give thee skill and understanding. At the beginning of thy supplications the commandment came forth, and I am come to shew thee; for thou art greatly beloved: therefore understand the matter, and consider the vision." *Daniel 9:21-23*.

It was because of his persistence in prayer and his faithful obedience that the angel Gabriel responded to Daniel's supplications. Over and over we see Daniel in prayer throughout the book, and here again it is the prayer of Daniel that brings his greatest vision:

> **"Then said he unto me, Fear not, Daniel: for from the first day that thou didst set thine heart to understand, and to chasten thyself before thy God, thy words were heard, and I am come for thy words."** Daniel 10:12.

Although Daniel did not receive an answer to his prayers immediately in this instance he persisted, and not one of his words was lost, "for from the first day…thy words were heard." How precious to know that our prayers will be answered when we earnestly seek the Lord. Had Daniel ceased to pray after a week or two the history of the Jewish nation might have been different, and the vision may have never been received. Jesus said, "that men ought always to pray, and not to faint." Luke 18:1. Persistence is essential for a powerful prayer life, and, to those who persist, the promise is given: "And it shall come to pass, that before they call, I will answer; and while they are yet speaking, I will hear." Isaiah 65:24.

A life of self-sacrifice and prayer coupled with faith is key to power and victory in the Christian experience. Men today will likely choose disobedience to God over lose of a job or persecution. However, when Daniel was threatened with death if he continued to pray he chose death. His example of prayer and faith is given to encourage and to instruct us. Here is his experience: In the days of king Darius the Mede a law was secured that required all people to pray solely to him for 30 days on pain of death. (See Daniel 6:1-9.) This law brought conflict to Daniel. He knew that he could not obey it because it would sever his connection with God, so Daniel ignored the law:

> "Now when Daniel knew that the writing was signed, he went into his house; and his windows being open in his chamber toward Jerusalem, he kneeled upon his knees three times a day, and prayed, and gave thanks before his God, as he did aforetime." *Daniel 6:10*.

Now human logic would say, "I will just shut the window, and they will never know. God understands!" However, it is only through faith that men can obey (see Romans 3:31) and therefore gain acceptance with God. The apostle Paul tells us that, "without faith it is impossible to please him: for he that cometh to God must believe that he is, and that he is a rewarder of them that diligently seek him." Hebrews 11:6. When confronted with a decision the true Christian will, in faith, always surrender to the will of God, even in the face of death. This then opens the door for God to work miraculously in man's behalf.

Daniel was cast into a den of lions, and his faith was tried to the uttermost. It was "because he believed in his God," and persisted openly in prayer, that he gained the victory and "stopped the mouths of lions." Daniel 6:16-23; Hebrews 11:33. Daniel new what God required and in faith obeyed. Thus it is to be with us. We also cannot hide our convictions in the time of danger and expect divine protection, for only when we exercise faith can we obtain the victory: "...and this is the victory that overcometh the world, even our faith." 1 John 5:4. Thus prayer is the key in the hand of faith that opens the wealth of heaven's storehouse to the child of God.

Michael and the Unseen Struggle

If our eyes could be opened we would behold a mighty conflict going on in the unseen world around us. The scriptures give many examples of this. In one instance, as the children of Israel were preparing to conquer the land of Canaan, Joshua, who had wondered off to pray, was greeted by the presence of the Lord "with his sword drawn in his hand." Wondering whom this person was Joshua questioned: "Art thou for us, or for our adversaries?" The Lord's reply revealed who He was: "Nay; but as captain of the host of the LORD am I now come… Loose thy shoe from off thy foot; for the place whereon thou standest is holy." Joshua 5:13-15. Joshua was assured of victory by the presence of the Lord dressed for war. The armies of Jesus had come to assist him in his mission.

That the Lord is interested in the events that transpire upon this earth is clear. It was Jesus that was with the three Hebrews when they were cast into the fiery furnace, and His angel was sent to shut the lion's mouths when Daniel was thrown into their den. (See Daniel 3:25; 6:22.) The vision by the Tigris also gives us ample proof that divine agencies are continuously working in the background for God's people:

> **"But the prince of the kingdom of Persia withstood me one and twenty days: but, lo, Michael, one of the chief princes, came to help me; and I remained there with the kings of Persia."** *Daniel 10:13.*

The full "one and twenty days" of Daniel's fast were absorbed by the angel in his struggle with "the prince of the kingdom of Persia." Daniel was doubtless praying about some action of the king connected with the restoration of the Israelites to Jerusalem and the decree that Cyrus had recently made. (See Ezra 1:1-4.) He was completely ignorant of the struggle that was taking place in the heart of the king, but his faith in God caused him to persist. That which is going on in the unseen world is brought to our view. The curtain is drawn aside for the moment that we may catch a glimpse of the heavenly conflict that prayer brings. The struggle was so intense that Michael had to come to Gabriel's aid.

Who is Michael? He is "the archangel" and the "great prince" that stands for Daniel's people. Jude 9; Daniel 12:1. Michael means "He who is like God," and archangel signifies "head" or "chief" of the angels. It is Michael the archangel's voice that awakes the dead, which Jesus claims is his office. (See 1 Thessalonians 4:16; John 5:25-29.) In the verse under discussion the phrase "one of the chief princes" is also translated as "one of the first princes." (See the margin.) This phrase is similar to that used by Gabriel in chapter eight where Jesus is called the "Prince of princes." Daniel 8:11, 25. It also resembles the phrase used in the Revelation where He is entitled "KING OF KINGS, AND LORD OF LORDS." Revelation 19:16. (See also Psalm 136:3; Deuteronomy 10:17; 1 Timothy 6:15.) Moreover the apostle Peter declares that Jesus is "the Prince of life," and "a Prince and a Saviour." Acts 3:15; 5:31. Thus we conclude that Michael is Jesus! It was Jesus, the "Prince of Peace" (Isaiah 9:6) that came to the aid of Gabriel in his struggle with "the prince of the kingdom of Persia," and it was Jesus that was standing with Gabriel before Daniel in this vision by the Tigris River. Thus Jesus is set forth as the divine helper and sustainer of His people working in the unseen world. (See also in this chapter the section: The Rise and Fall of Nations.)

This earth is the battleground where the forces of good and evil have been waging war for 6000 years, and the climax of this war is just before us. Divine agencies are now preparing for the last great conflict upon this earth, and the hosts of darkness will not give up the fight without a struggle. It is Michael, the "captain of the Lord's host" (Joshua 5:15), that leads the armies of heaven to battle against the devil and his followers in the last battle: "And there was war in heaven: Michael and his angels fought against the dragon; and the dragon fought and his angels, and prevailed not…" Revelation 12:7-11. The conflict will take place and it is only as God's children are connected to Him through pray and the experience of faith that their victory is guaranteed, and through that experience Satan will finally be defeated.

Daniel's Faithful People

Many make the mistake of believing that Daniel's people are only those of the bloodline of the Jewish nation, but this is a great error. Throughout the New Testament we have many instances where Christians are declared to be the children of God and are united with the Jewish believers in one body called the Church. Consider the words of the apostle Paul:

> "Wherefore remember, that ye being in time past Gentiles in the flesh, who are called Uncircumcision by that which is called the Circumcision in the flesh made by hands; That at that time ye were without Christ, being aliens from the commonwealth of Israel, and strangers from the covenants of promise, having no hope, and without God in the world: But now in Christ Jesus ye who sometimes were far off are made nigh by the blood of Christ." *Ephesians 2:11-13.*

Through faith in Jesus we enter into the family of God. Daniel was a man of faith as much as Abraham or the apostles were, and all those who walk by faith can confidently say that they are among Daniel's people: "For ye are all the children of God by faith in Christ Jesus." Galatians 3:26. "And it shall come to pass, that in the place where it was said unto them, Ye are not my people; there shall they be called the children of the living God." Romans 9:26. Thus when the vision by the Tigris speaks of Daniel's people in the last days we can know that it includes all those then living who walk by faith in Jesus.

"Now I am come to make thee understand what shall befall thy people in the latter days: for yet the vision is for many days. And when he had spoken such words unto me, I set my face toward the ground, and I became dumb." *Daniel 10:14-15.*

As Daniel pleaded for the king of Persia his prayer was heard and answered, however, the Lord had a greater purpose for him. Daniel was to receive and record information about the struggles that would befall his people in "the latter days." That is, Daniel received divine warnings about the things that would come upon the Church at the end of time. These prophecies as well as the other scriptures were "written for our admonition, upon whom the ends of the world are come." 1 Corinthians 10:11. The Bible clearly links Daniel with all of the faithful people of God throughout the ages in Hebrews chapter 11 (see Daniel 6:20-22; Hebrews 11:33), and after describing the victories of these faithful people the apostle says:

> "And these all, having obtained a good report through faith, received not the promise: God having provided some better thing for us, that they without us should not be made perfect." Hebrews 11:39-40.

Paul here places the Christians and the Jews into one body through the experience of faith. God never intended for us to focus the prophecy upon the bloodline of the Jewish nation as is common today. The glorious truth of the whole scripture is illuminated when we understand that the focus of the prophecies is upon Christ and His faithful followers. The Church is the union of the Jewish and the Gentile believers into one body:

> "And when they were come, and had gathered the church together, they rehearsed all that God had done with them, and how he had opened the door of faith unto the Gentiles." *Acts 14:27.*

> "Know ye therefore that they which are of faith, the same are the children of Abraham. And the scripture, foreseeing that God would

justify the heathen through faith, preached before the gospel unto Abraham, saying, in thee shall all nations be blessed." *Galatians 3:7-8*.

"There is neither Jew nor Greek, there is neither bond nor free, there is neither male nor female: for ye are all one in Christ Jesus. And if ye be Christ's, then are ye Abraham's seed, and heirs according to the promise." *Galatians 3:28-29*.

Thus Daniel's people are those who walk by faith in Jesus Christ, "For there is no respect of persons with God." Romans 2:11. However, as Gabriel spoke, Daniel did not yet realize that his people would include more than just his Jewish brethren. Neither did he grasp the full significance of the vision, nor understand that the temple would shortly be restored in Jerusalem. Therefore, as in chapter eight, he became distressed when the angel told him that the vision was to last for "many days" and he says: "I set my face toward the ground, and I became dumb." Nevertheless, it is for us to understand that the trials discussed at the end of the prophecy are for those faithful children of God, both Jews and Gentiles, the spiritual nation of believers, that live in the last days.

The Divine Connection

In the creation of man, "God said, Let us make man in our image, after our likeness." Genesis 1:26. Man was created with the attributes of God both in outward form and in character. Hence, many times in scripture when the Lord is seen He has the appearance of humanity. When He met Abraham on the plains of Mamre He had the form of a man. (See Genesis 18:1-2.) When Jacob struggled with the Lord the Bible says that "there wrestled a man with him until the breaking of the day." Genesis 32:24. And, when the Lord appeared to Joshua to lead the armies of heaven before him into the land of Canaan He again had the form of a man dressed for war. (See Joshua 5:13-14.)

At times when Daniel saw the Lord he describes Him as a man with human form. As he beheld the judgment proceedings in chapter seven he says: "I saw in the night visions, and, behold, one like the Son of man came with the clouds of heaven…" Daniel 7:13. Daniel here used the same phrase, "Son of man," as John does in the book of the Revelation. (See Revelation 1:13; 14:14.) In chapter eight Daniel also declared that the Lord had "the appearance of a man." Daniel 8:15. Likewise in the vision that Daniel received by the Tigris River the Lord is again revealed in the likeness of a man:

> "And, behold, one like the similitude of the sons of men touched my lips: then I opened my mouth, and spake, and said unto him that stood before me, O my lord, by the vision my sorrows are turned upon me, and I have retained no strength. For how can the servant of this my lord talk with this my lord? for as for me, straightway there remained no strength in me, neither is there breath left in me." *Daniel 10:16-17.*

There is no doubt that the "one like the similitude of the sons of men" is Jesus, and is the same being as discussed in verses five and six. The distinct difference between the appearance of Jesus and that of the angels was evident to the prophet Daniel. Nevertheless, the connection between God and man cannot be ignored. Man was created to secure the universe from sin and rebellion by revealing the fullness of the attributes of God to the rest of His vast creation. Therefore, after man's creation, the scripture says that God "rested on the seventh day from all his work which he had made." Genesis 2:2-3. He did not rest because He was tired, but because His work was finished. He then had a people that would secure the universe from sin, which Lucifer introduced by his rebellion.

The Sabbath was to be a constant reminder to man of the high purpose of his creation — the outward sign of God's completed work. (See Exodus 31:12-17; Ezekiel 20:12.) Unfortunately, through the temptation of Satan, man rebelled and the purpose of God was thwarted for a time. Ever since then God has been working to restore man. Jesus said: "My Father worketh hitherto, and I work" (John 5:17), and the apostle Paul declared that God's people had not yet entered into "His rest." (See Hebrews 4:1-10.) The apostle then admonishes them to be diligent "to enter into that rest." Hebrews 4:11. Ultimately, the Church will give the "Revelation of Jesus Christ" to the universe, and "bruise Satan" under their feet when they reveal the fullness of God's character within themselves. Revelation 1:1; Romans 16:20. The Sabbath rest is the one thing that links man with his Creator, and it is still the divine reminder to man of his higher purpose. Is it any wonder that Satan has been trying to destroy it for six millennium?

In the verse under discussion we see Jesus touching Daniel on the lips, and his mouth was immediately opened. For the first time in the vision Daniel here speaks to the angel, and he then tells him of his weakened condition: "O my lord, by the vision my sorrows are turned upon me, and I have retained no strength…neither is there breath left in me." The faculties of man were created so that he could communicate with God and the angels. Yet, in his sinful condition the connection has been interrupted: "But your iniquities have separated between you and your God, and your sins have hid his face from you, that he will not hear." Isaiah 59:2. God has thus resorted to other methods in order to reveal Himself. Consequently, the scriptures were developed as the primary channel through which He could make His character known to sinful humanity and to convict him to fulfill the purpose of his creation.

The Power of God

The one thing that men seek after is power, and power is what the Lord wants them to have, but the power that men seek would destroy them. Even godly people tend to seek for the things that the Lord does not want them to have, and many times in His mercy He withholds it from them. The apostle Paul prayed that the Lord would remove a particular infirmity from his eyes (see Galatians 4:15), but the Lord did not want that infirmity removed, for it was the very thing that restrained the apostle and brought power to his experience:

> "For this thing I besought the Lord thrice, that it might depart from me. And he said unto me, My grace is sufficient for thee: for my strength is made perfect in weakness. Most gladly therefore will I rather glory in my infirmities, that the power of Christ may rest upon me. Therefore I take pleasure in infirmities, in reproaches, in necessities, in persecutions, in distresses for Christ's sake: for when I am weak, then am I strong." *2 Corinthians 12:8-10*.

Few respond the way the apostle did. Men do not naturally glory in infirmity and sickness, but the Lord knows what His people need. If they trust Him they will be strengthened to endure whatever trial is brought to them, and the Lord will turn it around to the salvation of their souls. Every situation is different, and the Lord uses His power as He sees fit, "For there is no power but of God." Romans 13:1. As for Daniel, the vision had taken away all of his strength, and he needed power that he did not have in order to continue receiving the vision. Thus the Lord comes to him and supplies his need:

> **"Then there came again and touched me one like the appearance of a man, and he strengthened me, And said, O man greatly beloved, fear not: peace be unto thee, be strong, yea, be strong. And when he had spoken unto me, I was strengthened, and said, Let my lord speak; for thou hast strengthened me."** *Daniel 10:18-19*.

In the verse under discussion we see Jesus, who has "the appearance of a man," again touch Daniel, and he was "strengthened." At certain times Jesus' touch produced miraculous things: those with leprosy were cleansed, violent fevers ceased, the eyes of the blind were opened, and the dead were raised back to life. (See Matthew 8:3, 15; 9:29-30; Mark 5:41-43; Luke 4:40.) Nevertheless, the power of Jesus is here also manifested as He spoke to Daniel. When men speak they must make good on their words because men's words have no power to accomplish anything, but when the Lord speaks His words have the power within them to accomplish the task that He sends them to do:

> "So shall my word be that goeth forth out of my mouth: it shall not return unto me void, but it shall accomplish that which I please, and it shall prosper in the thing whereto I sent it." *Isaiah 55:11*.

All power is available in the words of Jesus. It was Jesus that spoke the worlds into existence, and in the things of creation the power of Jesus can be seen if men would but open their eyes. (See Psalms 33:6, 9; 107:19-20; Colossians 1:16; John 1:1-3; Romans 1:19-20; Hebrews 11:3; 1 Peter 3:5.) When the Lord therefore spoke to Daniel saying, "O man greatly beloved, fear not: peace be unto thee, be strong, yea, be strong," a wave of peace came over Daniel, as he had never experienced before. All fear left him, and he was "strengthened" to receive the rest of the vision as the apostle John was similarly strengthened to receive the Apocalypse. (See Revelation 1:17.) Jesus knew the need of His prophet, and supplied what Gabriel could not. Likewise, the power of Jesus is available to all. Those who believe in the promises of the Bible have available to them all of the creative power of the Lord, for the Bible is His Word to man, and in His Word is manifested His power.

The Rise and Fall of Nations

The rise and fall of nations does not take place by the courage and ability of man, but by the will and power of God. When the kingdom of ancient Babylon became so corrupt that the Lord could no longer impress and move its leadership He overthrew the nation. (See Isaiah 45:1-3; Daniel 5:24-31.) When Rome ruled the world the Bible says that it was "ordained" or established by God. Romans 13:1. Consequently, those who think that the United States rules the world today because of its military might are wrong. It is God that has and will control the events upon this earth, for "he removeth kings, and setteth up kings." Daniel 2:21. Says the Lord:

> "At what instant I shall speak concerning a nation, and concerning a kingdom, to pluck up, and to pull down, and to destroy it; If that nation, against whom I have pronounced, turn from their evil, I will repent of

the evil that I thought to do unto them. And at what instant I shall speak concerning a nation, and concerning a kingdom, to build and to plant it; If it do evil in my sight, that it obey not my voice, then I will repent of the good, wherewith I said I would benefit them." *Jeremiah 18:7-10.*

The Lord suffers long with the leaders of the nations and does not quickly remove them from their positions of authority, but He gives them time to prove and to develop their characters. King Nebuchadnezzar was given many opportunities to know God and was finally converted after the Lord humbled him through seven years of insanity. (See Daniel 4.) Nevertheless, if a nation's leaders reject His pleadings, as king Belshazzar did (see Daniel 5:17-23), He will eventually replace them and possibly their nation as well. Hence, the sins or righteousness of a nation and its leadership will determine its final destiny. This principle is clearly revealed in the Lord's struggle with the Persian leadership:

"Then said he, Knowest thou wherefore I come unto thee? and now will I return to fight with the prince of Persia: and when I am gone forth, lo, the prince of Grecia shall come. But I will shew thee that which is noted in the scripture of truth: and there is none that holdeth with me in these things, but Michael your prince. Also I in the first year of Darius the Mede, even I, stood to confirm and to strengthen him." *Daniel 10:20-11:1.*

Once Daniel received enough strength to endure the vision Gabriel continued his narrative, and opened to Daniel the demise of the Persian Empire. Gabriel draws aside the curtain again to reveal to Daniel the future conflict with the hosts of darkness that transpire in the unseen world. When a nation responds to the promptings of heavenly messengers its existence is assured, but when it becomes corrupt beyond repair the messenger will unfold his wings and take his flight. The nation will then be left to its own ruin. Consequently, the angel plainly declared that "Grecia" would be the next empire to exist when heaven withdrew its protection from Persia.

The events related to the restoration of Daniel's people and the rise and fall of the nations involved in the prophecy are elsewhere: "noted in the scripture of truth." The book of Daniel does not exist on its own. The Bible was written for us, and truth is contained in "all scripture." 2 Timothy 3:16. All of the books of the Bible contain information for those "upon whom the ends of the world are come." 1 Corinthians 10:11. Therefore the Bible must be studied as God intended. Surface reading will only confirm men in deception, for they will feel secure in knowing a few passages of scripture.

God intends that men study to show themselves "approved unto God" that they might rightly divide "the word of truth." 2 Timothy 2:15. They need to be as the Bereans who "were more noble than those in Thessalonica, in that they received the word with all readiness of mind, and searched the scriptures daily" to see "whether those things were so." Acts 17:11. Anything less will prevent God's children from the preparation that they need for the coming conflict.

In our passage the angel Gabriel again speaks of Michael, and He is not just called "a prince," but the angel's words to Daniel were "your prince." This again forcefully places Michael as Jesus, "the Messiah the Prince." Daniel 9:25. It was Michael that assisted His messenger in the struggle with king Cyrus the Great of Persia, and it was Gabriel, aided by Michael, that went forth to struggle with "Darius the Mede." Thus we can be assured that Gabriel and Michael are struggling with our nation and its leaders. Heaven is in control of the events upon this earth, and nothing is done without the intimate knowledge of God. He will make sure that all things are done as the prophecy declares, for history and scripture will always agree.

Summary of Chapter One

Through Daniel's self-sacrifice, prayer, and faith he gained precious victories, which can be to all that are determined to live as he did. His experience enabled him to receive this incredible vision. Those who want to understand it as Daniel did must be willing to surrender to the will of God in all that they do by following his example. Their diets must consist of simple, natural foods so that their minds will be clear. They must spend time with Jesus in nature and behold Him in His Word to learn of Him, and any sins in their lives must be yielded to His will. They must learn to pray and exercise faith. Then they will be blessed by His presence and accepted of Him, and the prophecy will become clear, for Jesus said: "If any man will do his will, he shall know of the doctrine, whether it be of God…" John 7:17.

Without a complete surrender the natural heart will dislike the clear teaching of the prophecy, and the parts that require a decision will be rejected. Consequently, those who refuse to live godly lives will fail of eternal life, and will be among them that say to the mountains and rocks at Jesus Second Coming: "Fall on us, and hide us from the face of him that sitteth on the throne, and from the wrath of the Lamb." Revelation 6:16.

The vision by the Tigris covers a long period of history, a "great, long conflict," and Jesus and His angels are shown to be struggling in the unseen world against demons and with the leaders of the nations of this earth. Jesus is

Michael, and in His office as "archangel" the throngs of heavenly angels are at His command. In the last conflict He will guide the entire host of heaven against the powers of hell, and will be victorious. Therefore it is vital that we have a close connection with Him.

Jesus is central to this vision as He is to the rest of the scripture, and all that has and will transpire is in perfect control by the Monarch of heaven. The nations of earth do not exist because of the courage and ability of man. They are at His command, and when the nations have filled their cup of wickedness He will tare them down and set up His kingdom, which shall last forever and ever.

With this understanding from the experiences of Daniel we now turn to the narrative of the prophecy.

Chapter 2: From Persia to Rome

This chapter covers roughly 500 years of history. It reaches from Daniel's time in the days of the great Medo-Persian empire, covers the rise of Alexander the Great, reveals the division of the Greek empire, introduces the kings of the North and the South, and then announces the establishment of Rome.

The Medo-Persian Dominion

In Nebuchadnezzar's dream of the "great image" found in Daniel chapter two, the "head of gold," and the "breast and arms of silver" represent the kingdoms of Babylon and Medo-Persia. Daniel 2:31-32. (See also Daniel 2:36-39; 5:18-31.) In the dream of Daniel chapter seven the "four great beasts" that "came up from the sea" of humanity likewise represent kingdoms. Daniel 7:3. (Read also verses 1-2, 15-17, 23; and Revelation 17:15.) The "lion" that "had eagle's wings" and the "bear" that "raised up itself on one side" symbolize Babylon and Medo-Persia respectively. Daniel 7:4-5. (See also Jeremiah 4:6-13; 50:17; Habakkuk 1:6-8; Isaiah 13:17-19; 21:2, 9; 45:1; Jeremiah 51:11, 27-33.) In Daniel's vision by the "river of Ulai" he saw "a ram that had two horns," which "did according to his will, and became great." Daniel 8:2-4. This prophecy in chapter eight skips the account of Babylon, for the ram is clearly declared to be "the kings of Media and Persia." Daniel 8:20. The vision by the Tigris also parallels Daniel's other three prophecies, and opens its narrative as well in the days of Medo-Persia:

> **"And now will I shew thee the truth. Behold, there shall stand up yet three kings in Persia; and the fourth shall be far richer than they all: and by his strength through his riches he shall stir up all against the realm of Grecia."** *Daniel 11:2.*

Daniel was living "in the third year of Cyrus king of Persia." Daniel 10:1. (See the map on page 43.) Cambyses, son of Cyrus the Great, was the first king to stand up when his father died in 529 B.C., and an impostor called the False Smerdis was the second king to come to the throne in Persia in the spring of 522. (These two kings are mentioned in Ezra chapter four under different names: Ahasuerus and Artaxerxes. The difference in names between scripture and history is common.) The third king, Darius Hystaspes, had the False Smerdis slain and acceded the Persian throne later that same year. He is described in Ezra chapters five and six, and his works prepared the Persian Empire for the "fourth" king, Xerxes, who came to power when he died in 486 B.C. The Scripture under discussion says that Xerxes would be "far richer than they all," and a description of his wealth is found in the book of Esther where he is also called Ahasuerus. (See Esther 1:1-9.) In the year 480 B.C., "by his strength through his riches," Xerxes stirred up "all against the realm of Grecia," and amassed a great force:

> "The whole number of souls that followed of Xerxes in this expedition amounted to five millions two hundred and eighty-three thousand two hundred and twenty." Rollin, *Ancient History: History of the Persians and Grecians*, chap. 2, sec. 3, par. 5.

Xerxes first met the Greeks, in August, at the famous battle of Thermopylae, which is the pass between northern and central Greece. Three hundred Spartans held Xerxes' army there until the treacherous Ephialtes showed the Persians an unguarded passageway over the mountains. The Persians then attacked the Greeks from behind and overwhelmingly defeated them. Xerxes next took Athens on September 21; however, two days later the Greek navy defeated the Persian fleet at Salamis. The Persians lost two hundred ships in this battle, and with their defeat they lost the command of the sea and ultimately the war. Xerxes abandoned Greece and returned to Sardes shortly after his naval defeat at Salamis. He then spent the rest of his reign in idleness and sensuality in his palace at Shushan until Artabanus, one of the attendants of his court, murdered him in 464 B.C.

> "Never again was Persia to make a serious attempt against the liberty of European Greece. For the following century and a half, the dealings between Greece and Persia only affected the western fringe of Asia, and then Alexander of Macedon achieved against the Asiatic monarchy what Xerxes failed to achieve against the free states of Europe." Bury, *A Student's History of Greece*, p. 154.

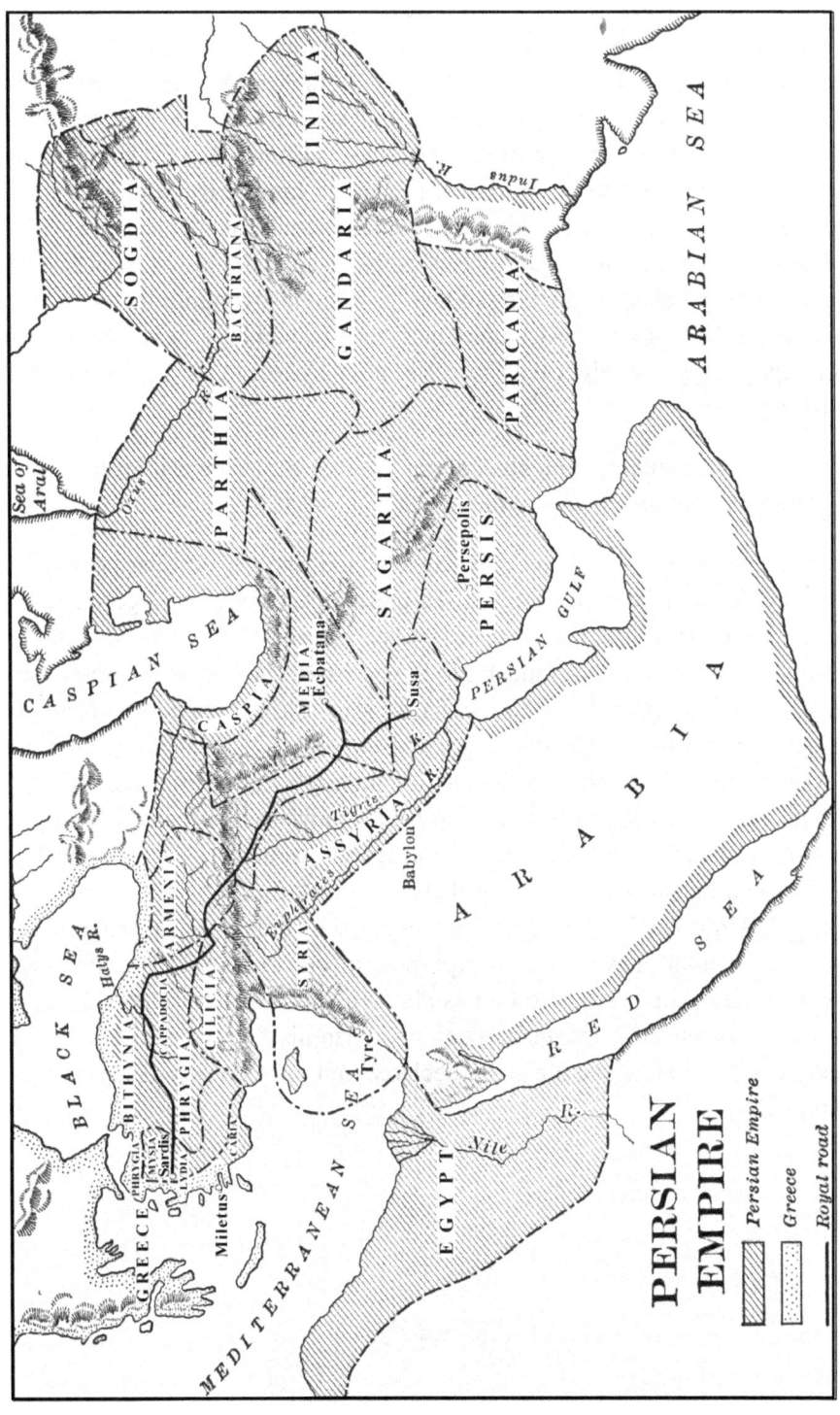

The Rise of Alexander the Great

In the prophecy of Daniel chapter two the "belly and thighs of brass," on the great image, illustrate the "third kingdom," the Greek empire. Daniel 2:32, 39. And in his dream in chapter seven Daniel sees Greece as a "leopard, which had upon the back of it four wings of a fowl." Daniel 7:6, 17. Daniel chapter eight strikingly represents the rise of the Greek Empire by "an he goat" that had "a notable horn between his eyes," which "came from the west on the face of the whole earth," and became "very great." Daniel 8:5-8. "The rough goat," as the angel reveals, "is the king of Grecia: and the great horn that is between his eyes is the first king," Alexander the Great. Daniel 8:21. Daniel's vision by the Tigris skips over eight Persian rulers after Xerxes to the beginning of the Greek Empire:

> **"And a mighty king shall stand up, that shall rule with great dominion, and do according to his will."** *Daniel 11:3.*

In the spring of 334 B.C., Alexander and his 35,000 men crossed the Dardanelles and invaded Persia. (See the map on the next page.) The first battle, which took place at Granicus, was a surprise to the Persians who lost nearly 40,000 men to Alexander. He next crossed the Taurus Mountains and met Darius Codomanus, king of Persia, at Issus. Darius was defeated and fled. Alexander then marched upon Tyre, and in July 332, after a siege of nearly seven months, it fell into his hands. He then left Parmenion, his second in command, to settle Syria from Damascus and advanced with his army toward Egypt. At Gaza, Alexander received a serious wound in his shoulder by a dart from a Persian catapult; nevertheless, he took the city after a tremendous struggle. Upon reaching Egypt, in November, the satrapies openly submitted to him. At Memphis he sacrificed to Apis and the other native gods; accordingly, the Egyptian people accepted him as Pharaoh. Upon his return to the coast he founded the city of Alexandria. Then he began his famous expedition to the temple of Ammon where the priest declared him to be the son of the god Zeus Ammon:

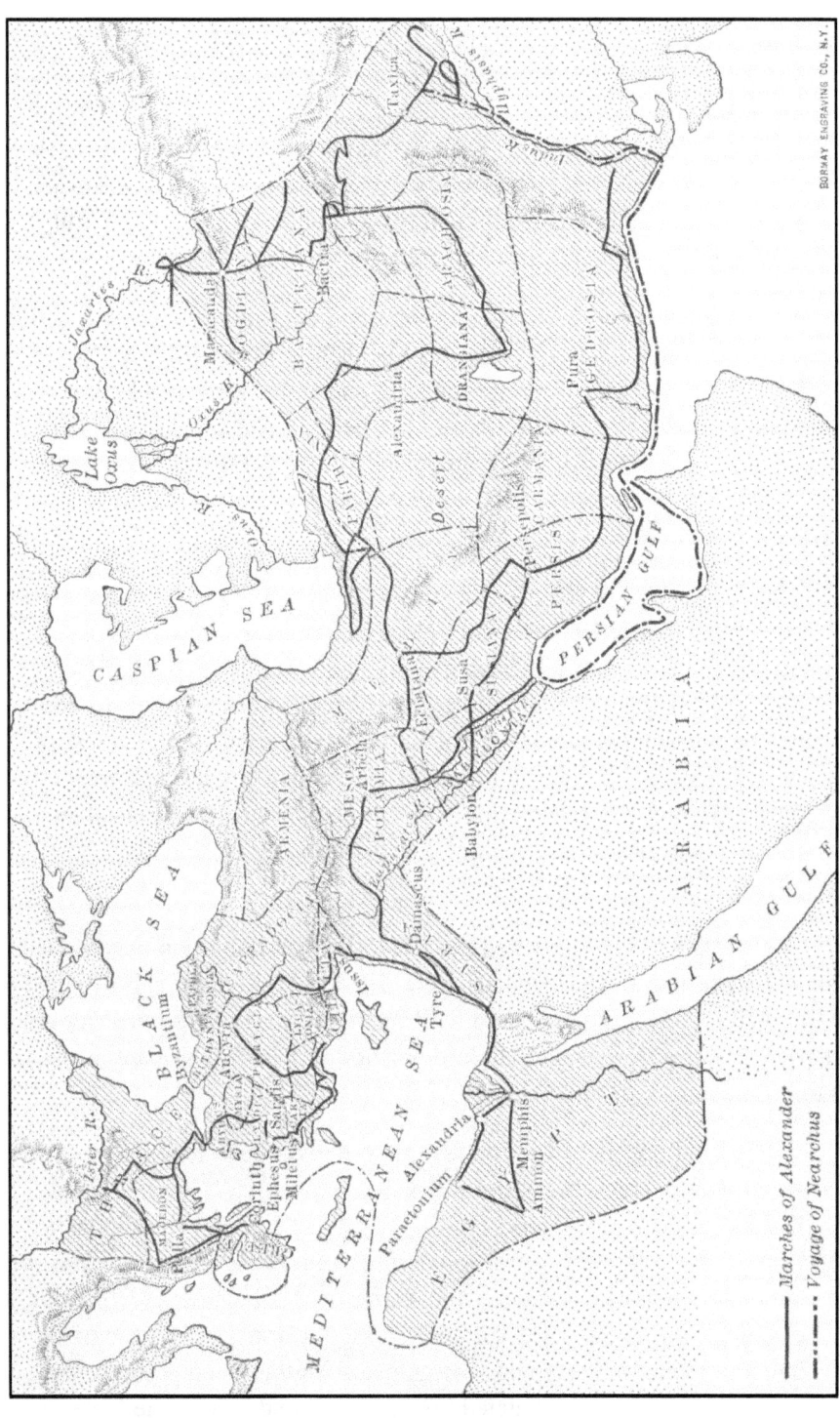

"In the official style of the Egyptian monarchy the Pharaohs were sons of Ammon, and as the successor of the Pharaohs Alexander assumed the same title. It was therefore necessary in order to regulate his position that an official assurance should be given by Ammon himself that Alexander was his son. To obtain this Alexander undertook a journey to the oracular sanctuary of Ammon in the oasis of Siwah. And this motive is alone sufficient to explain the expedition..." Bury, *A Student's History of Greece*, p. 329.

The following spring Alexander returned to Tyre and finished settling Syria by the appointment of a Macedonian satrap. In August he crossed the Euphrates and the Tigris rivers unopposed, and he camped with his army on a plain near Gaugamela, 56 miles west of Arbela. Darius prepared an immense army consisting of one million footmen and 40,000 horsemen, and on October 1, 331 B.C., the two armies met. Darius was again defeated and fled:

"The prodigious army of Darius was all either killed, taken, or dispersed at the battle of Arbela. No attempt to form a subsequent army ever succeeded; we read of nothing stronger than divisions or detachments. The miscellaneous contingents of this once mighty empire, such at least among them as survived, dispersed to their respective homes and could never be again mustered in mass. The defeat of Arbela was in fact the death-blow of the Persian empire. It converted Alexander into the Great King, and Darius into nothing better than a fugitive pretender." George Grote, *A History of Greece*, chap. 93, pars. 87, 88.

The wrath of Heaven visited the Medo-Persian dominion because it had cast off all restraint. The Persians were filled with gluttony and dissipation. Darius had lost all sense of that which constituted an army prepared for battle. Charles Rollin gives an incredible description of his effeminate army as it marched toward Issus and finishes by saying:

"Would not the reader believe, that he had been reading the description of a tournament, not the march of an army? Could he imagine that princes of the least reason would have been so stupid, as to incorporate with their forces so cumbersome a train of women, princesses, concubines, eunuchs, and domestics of both sexes? But the custom of the country was sufficient reason. Darius, at the head of six hundred thousand men, and surrounded with this mighty pomp, prepared for himself only, fancied he was great, and rose in the ideas he had formed of himself. Yet should we reduce him to his just proportion and his personal worth, how little would he appear!" *Ancient History: History Of Alexander*, book XV, sec. IV, par. 34.

The angel that God had sent to guide and protect the Persian monarchy had taken his flight that "the prince of Grecia" might come. Daniel 10:20. Alexander swept through the Persian Empire as if directed by an unseen hand, and a historian says of him: "I am persuaded that there was no nation, city, nor people then in being whither his name did not reach…there seems to me to have been some divine hand presiding both over his birth and actions." Arian, *Historical Library*, book 16, chap. 12. Alexander is truly the "mighty king" who was to "stand up" and "rule with great dominion, and do according to his will."

The Dividing of the Greek Empire

Daniel chapter two only typifies the Greek empire as the "belly and thighs of brass," it does not reveal its segmentation. The "leopard" beast of Daniel chapter seven had "four heads," a symbol of the four monarchs who fractured the Greek dominion after the death of Alexander. Daniel 7:6. (See Exodus 18:25; Psalm 110:6.) Daniel chapter eight reveals that when the Greek empire "was strong, the great horn," Alexander, "was broken; and for it came up four notable ones toward the four winds of heaven." "Now that being broken," says Gabriel, "four kingdoms shall stand up out of the nation, but not in his power." Daniel 8:8, 22. The vision by the Tigris also portrays the same events of the Greek empire, but with much greater detail:

> **"And when he shall stand up, his kingdom shall be broken, and shall be divided toward the four winds of heaven; and not to his posterity, nor according to his dominion which he ruled: for his kingdom shall be plucked up, even for others beside those."** *Daniel 11:4.*

On June 13, 323 B.C., at the age of 32, Alexander the Great died of a fever due to excessive alcoholic indulgence. He conquered the world, but he unfortunately could not conquer his own passions:

> "His sudden death was no freak of fate or fortune; it was a natural consequence of his character and his deeds. Into thirteen years he had compressed the energies of many lifetimes. Sparing of himself neither in battle nor at the feast, he was doomed to die young." *A Student's History of Greece*, pp. 362-363.

Upon his death Satrapies were assigned to the various generals with the idea of holding the empire together as one. War began in 321 when Perdiccas, general over the satrapies in Babylon, thought to make himself king. With this war commenced 20 years of non-stop fighting. In 310 Cassender murdered Alexander's "posterity," his son Alexander IV, and in 301 "his kingdom" was "broken" and "divided toward the four winds of heaven."

> "After the death of Antigonus, the four confederated princes divided his dominions between them; and hereby the whole empire of Alexander became parted, and settled into four kingdoms." Prideaux, *The Old and New Testament Connected in the History of the Jews*, Vol. 1, p. 415.

None of Alexander's successors ruled "according to his dominion which he ruled." Lysimachus became king over Thrace, and all Asia-Minor north of the Taurus except Pontus and Bithinia. Ptolemy controlled Egypt, Libya, Ethiopia, Ceole-Syria, Palestine, Phoenicia, and Arabia. Seleucus reigned over Syria, Babylon, and all the countries to the East as far as Bactria and Sogdiana. And lastly, Cassender was ruler of Macedonia and parts of Greece.

Even though four smaller kingdoms fragmented Alexander's empire, the wars continued for 24 more years before their dominions, in 277 B.C., assumed their final forms: "for his kingdom shall be plucked up, even for others beside those." The empire was finally settled into three distinct divisions: Macedonia under Antigonus, the Seleucid Empire ruled by Antiochus Soter, and the Ptolemaic governed by Ptolemy Philadelphus. Once established history proves that these three were destined to endure:

> "Frontiers might change, but the Antigonid, Seleucid, and Ptolemaic kingdoms remained until the coming of Rome." Botford and Robinson, *Hellenic History*, p. 385.

The next eight verses of the prophecy deal with two of these three major powers. To assume that there were only two empires in existence at this time would be a mistake. Only the Seleucid and the Ptolemaic powers are considered because of their close connection with the people of God. (See Daniel 10:14.) Verse 14 reintroduces the third power, Macedonia, into the prophecy, and it will be discussed at that time. Thus we can see that the vision that Daniel received by the Tigris River is a very accurate representation of the events of history. It should awe us to realize that Daniel obtained his account before the events occurred!

The Kings of the North and South

The king of the North and the king of the South occupy the rest of the prophecy. Scripture identifies Egypt as being in the South. (See Genesis 12:9-10; Daniel 11:7-8.) Verse eight reveals to us the importance of Egypt to the "king of the south." It was there that he carried captive the "gods" of the North. Whoever, therefore, governs the land of Egypt is the "king of the south." Likewise, the scripture refers to Babylon as being in the North. (See Jeremiah 25:9; Ezekiel 26:7; Zechariah 2:6-7.) We must therefore keep in mind that before any monarch could be termed "the king of the north" he must be in control of the land of Babylon. The titles of these kings reflect the positions they held geographically in relation to Jerusalem, for God said through the prophet Ezekiel that He set Jerusalem "in the midst of the nations." His purpose was that they witness to the heathen of His goodness, mercy, and love, but instead He declares: "she hath changed my judgments into wickedness more than the nations, and my statutes more than the countries that are round about her: for they have refused my judgments and my statutes, they have not walked in them." Consequently, the Lord laments: "Behold, I, even I, am against thee, and will execute judgments in the midst of thee in the sight of the nations." Ezekiel 5:5-8. As these two kingdoms made war they traversed through the land of Israel, as can be seen in the map on the next page, and the Jews were greatly oppressed by them. The vision by the Tigris River next describes the king's that ruled these two geographical areas:

> "And the king of the south shall be strong, and one of his princes; and he shall be strong above him, and have dominion; his dominion shall be a great dominion." *Daniel 11:5.*

Ptolemy, being the ruler of Egypt, was obviously "the king of the south." He is the king that was to "be strong." But Seleucus was "one of his princes," that is, one of Alexander's princes, and he was to "be strong above him, and have dominion; his dominion shall be a great dominion." The Seleucid Empire stretched from Thrace in Europe to the Indus River in the East, and its existence began with the reinstatement of Seleucus to the land of Babylon. It happened while Ptolemy was at war in Syria that Seleucus took the opportunity to gain the territory:

> "Seleucus, however, seized this moment to dash across the desert to Babylon and reinstate himself in his old satrapy. The Seleucids dated their Era from this event (October, 312 B.C.)." Botsford and Robinson, *Hellenic History*, p. 375.

Shortly after Seleucus took back the land of Babylon, "He founded, and built with great rapidity, the city of Seleucia upon the Tigris, at a distance of about forty miles from Babylon." George Rawlinson, *The Sixth Great Oriental Monarchy*, ch. 3, p. 35. This city became the capital of his empire and it lasted until Rome destroyed it.

The importance of the lands of Babylon and Egypt to the understanding of the prophecy cannot be over emphasized. These names are meant to be interchangeable with the two terms: the king of the North and the king of the South respectively. They are the link between the book of Revelation and Daniel's greatest vision. The great apostate system spoken of in the Revelation is called "Babylon," and must be considered when we come to the climax of this prophecy in verse 40.

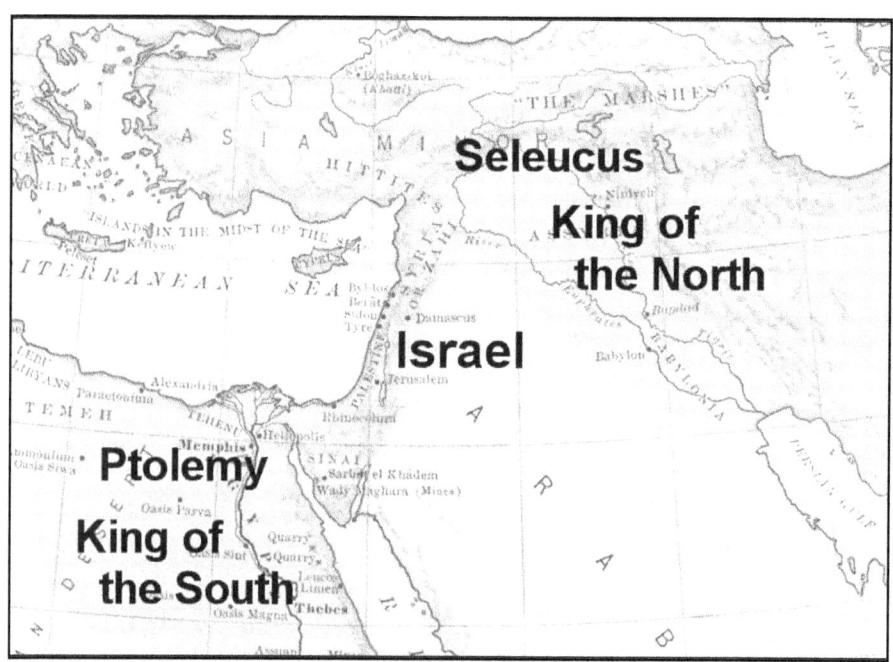

The Kings Attempt Peace through Marriage

Men will at times try desperate measures to achieve peace. One of these attempts that has always proved to be unsuccessful is the endeavor to make peace through the marriage contract. Solomon in all of his wisdom attempted it as the scripture says: "And Solomon made affinity with Pharaoh king of Egypt, and took Pharaoh's daughter..." 1 Kings 3:1. This he tried with many of the nations, but the attempt only brought about his downfall: "And he had seven hundred wives, princesses, and three hundred concubines: and his wives turned away his heart." 1 Kings 11:3-4. Such a thing is an abomination in the sight of a pure and holy God, and can only bring about ruin to those who try it. Nevertheless the prophecy tells us that this is what the kings of the North and South did:

> **"And in the end of years they shall join themselves together; for the king's daughter of the south shall come to the king of the north to make an agreement: but she shall not retain the power of the arm; neither shall he stand, nor his arm: but she shall be given up, and they that brought her, and he that begat her, and he that strengthened her in these times."** *Daniel 11:6.*

In 253 B.C. an "agreement" was made between Ptolemy Philadelphus and Antiochus Theos, the son of Antiochus Soter. Antiochus was to put away his wife Laodice and marry Berenice, Ptolemy's daughter. The son who was to be born to Antiochus was then to become king in the North. The following year Laodice was sent away into Asia Minor and the marriage was consummated with Berenice. The new heir was soon born. All was not well, however, for Antiochus made a visit to Laodice at Ephesus in 247 B.C. and announced his oldest son Seleucus as heir. Antiochus then unexpectedly died:

> "During his stay in this city the king suddenly fell ill and died, but not before he had declared Seleucus II, his eldest son by Laodice, as his successor." Cary, *A History of the Greek World 323-146 B.C.*, p. 87.

The events of the marriage and suspicious death of Antiochus, and the accession of Seleucus Callinicus to the throne in the North only brought strife. In 246 Laodice had Berenice, her infant son, and her attendants killed. Thus the prophecy was fulfilled that says: "but she," Berenice, "shall not retain the power of the arm; neither shall he," Antiochus, "stand, nor his arm: but she shall be given up," put to death, "and they that brought her," the Egyptians that came with Berenice, "and he whom she brought forth" (margin), Berenice's son, "and he that strengthened her in these times," the northern attendants supporting her. Thus the prophecy was fulfilled in every detail.

Ptolemy Euergetes Stands Up

With every action there is a reaction. In this case the death of Berenice stirred up great wrath from the kingdom of the South. The relatives of Berenice were provoked to war. Thus it caused the very thing that the marriage was intended to prevent:

> "But out of a branch of her roots shall one stand up in his estate, which shall come with an army, and shall enter into the fortress of the king of the north, and shall deal against them, and shall prevail: And shall also carry captives into Egypt their gods, with their princes, and with their precious vessels of silver and of gold; and he shall continue more years than the king of the north. So the king of the south shall come into his kingdom, and shall return into his own land." *Daniel 11:7-9.*

In 246 B.C., after Philadelphus died Ptolemy Euergetes came to the throne in the South. Ptolemy, "the branch of her roots," deciding to avenge his sister's death assembled "an army" and marched unopposed through the Seleucid dominion. He made it all the way to the land of Babylon and entered "into the fortress of the king of the north," Seleucia on the Tigris. That Ptolemy captured an array of treasures while in the land of Babylon is clear from the following quote:

> "In the taking of Babylon, Ptolemy secured about thirty million dollars in clear gold, untold quantities of gold and silver vessels; twenty-five hundred statues, among which were the gods which Cambyses of Persia had carried away when he had invaded Egypt. When Ptolemy had brought back these gods to their own land, the people of Egypt expressed their gratitude by bestowing upon him the title of Euergetes — Benefactor." Jones, *The Great Empires of Prophecy*, chap. XVIII, par. 25.

The last part of verse eight and all of verse nine are more correctly translated: "And for years he shall stand from the king of the North. And he shall come into the kingdom of the king of the South, and shall retreat into his own land." Seleucus was unready for Ptolemy's invasion and could offer no resistance. He therefore sought the aid of his brother, Antiochus Hierax, and in return declared him ruler of Asia Minor as an independent kingdom. Ptolemy, being satisfied with his conquest into Babylon, and fearful of fighting the two Seleucid brothers at once, ruled or stayed away "from the king of the North" the rest of his reign.

Seleucus crossed the Taurus Mountains in the spring of 244 B.C., and made war against the Egyptians. The Egyptian rule, in Babylon and northern Syria, crumbled as fast as it had arisen. He next attacked the Egyptians in southern Syria, but was defeated and forced to "retreat into his own land." Finally in 241 B.C. Seleucus and Ptolemy concluded a treaty. The old boundary in Syria, between Egypt and Babylon, was reestablished except for Seleucia in Pieria and the whole of Phoenicia, which fell to the lot of Ptolemy. In the war with Ptolemy, Seleucus lost, not only parts of Syria and all of Asia Minor north of the Taurus, but he also lost his far Eastern provinces that had rebelled: Bactria, Sogdiana, Hyrcania, and Parthia. Thus the kingdom of the North was restricted mainly to the land of Babylon.

Antiochus becomes King of the North

In 228 B.C. Attalus, king of Pergamum, overthrew Antiochus Hierax and became ruler over all of Asia Minor north of the Taurus Mountains. The Seleucid monarchy did not recover Asia Minor, the Far East, or southern Syria until later in the reign of Antiochus the Great (Magnus). However, the term "king of the north" refers to Antiochus during his entire reign. The next few verses cannot be reconciled to the reign of Antiochus the Great unless Babylon is understood as the land of "the king of the north" because he was limited to that region in the following passages of the prophecy.

> **"But his sons shall be stirred up, and shall assemble a multitude of great forces: and one shall certainly come, and overflow, and pass through: then shall he return, and be stirred up, even to his fortress."** Daniel 11:10.

The two "sons" of Seleucus Callinicus who were to be "stirred up" and "assemble a multitude of great forces" were Seleucus Ceraunus and Antiochus Magnus. Seleucus first took the throne in the North when his father died (226 B.C.). He assembled an army in an attempt to recover Phoenicia and Asia Minor. However, he was poisoned by his generals and died in the year 223. Achaeus, an able Seleucid general, took control, placed Antiochus Magnus upon the throne in Babylon, and went to make war with Attalus:

> "Achaeus drove his adversary Attalus back over the frontiers of his own principality, pressed hard upon him in his own capital, and, by a policy of mingled conciliation and coercion, prevailed upon the Greek cities of the western coast to submit to annexation. But, rendered presumptuous by success, he next attempted to set up an independent kingdom in Asia Minor, and thus again prevented the complete restoration of the Seleucid dominion." Williams, *Historians' History of the World*, p. 558.

Antiochus, knowing that Achaeus and his men would not attack him, assembled another "great" army and made war with the king of the South. He first attacked Seleucia in Pieria, which quickly fell into his hands. He then by force of arms took back all of Phoenicia, overthrew much of Palestine, and marched quickly toward Egypt. Here is the "one" who was to "certainly come, and overflow, and pass through." However, Antiochus made the mistake of believing a rumor started by Sosibius, the Prime Minister of Egypt, that the Egyptian army, which did not exist, was in full strength at Pelusium, and he agreed to a four-month truce. After Antiochus established garrisons to hold the country he decided to "return" to Seleucia on the Orontes, "his fortress," and for a time awaited negotiations for the full surrender of Palestine. During this interval Ptolemy Philopator, the son of Ptolemy Euergetes, prepared his army. Nothing was settled by the negotiations. Hence, in the spring of 218 B.C., Antiochus became "stirred up," recalled his army, and prepared for war.

The Battle of Raphia

The preparations for war on both sides culminated in one of the famous encounters of history. The battle of Raphia that followed is forcefully brought to our attention by the prophecy, and encompasses the next two verses. The reason for the focus of the prophecy upon this battle has evaded the minds of many Bible scholars, but shall become apparent as we proceed.

> **"And the king of the south shall be moved with choler, and shall come forth and fight with him, even with the king of the north: and he shall set forth a great multitude; but the multitude shall be given into his hand. And when he hath taken away the multitude, his heart shall be lifted up; and he shall cast down many ten thousands: but he shall not be strengthened by it."** *Daniel 11:11-12.*

Ptolemy Philopator, "the king of the south," was "moved with choler" at the losses that he had sustained to Antiochus, and assembled an army of 75,000 men and 73 elephants. Antiochus also assembled a "great multitude." He had 78,000 men and 102 elephants. Ptolemy came "forth" to "fight with him" on June 22, in the year 217 B.C., at Raphia. He slew 14,000 of Antiochus' soldiers in this battle, and he took 4,000 captives. The "multitude" of Antiochus' army was truly "given into his hand."

> "Humbled by this defeat, and alarmed at the progress of Achaeus in Asia Minor, Antiochus was anxious to make peace with Ptolemy; and the Egyptian king, although he had every inducement to prosecute the war, being equally anxious to return to his licentious pleasures, was ready to receive his overtures. A peace was in consequence con-

cluded, by which Coele-Syria and Palestine were confirmed as belonging to Egypt." *Historians' History of the World*, p 572.

Ptolemy, recovering all that he had lost to Antiochus, was "lifted up" by his success and held processions through the provinces he had reclaimed. During his march he entered Jerusalem, offered sacrifices, and tried to penetrate the Most Holy place of the Jewish sanctuary. Nevertheless, he met determined resistance and after this he began a hateful persecution against the Jewish nation. In 213 B.C. he "cast down" 40,000 of them in the city of Alexandria. Also, in his war with Antiochus, Ptolemy used native Egyptians in his army; it was the first time in nearly a century that they had fought for their own country. They had saved Egypt from Antiochus, what need had they then of Greek rule? Thus, after the war, many of his citizens, both Jews and Egyptians, rebelled against him and his kingdom was not "strengthened" by his victory.

Interestingly, it was not until after his war with Ptolemy that Antiochus marched upon Achaeus and recovered Asia Minor. The focus of the prophecy here on the battle of Raphia is to establish for us the exact identity of the king of the North. The scripture says that, "the king of the south," Ptolemy, "shall be moved with choler, and shall come forth and fight with him, even with the king of the north." The term "king of the north" can only fit Antiochus Magnus that controlled the land of Babylon. Therefore Babylon is again forcefully impressed upon us as the land where the king of the North reigns. No other kings or events even come close to fulfilling this passage. Let this point sink deep into the mind, for the end of the prophecy requires that we understand it clearly. Those that skip this part of the prophecy and begin their interpretation in verse 40 will undoubtedly fail to understand the vision, and will accept and teach some interpretation that has its foundation in speculation.

Rome Establishes the Vision

In the dream of the "great image" of Daniel chapter two the last earthly kingdom to come to power, represented by the "legs of iron," is Rome. Daniel 2:33, 40. In Daniel seven the "fourth beast, dreadful and terrible," which had "great iron teeth," also symbolizes Rome (Daniel 7:7, 23), and in chapter eight Rome is portrayed as a "little horn, which waxed exceeding great," and "came forth" from one of the "four winds of heaven." Daniel 8:8-9. All the prophecies of Daniel reveal the last earthly power as rising after Greece. Paul tells us that Rome is one of the powers "ordered by God" to rule the world.

Romans 13:1, margin. This ordering is done only in the book of Daniel. The first three powers were Babylon, Medo-Persia, and Greece as clearly described by Daniel. Paul then defines the last kingdom for us and history establishes the fact. The first three prophecies end with Rome, and as we shall see from this revelation before us, when Rome cast itself upon the scene of prophecy, it likewise established this vision by the Tigris River:

> **"For the king of the north shall return, and shall set forth a multitude greater than the former, and shall certainly come after certain years with a great army and with much riches. And in those times there shall many stand up against the king of the south: also the robbers of thy people shall exalt themselves to establish the vision; but they shall fall."** *Daniel 11:13-14.*

After his victory over Achaeus, Antiochus rushed off to the East and left Asia Minor in a broken state with some of the coastal regions controlled by Ptolemy. He spent the following years subduing and securing his eastern dominions, and returned with riches beyond measure. "After certain years," in the fall of 203 B.C., Antiochus, "the king of the north," gathered "a multitude greater than the former," and came "with a great army and with much riches" against the Egyptian dependencies along the coasts of Asia Minor. Egypt had deteriorated under it sluggish leader, and Antiochus set out to recover his lost territories.

> "One thing surely was possible: with the resources of Asia to his hand, he might recover from the Ptolemies the countries they had stolen from his ancestors." *The Cambridge Ancient History*, vol. 8, chap. VI, sec. I. par. 9.

Not long after Antiochus began his offensive Philopator died, and upon hearing the news Antiochus and Philip of Macedonia contracted an agreement to divide the young Ptolemy Epiphane's kingdom between them. In performing this transaction they fulfilled the words of our passage that says, "there shall many stand up against the king of the south." In the spring of 201 Antiochus resumed his assault upon Egypt by invading southern Syria and making it all the way to Gaza. Philip also stormed Samos, an Egyptian dependency, capturing it and many Egyptian vessels, but Philip's attack upon the independent cities and kingdoms of the Aegean brought another power to the prophetic seen: "In autumn 201 the Rhodians and Pergamenes…sent envoys to Rome to solicit the help of the Republic." Cary, *A History of the Greek World 323-146 B.C.*, p. 188. The Romans quickly responded to their request:

"During the Hannibalic War, Philip V. (III.) of Macedonia had aided the Carthaginians... He was now troubling the Greek cities which were under the protection of Rome. For these things the Roman Senate determined to punish him." Myers, *A General History*, p. 267.

At this time Rome enters the prophecy. "The robbers of thy people," or translated more correctly, "the young breakers of your people," refers to Rome. It is the same as the last kingdom revealed in Daniel's other three prophecies. "And the fourth kingdom shall be strong as iron: forasmuch as iron breaketh in pieces and subdueth all things: and as iron that breaketh all these, shall it break in pieces and bruise." Daniel 2:40. "After this I saw in the night visions, and behold a fourth beast, dreadful and terrible, and strong exceedingly; and it had great iron teeth: it devoured and brake in pieces, and stamped the residue with the feet of it." Daniel 7:7. "And out of one of them came forth a little horn, which waxed exceeding great, toward the south, and toward the east, and toward the pleasant land. And it waxed great, even to the host of heaven; and it cast down some of the host and of the stars to the ground, and stamped upon them." Daniel 8:9-10.

Here Rome is first introduced into this vision as a young devastating power thrusting itself upon the seen of prophecy. Macedonia is re-introduced into the prophecy at this time to direct us to Rome. In the late summer of 201 Rome declared war upon Philip, and the following October they sent two legions, about 25,000 men, to Illyria to oppose him. Philip did not present a threat to Rome and they had no reason to make war with him except that the senate willed it:

"To cripple, or at least to stay the growth of Philip's power was in the eyes of the senate a necessity; but it was only by representing a Macedonian invasion of Italy as imminent that they persuaded the assembly, which was longing for peace, to pass a declaration of war (200 B.C.), an ostensible pretext for which was found in the invasion by Macedonian troops of the territory of Rome's ally, Athens." Pelham, *Outlines of Roman History*, p. 142.

This statement clearly shows that Rome is the power that fulfills the prophecy. Our passage says that they "shall exalt themselves to establish the vision." The Roman leadership did indeed "exalt themselves." Yet, God did not leave His people without reassurance, for the prophecy says that: "they shall fall," briefly wrapping up Rome's existence.

Rome Overthrows Antiochus the Great

Antiochus was making much headway in his war with Egypt, but failed to come to the aid of his ally when Rome declared war against Philip. If he had, history may have been written much differently. Nevertheless, the prophecy declared that Rome would be the last great power in history, and would last until the end of time. Rome is introduced into the prophecy in verse 14, but the narration continues in the next verse with the final conflict between Antiochus the Great and the armies of the king of the South. The prophecy then centers upon the events of the establishment of Rome as it attacks the king of the North and its assault upon the Jewish people in Palestine:

> **"So the king of the north shall come, and cast up a mount, and take the most fenced cities: and the arms of the south shall not withstand, neither his chosen people, neither shall there be any strength to withstand. But he that cometh against him shall do according to his own will, and none shall stand before him: and he shall stand in the glorious land, which by his hand shall be consumed."** *Daniel 11:15-16.*

Egypt sent Scopas and an army of Aetolian mercenaries in retaliation against Antiochus. After making it as far north as the sources of the Jordan River, Scopas suffered a defeat at Panion and fled with a remainder of 10,000 men to Sidon, "the most fenced cities" (Hebrew — "a fortified city"). In the summer of 200, Antiochus "cast up a mount" and began a siege by land and by sea. The following spring Antiochus defeated an Egyptian army sent to assist Scopas at Sidon, and after a siege of nearly nine months starved Scopas and his men into surrender and took the city. So "the arms of the south," the Egyptian army, could "not withstand, neither his chosen people," Scopas and his Aetolians mercenaries. Antiochus then retook Jerusalem, all of Palestine as far as the Sinai desert, and was ready to invade Egypt by 198. The armies of the king of the South, as the scripture says, had no "strength to withstand." Ptolemies' "…empire had collapsed under the blows of the Syrian king." *The Cambridge Ancient History, vol. 8*, chap. VI, sec. IX, par. 6.

> "Antiochus III. of Syria, Philip's accomplice in the proposed partition of the dominions of their common rival, Egypt, returned from the conquest of Coele-Syria (198 B.C.) to learn first of all that Philip was hard pressed by the Romans, and shortly afterwards that he had been decisively beaten at Cynoscephalae. It was already too late to assist his former ally, but Antiochus resolved at any rate to lose no time in secur-

ing for himself the possessions of the Ptolemies in Asia Minor and in eastern Thrace, which Philip had claimed, and which Rome now pronounced free and independent." Pelham, *Outlines of Roman History*, pp. 145-146.

The Romans saw this movement by Antiochus as the first step of an assault calculated to force them from Greece. After negotiations failed with the Romans, in 193 B.C., Antiochus became irritated by their obstinacy, stirred up by Greek overtures to deliver them from the hand of Roman oppression, and prepared for war if Rome demanded it. In the autumn of 192 Antiochus entered Greece, but the following February the Romans, in a single battle at Thermopylae, expelled him. In September 190 Antiochus lost 42 ships, between Myonnesus and Corycus, in a decisive naval battle to Rome. The following January the two armies met at Magnesia, and Antiochus lost 50,000 men! Thus God, through Rome, abased the pride of the king of the North as the scripture forecast: "he that cometh against him, shall do according to his own will, and none shall stand before him."

> "With the day of Magnesia Asia was erased from the list of great States; and never perhaps did a great power fall so rapidly, so thoroughly, and so ignominiously as the kingdom of the Seleucidae under this Antiochus the Great... it alone, of all the great States conquered by Rome, never after the first conquest desired a second appeal to the decision of arms." Theodor Mommsen, *History of Rome*, p. 272, 274.

First Philip of Macedonia and then Antiochus, "the king of the north," could not stand before the Romans. Moreover, during the second century B.C., the Seleucid Empire became broken into a number of local kingdoms; among them was the Hasmonaean dynasty, a Jewish State. Under Jannaeus, who reigned from 103 to 76 B.C., the empire expanded until it nearly corresponded with the kingdom of David. In 63 B.C. Pompey made war against Aristobulus, entered Jerusalem, and laid siege to the Temple hill where his followers were holding out. Pompey overthrew the Jews after a siege of three months, and the Hasmonaean kingdom collapsed:

> "This was the end of the Hasmonaean kingdom. King Aristobulus was carried off to Rome, to walk in Pompey's triumph. Thousands of other Jews were sent to slavery in the West. In Palestine the kingdom was broken up..." *The Cambridge Ancient History*, vol. 9, chap. IX, sec. I, par. 11.

This is the obvious fulfillment of the prophecy under consideration: "and he shall stand in the glorious land, which by his hand shall be consumed." The Hebrew word here translated "consumed" means to "end" or to "finish." The Jews had enjoyed a brief period of freedom after the king of the North was overthrown until Rome entered their land and forced them to submit as well.

Rome and the King of the North

In the beginning of Roman history, "For nearly two and a half centuries after the founding of Rome (from 753 to 509 B.C., according to tradition), the government was a monarchy." Myers, *A General History*, p. 225. Rome, however, was destined to become a great republic: "Upon the overthrow of the monarchy, the Romans set up a republican form of government..." Boak and Sinnigen, *A History of Rome to A.D. 565*, p. 43. The Roman Republic was a government of the people, by the people, and for the people. It was Rome during the Republic that overthrew Philip and Antiochus and then consumed the Jewish State that was under the leadership of Aristobulus.

Rome eventually acquired Syria after the defeat of Antiochus. Nevertheless, Rome never obtained control of the land of Babylon. It was absorbed by Parthia, and "the king of the north" passed off the seen of prophecy at that time until verse 40. (Some modern Bibles add the phrase "the king of the north" into the text of the prophecy between verses 16 and 40, but the phrase is not in the original language. The NIV does this in verse 28, but this is incorrect.) The pagan Roman Empire is not, and never has been, the king of the North because it never controlled the land of Babylon. Consider the clear and obvious statement made by a historian on this subject:

> "One thinks of the Roman Empire as including the whole ancient civilized world, except distant China and India. But it should be remembered that, if the Romans had spread Greek culture to Western lands like Gaul and Britain, they had lost a large part of the empire of Alexander the Great, and that their frontier went no farther east than the Euphrates River and the Arabian Desert. They were unable to conquer and hold the Tigris-Euphrates Valley, once the most civilized and influential region on earth. Here they were successfully opposed, first, by the Parthian, and then, after 227 A.D., by the Persian Kingdom." Thorndike, *The History of Medieval Europe*, p. 40.

Thus it is clear that although Rome overthrew Antiochus the Great it does not become the king of the North. It is the king over the land of Babylon that comes back into focus at the end of time. Therefore we must yet develop other principles before we can correctly interpret who the king of the North is at the end of the prophecy. Many have made the mistake of believing that Rome is the king of the North at the end of the prophecy because the Romans overthrew Antiochus, but this is not true since Rome never ruled the land of Babylon.

Summary of Chapter Two

It is obvious to anyone that the prophecy points to the most well known events and greatest leaders of human history. Daniel was living in the days of king Cyrus the Great of Persia when he received this prophecy. It quickly transitions to Alexander the Great and the rise of the Greek Empire, and then to Alexander's successors. The focus of the prophecy then centers upon the two divisions of the Greek Empire, the kings of the North and South, which were in conflict over the territory around Palistine. The prophecy next places the spotlight on Antiochus the Great and his battles with the Ptolemies in Egypt, particularly the battle of Raphia. The reason for the focus upon Antiochus during this time is to establish for us the exact territory of the king of the North — Babylon. Thus Babylon is inseparably connected with the king of the North and is the focus in the last great conflict discussed in verse 40.

The establishment of the great pagan Roman Empire in its republican form commences in verse 14, and Rome is the last earthly power mentioned in the book of Daniel. Therefore it must be understood that the rest of the prophecy has much to do with Rome and its connection with the people of God. This must be considered, and will be obvious as the narration of the prophecy continues. Nevertheless, pagan Rome is never termed the king of the North because it never controlled the land of Babylon. However, the king of the South is included in the prophecy in the intervening verses, and will be discussed when the passages are considered.

Chapter 3: Rome and the Prince

In this chapter we will witness the transformation of Rome from a republic into a principate. This development in Rome came through greed, human passion and civil war. The Principate was the established form of government that controlled Rome when Jesus, the "prince of the covenant," was born.

Julius Caesar Asserts his Authority

As the Roman people grew in power and expanded across the world they began to live for pleasure and luxury. The war with Antiochus brought wealth as well as depravity into Rome:

> "It is from this victory over Antiochus, and the conquest of Asia, that Pliny dates the depravity and corruption of manners in the republic of Rome, and the fatal changes which ensued it. Asia, vanquished by the Roman arms, afterwards vanquished Rome by its vices. Foreign wealth extinguished in that city a love for the ancient poverty and simplicity, in which its strength and honor consisted. Luxury, that in a manner entered Rome in triumph with the superb spoils of Asia, brought with her, in her train, irregularities and crimes of every kind, made greater havoc in the city than the mightiest armies could have done, and in that manner avenged the conquered globe." Rollin, *Ancient History: History Of Alexander's Successors*, chap. 5, sec. VII, par. 58.

As wealth and luxury increased in Rome there came "irregularities and crimes of every kind," and the Roman people lost all ability to rule themselves. In 60 B.C., Pompey, Julius Caesar, and Crassus formed the "First Trimvirate," a triple dictatorship. Nevertheless, the Parthians killed Crassus in 53 B.C., and the Triumvirate was dissolved. The Senate won Pompey to themselves, and together they plotted the destruction of Caesar. In March, 49 B.C., when Julius Caesar, who had become a powerful general in Gaul, marched his army into Italy many of the Senators fled to Pompey in Epirus. (See the map of Rome on page 65.) When this civil war broke out, Pompey lost the famous battle of Pharsalus on August 9, 48 B.C., and then fled to Egypt where Ptolemy murdered him.

"The death of Crassus and the battle of Pharsalia left Caesar the master of the world." Draper, *History of the Intellectual Development of Europe*, vol. 1, chap. 8, part. 1, par. 18.

With Pompey's death, September 28, 48 B.C., Caesar became master of the Roman Empire, and his experience in Egypt is next discussed by the vision by the Tigris River:

"He shall also set his face to enter with the strength of his whole kingdom, and upright ones with him; thus shall he do: and he shall give him the daughter of women, corrupting her: but she shall not stand on his side, neither be for him." Daniel 11:17.

The Hebrew word translated "strength" in this verse is also translated "authority" (Esther 9:29) and "power" (Esther 10:2). In these two references the word obviously means the political power or authority of Mordecai the Jew, and not his military might. So here too, the word is clearly talking about the political authority of a Roman ruler bringing "equal conditions." Daniel 11:17, margin. Thus when Caesar, who was following Pompey, landed in Egypt his "authority" as consul of Rome, "his whole kingdom," was quickly asserted:

"To make it quite clear that he [Caesar] was not coming to Alexandria in his military capacity but as the government representative of the Republic to negotiate in the name of Rome solely with regard to an affair of state, he assumed the insignia of his consular office and stepped ashore preceded by his fasces." Waltar, *Caesar a Biography*, p. 418.

Because of strife between Ptolemy and his sister Cleopatra, who were setup as joint rulers in Egypt, Caesar stated his intentions, as consul of the Republic, to decide the fate of the Egyptian throne. He ordered them to disband their armies and appear before him.

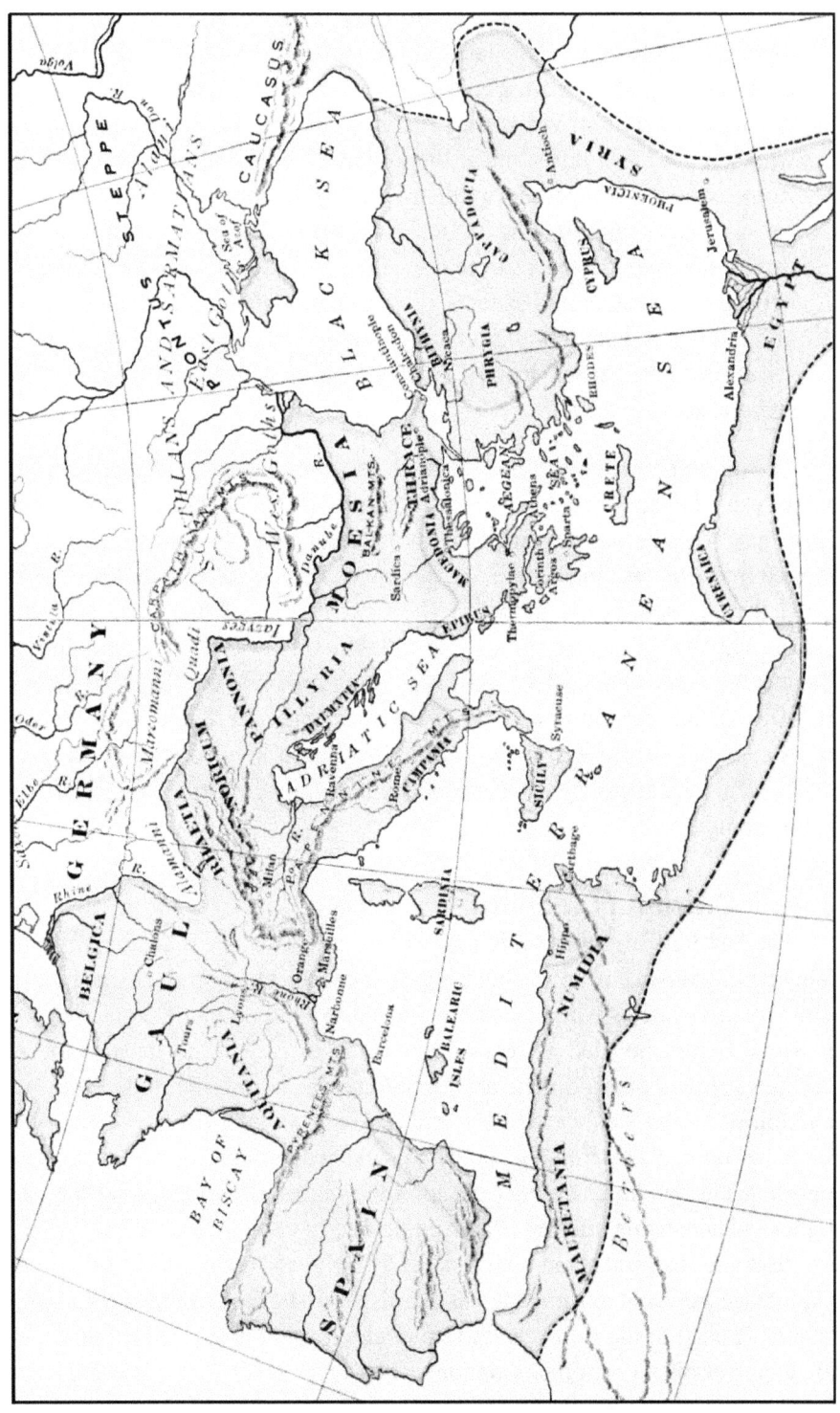

"This order was looked upon in Egypt as a violation of the royal dignity, which being independent, acknowledged no superior, and could be judged by no tribunal. Caesar replied to these complaints, that he acted only in virtue of being arbitrator by the will of Auletes, who had put his children under the tuition of the senate and people of Rome, whose whole authority then vested in his person, in quality of consul; that as guardian, he had a right to arbitrate between them; and that all he pretended to, as executor of the will, was to establish peace between the brother and sister. This explanation having facilitated the affair, it was at length brought before Caesar, and advocates were chosen to plead the cause." Rollin, *Ancient History: The History of Egypt*, chap. 1, sec. 2, par. 11.

The quote above clearly reveals the meaning of the passage of scripture before us: "He shall also set his face to enter with the authority of his whole kingdom." This passage clearly refers to Caesar when he entered Egypt. He entered by virtue of "the senate and people of Rome, whose whole authority [was] then vested in his person." The next phrase of the verse says that Caesar had "equal conditions with him," which is also clearly explained in the quote. Caesar being setup as the guardian of the two children "by the will of Auletes…had a right to arbitrate between them; and that all he pretended to, as executor of the will, was to establish peace between the brother and sister." Thus the accuracy of the prophecy is readily confirmed by the history of the events!

Caesar Corrupts Cleopatra

The last half of verse 17 is now before us: "And he shall give him the daughter of women corrupting her." It was Caesar that had originally negotiated with Ptolemy Auletes who placed his son and daughter under the guardianship of Rome before he died. When Caesar came to Egypt and called Ptolemy and Cleopatra to disband their armies and appear before him, Cleopatra was determined to get her way. She found a friend to take her to Caesar, who rolled her up in a carpet like a bundle, and carried her into his presence. Upon unrolling the bundle Caesar gazed upon the young Cleopatra, and that very night she became his mistress, "corrupting her."

"But she shall not stand on his side." The phrase "on his side" is not in the original Hebrew and has no place in our discussion of the prophecy. The word "stand" is used in many places in Daniel eleven, and is applied to those who rise to power over a nation or kingdom. (See verses 2-4, 6-7, 14-16, 20-21, 25.)

To what kingdom does the prophecy refer when it says, "she shall not stand?" History proves that she did gain control of Egypt, but Rome is the kingdom to which the prophecy is now speaking. Cleopatra obviously intended to gain control of the entire Roman world through Caesar.

> "The keynote of her [Cleopatra's] character was not sex, but ambition... Alone of Alexander's successors she became a legend: she was the daughter of Re, as he was the son of Ammon, and like him she dreamt of becoming a world ruler." Fuller, *Julius Caesar: Man, Soldier, and Tyrant*, p. 245.

Cleopatra had an incorrigible lust for power. Her affair with Caesar resulted in the birth of his son. She quickly took advantage of this situation in which she found herself, for Caesar's legitimate wife was childless. When he later returned to Rome Cleopatra followed him there, and sought to become legally recognized as his wife. This would guarantee that her dreams would be fulfilled. Consider the following:

> "She [Cleopatra] had believed that her marriage to Caesar had been imminent and she had never for a moment doubted that she would presently be seated at his side on the throne of an Egypto-Roman kingdom whose bounds would be the ends of the earth." Weigall, The *Life and Times of Marc Antony*, p. 230.

Knowing his age and her own she was certain to ascend to power when he died: "At his death...she would have the world at her feet." Waltar, *Caesar: a Biography*, p. 524. The fact that Cleopatra intended to control the entire Roman world, as well as Egypt, is clear. However, she never married Caesar because he was murdered before it could take place. And after his death we read:

> "When Caesar was assassinated, she was still at Rome, and had some wild hopes of having her son recognized by the Caesareans. But failing in this she escaped secretly, and sailed to Egypt..." Mahaffy, *Cleopata's Conquest of Caesar and Antony*, part. 1, B.C. 52-30, par. 12.

The fact that Cleopatra tried to have her son recognized as Caesar's legitimate heir indicates how deeply her desire was for world power. Nevertheless, it is clear that Cleopatra did not "stand." Moreover, the last phase of the verse "neither be for him" reveals the true purpose of Cleopatra's affair with Caesar — she was solely living to fulfill her selfish ambition. The

Word of God obviously brings out the motives as well as the actions of the participants involved in the prophecy.

Caesar Takes the Isles

Not all things were easy for Caesar in Egypt as his affair with Cleopatra might suggest. Those in sympathy with Ptolemy were plotting his destruction, and the next verse reveals his further struggles in Egypt and along the coasts of the Mediterranean Sea:

> **"After this shall he turn his face unto the isles, and shall take many: but a prince for his own behalf shall cause the reproach offered by him to cease; without his own reproach he shall cause it to turn upon him."** Daniel 11:18.

Caesar's first war was in Egypt against Ptolemy. He ruined any chance of reconciliation between Ptolemy and Cleopatra when he entered into an affair with her. Ptolemy became infuriated when he found that Cleopatra was with him in his apartment. The war that followed taxed Caesar to the uttermost of his abilities, and reinforcements from the neighboring countries came to his aid. A number of small battles were fought near the Delta, and the allied armies friendly to Caesar were victorious. Ptolemy, in attempting to escape in a boat, was drowned in the Nile River, after which Alexandria and all Egypt then submitted to Caesar.

To appease the Egyptians Caesar had Cleopatra married to her other younger brother, Ptolemy XIII. (She later murdered him.) They were both then to rule jointly on the throne in Egypt. He also substituted a Roman garrison and a legion from Syria for the former royal army and appointed one of his soldiers to command them. All things were completed in Egypt by the end of January 47 B.C., but Caesar did not then leave. He spent whole nights in feasting with Cleopatra and remained in Egypt until she brought forth to him a son called Caesarian.

It was the end of June 47 B.C. before Caesar left Egypt. He first stopped at Ptolemais, had a meeting with the Jew Hyrcanus and his counselor Antipater, and bestowed special privileges upon them for the help he received in Egypt. Next Caesar went to Tyre, imposed a large war contribution upon it, and took all the money from the temple of Hercules because they had harbored Pompey during his flight. He then continued to stop at all the maritime towns he passed on his way, and collected considerable sums of money from them. Finally, Caesar embarked upon his famous battle against Pharnaces:

> "Caesar immediately marched against him with three legions, fought him near Zela, drove him out of Pontus, and totally defeated his army. When he gave Amantius, a friend of his at Rome, an account of this action, to express the promptness and rapidity of it, he used three words, I came, saw and conquered, which in Latin having all the same cadence, carry with them a very suitable brevity." Plutarch, *Lives: Caesar*, part 3, par. 17.

Caesar reached Rome in late September 47 B.C., and attended to the problems that had been developing there while he was absent and of which we shall yet speak. He next left for the coast of Africa early the following year where his enemies were making headway against him. The African campaign ended in April 46 B.C. with the successful battle of Thapsus. In November he found himself in southern Spain to subdue the opposing forces that had found refuge there after Pharsalus. The last of his victories was then won at Munda, on March 17, 45 B.C. Thus history clearly confirms that Caesar did "turn his face unto the isles," and took "many."

Antony Speaks on Caesar's Behalf

Verse 18 describes two simultaneous events. The first half clearly revealed the wars that Caesar fought along the coasts of the Mediterranean Sea. The last part of the verse is now before us, and helps give support to the accuracy of the vision that Daniel received: "But a prince for his own behalf shall cause the reproach offered by him to cease; without his own reproach he shall cause it to turn upon him." About the time that Caesar landed in Egypt, October 48 B.C., Antony arrived in Rome with the legions that he was placed in charged of after Pharsalus. Antony was the "prince" who was sent to Rome to speak on Caesar's "own behalf." (The word prince in the original language "is a military term. It signifies the man responsible for recruiting, an administrator in the army. It appears to denote the one at the head of an army, or people." *Theological Wordbook of the Old Testament*, No. 2054a.) Consider the extent to which Antony served under Caesar:

> "There was not one of the many engagements that now took place one after another in which he [Antony] did not signalize himself; twice he stopped the army in its full flight, led them back to a charge, and gained the victory. So that not without reason his reputation, next to Caesar's, was greatest in the army. And what opinion Caesar himself had of him well appeared when for the final battle in Pharsalia, which was to determine every thing, he himself chose to lead the right wing,

committing the charge of the left to Antony, as to the best officer of all that served under him. After the battle, Caesar, being created dictator, went in pursuit of Pompey, and sent Antony to Rome, with the character of Master of the Horse, who is in office and power next to the dictator, when present, and in his absence is the first, and pretty nearly indeed the sole magistrate. For on the appointment of a dictator, with the one exception of the tribunes, all other magistrates cease to exercise any authority in Rome." Plutarch, *Lives: Antony*, part I, par. 8.

Caesar's victory at Pharsalus and Antony's arrival in Rome caused "the reproach" which was being cast upon Caesar by the Roman Senate "to cease." The senate had refused to allow Caesar to run for offices while he was absent from Rome, for they hated him and his policies. However, with Antony's arrival they became his greatest supporters and named him dictator for a whole year:

"Finding that Pompey was dead, and that all hope of support from him was gone, Caesar's enemies in Rome became his most servile flatterers. Those who had plunged the State into civil war rather than allow him while absent to be even a candidate for the consulship, now in his absence made him dictator for a whole year, and were ready to heap upon him other preferences without limit." Jones, *The Two Republics*, p. 63.

While Caesar was in Egypt and settling affairs in the East Antony had full sway in Rome, and he proved himself less capable of running an empire then commanding an army. When Caesar returned to Rome in the autumn of 47 B.C., he found the political affairs of the state in crisis proportions, and his legions ready to mutiny because they had not been paid and discharged.

"Antony, though officially a good servant, had subjected himself to grave reproach for many breaches of decorum, legal, social and political, and there was widespread discontent." Dodge, *Great Captains: Caesar*, Vol II, p. 616.

The widespread discontent gave Caesar the opportunity to make a scapegoat out of Antony, and Caesar permitted the rabble to disgrace him without mercy. He caused the "reproach" to "turn upon" Antony, and deposed him of his position for a time. When Caesar finally finished his battles in Spain Antony was again by his side, and Caesar could then rest from war.

The Murder of Julius Caesar

Things had gone well for Caesar since his battle at Pharsalus. He had triumphed over Pompey, enjoyed an affair with Cleopatra who gave birth to his son, overthrew Ptolemy, crushed Pharnaces, suppressed the mutiny of his troops, stomped out the rebellion in Africa, brought farther Spain into submission, and received honor after honor from the senate in his absence:

> "All this time the Senate was heaping upon him titles and honors in the same extravagant profusion as before. One decree made him the father of his country; another liberator; another made him imperator, and commander-in-chief of the army for life with the title to be hereditary in his family. They gave him full charge of the treasury; they made him consul for ten years, and dictator for life. A triumphal robe and a crown of laurel were bestowed on him, with authority to wear them upon all occasions. A figure of his head was impressed upon the coin. His birthday was declared to be a holiday forever; and the name of the month, Quinctilius, was changed to Julius, and is still our July. Next his person was declared sacred, and any disrespect to him in word or action was made to be sacrilege. It was decreed that the oath of allegiance should be sworn by the Fortune of Caesar. The Senate itself took this oath, and by it swore sacredly to maintain his acts, and watch over the safety of his person. To complete the scale, they declared that he was no more Caius Julius, a man, but Divus Julius, a god; and that a temple should be built for the worship of him, and Antony should be the first priest." *The Two Republics*, pp. 66-67.

Nevertheless, in the midst of all his victories and the profusion of flattery being heaped upon Caesar, the members of the senate were secretly conspiring to murder him, and to this the prophecy next turns:

"Then he shall turn his face toward the fort of his own land: but he shall stumble and fall, and not be found." *Daniel 11:19.*

Upon his return to Rome, "the fort of his own land," Caesar began to make reforms to the government and war preparations for his expedition to Parthia. However, 60 members of the Senate were planning the assassination on March 15, 44 B.C. The conspirators had chosen the use of daggers as their instruments of execution, which they could easily hide under their garments. One of the conspirators, Trebonius, was to occupy Antony who generally accompanied Caesar wherever he went. Tillius Cimber, whose brother had been banished, was to approach Caesar and appear to be soliciting pardon for his brother's exile. This man was to give the signal for the assassination by pulling on Caesar's garment and baring his shoulder. The first blow was to go to the tribune Casca after which the rest were to rush upon him. The senate was powerless to implement their desires while Caesar lived, and they hated his power and control over them:

> "His [Caesar's] dazzling successes, and still more the avowed, though humane, absolution of his government, were intolerable to the Roman nobles, who could see in his rule only degradation of their order, and in the ruler nothing but a tyrant of the Greek type." Pelham, *Outlines of Roman History*, pp. 344-345.

When the Ides of March had finally arrived Caesar's legitimate wife, Calpurnia, awoke in a frantic terror because of a dream. She dreamed that Caesar was assassinated! Calpurnia pleaded with Caesar not to go to the senate that day, but when Brutus arrived he persuaded Caesar to go. Upon reaching the senate Spurinna, the diviner, warned Caesar of danger, but Caesar shrugged it off as superstitious. After entering the building Tillius performed his duty. At the right moment he gave a forceful tug on Caesar's garment and Casca lunged at him with his dagger, which only grazed his shoulder. Caesar turned in horror and shouted "Vile Casca, what does this mean?" At this the remainder of the conspirators enclosed Caesar and with their bare daggers in their hands they thrust at him. Caesar received 23 wounds from them and died at the foot of Pompey's statue. The scripture is clearly fulfilled when it says that "he," Caesar, "shall stumble and fall, and not be found" — he was murdered.

Augustus Caesar Stands Up

After Caesar died Antony determined to take his position. However, a serious check was soon put upon his ambitions. Octavius, the grandson of one of Caesar's sisters, was left as heir and adopted son according to Caesar's will. Caius Octavius, a young and ambitious man of only nineteen years of age came forward as soon as he learned of Caesar's death. In November of 43 B.C. Octavian, Antony, and Lepidus formed a triple dictatorship, and divided the Roman Empire between them. Lepidus soon lost power and resigned from his office of Triumvir, which left Octavius and Antony as joint rulers. Antony controlled the East and Octavius reigned in the West. Cleopatra's plan to rule the world had become revived with her marriage to Antony, and she immediately sought to influence his decisions. However, it was not possible that her desire could ever be fulfilled, for the prophecy tells us that there would be one to take Caesar's place that would institute taxes upon the world:

"Then shall stand up in his estate a raiser of taxes in the glory of the kingdom: but within few days he shall be destroyed, neither in anger, nor in battle." Daniel 11:20.

In November of 33 B.C., with the return of Antony's army from Armenia, and being compelled by Cleopatra, he decided upon war with Octavian and began his preparations. They assembled 500 warships with as many as 150,000 sailors. Their land forces numbered 70,000 footmen and 12,000 horsemen. In the fall of 32 B.C., Octavian, sensing the inevitable, declared war upon Antony. He than assembled a navy of 400 warships and a land force of 80,000 footmen and 12,000 horsemen. Octavian attacked Antony and Cleopatra at Actium in the early spring of 31 B.C., but before any battles were fought the eastern army deserted to Octavian. As a last resort they engaged their navy, but many of their ships forsook them in the battle. Cleopatra hastily lifted sail and headed to Egypt with lovesick Antony close to follow.

When Octavian attacked Egypt, Antony, not being with Cleopatra, heard a rumor that she was dead, and not wanting to live without her he stabbed himself. When he found that she was still alive, he was taken to her, where he died in her arms. Cleopatra and her treasure were captured and taken by Octavian to Rome were Cleopatra also committed suicide.

> "At this moment nothing could have prevented the inevitable result. The dagger of Brutus merely removed a man, but it left the fact. The battle of Actium reaffirmed the destiny of Rome, and the death of the republic was illustrated by the annexation of Egypt. The circle of conquest around the Mediterranean was complete; the function of the republic was discharged: it did not pass away prematurely." Draper, *History of the Intellectual Development of Europe*, vol. 1, chap. 8, part. 1, par. 18.

With the overthrow of Egypt by Octavian, also known as Caesar Augustus, the destiny of the Republic was forever decided. In 27 B.C. Augustus set up a new form of government, and the title that he took reflected his high position. Princeps was a term previously used to designate the leader of the Senate under the Roman Republic, but Augustus used the term to refer to himself as the single or highest leader of the Empire. The Roman word princeps later gave rise to the English word "prince" in medieval Europe. Nevertheless, we now use the term Principate to refer to the new system of government that Augustus set up:

> "From the word princeps arose the term principate to designate the tenure of office of the princeps, a term which we now apply also to

the system of government that Augustus established for the empire." Boak and Sinnigen, *A History of Rome to A.D. 565*, p. 272.

Thus Augustus established a new system of government for Rome. He is also the one who, just prior to the birth of Christ, decreed, "that all the world should be taxed." Luke 2:1. It was this decree that brought Joseph and his pregnant wife, Mary, to Bethlehem were Jesus was born. Rome was at the height of its "glory" during the reign of Augustus, and his rule is often termed "the Golden Age." It can easily be seen, then, that Augustus was the one that was to "stand up in his [Julius Caesar's] estate a raiser of taxes in the glory of the kingdom."

"But within few days he shall be destroyed, neither in anger, nor in battle." The time period mentioned here is an indefinite but short length of time. (See principle number 10 in appendix A.) Although the reign of Caesar Augustus is considered to be a long one in man's terms, it is but a few days to the God of heaven: for "one day is with the Lord as a thousand years, and a thousand years as one day." 2 Peter 3:8. Caesar Augustus died on August 19, A.D. 14, at the age of 76 in a time of peace.

Tiberius Caesar Stands Up

Before Augustus died, with much hesitation, he elected Tiberius to succeed him on his throne. But, for Tiberius to accept the throne immediately upon the death of Augustus signaled great danger for him, for there were many who did not like him and many candidates for the imperial throne. The prophecy at this point gives the most accurate description of Tiberius:

> **"And in his estate shall stand up a vile person, to whom they shall not give the honour of the kingdom: but he shall come in peaceably, and obtain the kingdom by flatteries. And with the arms of a flood shall they be overflown from before him, and shall be broken; yea, also the prince of the covenant."** Daniel 11:21-22.

After the death of Caesar Augustus, Tiberius immediately assumed the imperial authority, but he refused to accept the title at first. However, after long pleading and flatteries from the senate and people he finally conceded:

> "Though he made no scruple to assume and exercise immediately the imperial authority, by giving orders that he should be attended by the guards, who were the security and badge of the supreme power; yet he affected by a most impudent piece of acting to refuse it for a long time; one while sharply reprehending his friends who entreated

him to accept it, as little knowing what a monster the government was; another while keeping in suspense the senate when they implored him and threw themselves at his feet, by ambiguous answers and a crafty kind of dissimulation; in so much that some were out of patience, and one cried out, during the confusion, 'Either let him accept it or decline it at once;' and a second told him to his face: 'Others are slow to perform what they promise, but you are slow to promise what you actually perform.' At last as if forced to it, and complaining of the miserable and burdensome service imposed upon him, he accepted the government." Suetonius, *Lives of the Caesars: Tiberius*, chap. xxiv.

Thus Tiberius was not given "the honour of the kingdom," but he came in "peaceably," and obtained the kingdom by "flatteries." Hence, Tiberius became the next Caesar of prophecy on September 17, A.D. 14. (Some date the beginning of the reign of Tiberius on August 19 when Augustus died. Nevertheless, the first year of Tiberius was short; only lasting until the New Year began sometime in October.)

That Tiberius was "a vile person" and cruel in the extreme, let us consider the words of Suetonius again:

"It would be tedious to relate all the numerous instances of his cruelty; suffice it to give a few examples, in their different kinds. Not a day passed without the punishment of some person or other, not excepting holidays, or those appropriated to the worship of the gods. Some were tried even on New Year's Day. Of many who were condemned, their wives and children shared the same fate; and for those who were sentenced to death, the relations were forbid to put on mourning... The information of any person, without exception, was taken, and all offences were capital, even speaking a few words, though without any ill intention... Many persons, when summoned to trial, stabbed themselves at home, to avoid the distress and ignominy of a public condemnation, which they were certain would ensue. Others took poison in the Senate house. The wounds were bound up, and all who had not expired, were carried, half-dead, and panting for life, to prison. Those who were put to death, were thrown down the Gemonian stairs, and then dragged into the Tiber... Those who were desirous to die, were forced to live." *Lives of the Caesars: Tiberius*, chaps. lxi.

The first part of verse 22, "And with the arms of a flood shall they be overflown from before him, and shall be broken" refers to the multitudes who lost their lives by the hand of Tiberius. Clearly then, Tiberius fits the prophecy's description of the vile person that was to take the place of Augustus.

The Prince of the Covenant

The prophecy now brings us to the last phrase of verse 22, which is the core of Daniel's vision by the Tigris: "yea, also the prince of the covenant." The Bible specifically mentions the reign of Tiberius in the book of Luke: "Now in the fifteenth year of the reign of Tiberius Caesar" John the Baptist was baptizing people in the Jordan River when Jesus came to him and was also baptized. Luke 3:1, 21-22. Luke then tells us that "Jesus himself began to be about thirty years of age" (Luke 3:23), and after that he gives the narrative of His Gospel ministry. (See Luke 4.) The beginning of Jesus' ministry therefore commences in the 15th year of the reign of Tiberius. Moreover, we have already seen that Jesus is declared to be our Prince in Daniel chapter 10, and the book of Acts says that Jesus is "the Prince of life" and "a Prince and a Saviour." Acts 3:15; 5:31. Thus the focus of the prophecy upon the Caesars is meant to lead us to Jesus Christ and the Covenant that He made for the world.

The character of Tiberius gives force to the words of the Jews to Pilate at Jesus' trial: "If thou let this man go, thou art not Caesar's friend: whosoever maketh himself a king speaketh against Caesar." John 19:12. Their words must have struck fear into Pilate's mind, for anyone who crossed Tiberius could expect a cruel death, so he gave the Jews what they wanted:

> "When Pilate saw that he could prevail nothing, but that rather a tumult was made, he took water, and washed his hands before the multitude, saying, I am innocent of the blood of this just person: see ye to it." *Matthew 27:24.*

Pilate knew that Jesus was innocent. His wife even sent word to him saying, "Have thou nothing to do with that just man: for I have suffered many things this day in a dream because of him." Matthew 27:19. Nevertheless, because of his cowardice, Pilate sent the Lord of glory to the cross. Moreover, the last sentence in the passage under discussion signifies that Jesus would be put to death in the days of Tiberius, which is clearly the case. Thus the prophecy once again is proved to be an exact description of history.

That Jesus made "the covenant" of which the prophecy is speaking is obvious to anyone who will take the time to consider the simple statements of scripture. The book of Hebrews clearly says that Jesus is "the mediator of the new covenant," and that, "he obtained a more excellent ministry, by how much also he is the mediator of a better covenant." Hebrews 12:24; 8:6. It was the "blood" of Jesus that ratified this better Covenant as He sacrificed His life for the sins of the world, and it is declared to be an "everlasting covenant." Hebrews 10:29; 13:20. (See also John 1:29; Hebrews 9:26.) Thus the scripture is clear that Jesus came to make the Covenant, and it is He that is being described in the vision by the Tigris.

The Time of the Prince

Verse 22 is parallel with chapter eight where the Roman civil power "magnified" itself "even against the prince of the host." Daniel 8:11, margin. That is, it crucified Jesus. In Daniel chapter nine we are given a fuller explanation of "the prince of the host" where He is called "the Messiah the Prince." The prophecy says that 70 weeks were "determined" for the Jewish people, and that the Prince would come after "seven weeks, and threescore and two weeks" had been fulfilled. Daniel 9:24-25. A day in symbolic prophecy represents a year. (See Numbers 14:34; Ezekiel 4:6.) Thus the 70 prophetic weeks represent 490 literal years. At the end of 69 (7 + 62) prophetic weeks, or 483 years, Prince Jesus, the "Messiah," was to come.

The beginning of the time period started with "the going forth of the commandment to restore and to build Jerusalem…the street shall be built again, and the wall, even in troublous times." Daniel 9:25. King Cyrus of Persia was the first to issue this command (see Isaiah 44:28; 2 Chronicles 36:20-23; Ezra 1:1-4), but his command was incomplete. According to Ezra the commandment was issued in three parts by different Persian kings, and is called: "the commandment of Cyrus, and Darius, and Artaxerxes king of Persia." Ezra 6:14. The 483-year time period commenced in the fall of the year 457 B.C. with the last and most complete form of the commandment issued by Artaxerxes. (See Ezra 7.) Ezra also acknowledges that: "our God hath extended mercy unto us in the sight of the kings of Persia…to give us a wall in Judah and in Jerusalem." Ezra 9:9. Thus the beginning point of the time prophecy is clearly pointed out in the book of Ezra. That "the going forth of the commandment" originated in 457 B.C. is proved by the excellent work of professors Siegfried Horn and Lynn Wood:

> "…Ezra's journey, which began in the month of Nisan of the 7th year of Artaxerxes and ended in Ab (5th month), took place from late March to late July in 457 B.C., and the decree of Artaxerxes I went into effect after Ezra's arrival in Palestine in late summer or early fall of that same year." *The Chronology of EZRA 7*, p. 117.

The 69 weeks ended in A.D. 27 with the anointing of Jesus by baptism. (The 15th year of Tiberius began in the fall of A.D. 27; Jesus was also baptized shortly after that in the same year. Messiah means "the Anointed One," thus the phrase "unto the Messiah" directs us to His anointing by baptism.) The reason that John the Baptist came "baptizing with water," was that the Messiah "should be made manifest to Israel." John 1:31. Jesus said of Himself: "The Spirit of the Lord is upon me, because He hath anointed me..." Luke 4:18. And the apostle Peter declared: "God anointed Jesus of Nazareth with the Holy Ghost and with power." Acts 10:38. After He was baptized He began His preaching of the gospel by proclaiming: "the time is fulfilled." Mark 1:15. The end of the 69 prophetic weeks had come.

"And after threescore and two weeks shall Messiah be cut off, but not for himself... And he shall confirm the covenant with many for one week: and in the midst of the week he shall cause the sacrifice and the oblation to cease." Daniel 9:26-27. Three and a half years after Jesus was anointed, in the midst of the 70th week, in the spring of A.D. 31, He was "cut off," or crucified by the Roman civil power. With His great sacrifice the long years of sacrificial offerings were finished. The Jewish temple was left "desolate," and the tearing of the "veil in the temple" symbolized its end. Matthew 23:38; 27:50-51. The covenant was confirmed with many of the Jewish people during the last prophetic week, which ended in A.D. 34 with the Jewish nation's rejection of Christianity by the stoning of Stephen. The Christians were then scattered throughout the Roman Empire and the apostle Paul was converted and began proclaiming the gospel to the Gentile world. (See Acts 7:59-8:1; 9:1-22; 13:44-49 and the timeline below.) Thus "the prince of the host," "the Messiah the Prince" that "confirms the covenant with many," and "the prince of the covenant" are all speaking of Jesus Christ. He is placed at the center of the prophecy, and "to him give all the prophets witness." Acts 10:43.

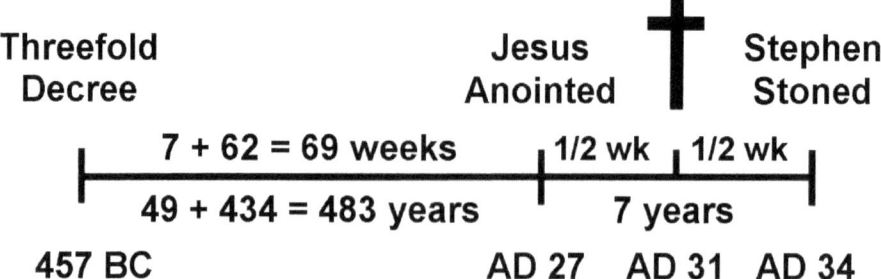

The Purpose of the Covenant

Daniel's vision by the Tigris speaks of the Covenant again in verses 28-32. Therefore we must have a correct understanding of it. The apostle Paul tells us that Jesus "is the mediator of a better covenant, which was established upon better promises." Hebrews 8:6-7. This passage presupposes that the Old or First Covenant had promises as well. In Deuteronomy the fifth chapter Moses narrates the establishment of the Old Covenant and its promises. In this passage he reiterates the giving of God's Law of Ten Commandments in the audience of the people after which he repeats their promise to God to obey Him. They said to Moses:

> "Go thou near, and hear all that the LORD our God shall say: and speak thou unto us all that the LORD our God shall speak unto thee; and we will hear it, and do it." *Deuteronomy 5:27.*

The people became afraid after hearing the Lord speak the Ten Commandments from mount Sinai. Therefore they asked Moses to go and speak to the Lord, and whatsoever the Lord said to do the people declared that they would do. This is an Old Covenant promise — men's promise to obey the Commandments of God in their own strength. Notice the Lord's reply to the people:

> "And the LORD heard the voice of your words, when ye spake unto me; and the LORD said unto me, I have heard the voice of the words of this people, which they have spoken unto thee: they have well said all that they have spoken. O that there were such an heart in them, that they would fear me, and keep all my commandments always, that it might be well with them, and with their children for ever!" *Deuteronomy 5:28-29.*

The Lord acknowledged the promise of the people to obey His commandments, and then in verse 29 He uncovers the real problem — that it was not in their heart to obey Him. Men do not realize the inability of their heart to obey God: "The heart is deceitful above all things, and desperately wicked: who can know it?" Jeremiah 17:9. (See also Proverbs 4:23; Matthew 12:35; 15:19.) The apostle Paul speaking plainly about the people said that the fault was with "them," and then, quoting the Lord, he declared: "I will make a new covenant..." Hebrews 8:8. This New Covenant is based upon God's Law of Ten Commandments just as the Old Covenant was, but it is only through the New Covenant's "better promises" that God's people can become obedient to His Commandments:

> "For this is the covenant that I will make with the house of Israel after those days, saith the Lord; I will put my laws into their mind, and write them in their hearts: and I will be to them a God, and they shall

be to me a people: And they shall not teach every man his neighbour, and every man his brother, saying, Know the Lord: for all shall know me, from the least to the greatest. For I will be merciful to their unrighteousness, and their sins and their iniquities will I remember no more." *Hebrews 8:10-12.*

Here are clearly the "better promises" of the New Covenant. First the Lord promises to put His Laws into the minds and write them in the hearts of His people, and then He promises to blot out every remembrance of their sins. God has promised to give them His righteousness! This is not just something written into a book and placed to their account, but it is "unto all and upon all them that believe." Romans 3:22. His righteousness is imputed to the life of the believer as well as imparted to them. Through faith then in His promises God's children can partake of His righteousness, and this righteousness is made manifest in obedience to all of His Commandments. This purpose of the New Covenant is reiterated throughout the scriptures:

> "A new heart also will I give you, and a new spirit will I put within you: and I will take away the stony heart out of your flesh, and I will give you an heart of flesh. And I will put my spirit within you, and cause you to walk in my statutes, and ye shall keep my judgments, and do them." *Ezekiel 36:26-27.*

> "For this is my covenant unto them, when I shall take away their sins." *Romans 11:27.*

> "Ye are the children of the prophets, and of the covenant which God made with our fathers, saying unto Abraham, And in thy seed shall all the kindreds of the earth be blessed. Unto you first God, having raised up his Son Jesus, sent him to bless you, in turning away every one of you from his iniquities." *Acts 3:25-26.*

The first part of the New Covenant is fulfilled to God's people when they accept Jesus as their Lord and Savior, and as they continue to walk with Him. They are forgiven and accepted of God, and they are daily cleansed from their unrighteous works by the blood of Jesus. The second part of the New Covenant, "and their sins and their iniquities will I remember no more" (Hebrews 8:12), is fulfilled to them in the judgment, as we shall discuss in chapter six. (See chapter 6: The Sealed Remnant.)

The Application of the Covenant

The Old Covenant promise is repeated in many places in the scripture. After Moses read the Commandments of the Lord to the people they replied: "All that the LORD hath said will we do, and be obedient." Exodus 24:3, 7. Joshua also made an Old Covenant with the people in his day: "And the people said unto Joshua, The LORD our God will we serve, and his voice will we obey. So Joshua made a covenant with the people that day, and set them a statute and an ordinance in Shechem." Joshua 24:24-25. These promises and the words of the Lord were written in the book of the Law or book of the Covenant, and they were placed there as a witness against them. (See Exodus 24:3-7; Joshua 24:24-27; 2 Kings 22:8; 23:2; Deuteronomy 31:24-26.)

Once the Old Covenant was agreed upon it was then ratified or sealed, and, as in the case of Moses, he "took the blood of calves and of goats, with water, and scarlet wool, and hyssop, and sprinkled both the book, and all the people," and then he said, "Behold the blood of the covenant, which the LORD hath made with you concerning all these words." Hebrews 9:19-20; Exodus 24:8. This service bound the people to obey the Lord, but "it is not possible that the blood of bulls and of goats should take away sins." Hebrews 10:4. Their hearts were not changed by the application of the animal's blood, and they could not obey. Therefore a New Covenant had to be made, and it is the blood of Christ that ratifies or seals the New Covenant:

> "How much more shall the blood of Christ, who through the eternal Spirit offered himself without spot to God, purge your conscience from dead works to serve the living God? And for this cause he is the mediator of the new testament, that by means of death, for the redemption of the transgressions that were under the first testament, they which are called might receive the promise of eternal inheritance. For where a testament is, there must also of necessity be the death of the testator. For a testament is of force after men are dead: otherwise it is of no strength at all while the testator liveth." *Hebrews 9:14-17.*

The purpose of the sacrifices from the beginning was to open men's minds to the reality of sin. Sin caused the death of the Son of God, the "Lamb slain from the foundation of the world." Revelation 13:8. Thus, in bringing sacrifices men would be led to see the ugliness of sin, and would understand how much suffering it caused God. They would be brought into sympathy with Him, their thoughts would be drawn to the true "Lamb of God, which taketh away the sin of the world" (John 1:29), faith would spring up in their hearts, and they would finally come to repentance of their transgressions. They would, in short, be "born again" and then could "enter into the kingdom of God." John 3:3-8.

Abel, Abraham and others came to a realization of the New Covenant through the animal sacrifices. They understood that the animal was a symbol or type of Jesus, the Lamb of God, who was to give His life for the sins of the world. The New Covenant was applied to their lives and they were enabled to obey the Law of Ten Commandments. (See Genesis 26:5; John 8:56; Hebrews 11:4; 1 John 5:1-5.) Nevertheless, the Jews became blinded to the sacrifices, and began to see them as a means by which they would be accepted by God and saved. The sacrificial system that was meant to be a blessing became a curse, and God had to remove it. The Old Covenant promise and its sacrifices were never an accepted means of salvation. The sacrifices were only meant to point men to the true sacrifice. Consequently, when Jesus died on the cross He forever did away with, in Himself, the Old Covenant promise written in the book of the Law:

> "Blotting out the against us handwriting in the decrees, which was contrary to us, and has taken it out of the midst, nailing it to the cross; having stripped the principalities and the powers, he exposed them publicly, triumphing over them in it." *Colossians 2:14-15*, literal translation.

The manmade, handwritten promises of obedience in the Old Covenant, which were placed in the book of the Law, were "taken out of the midst" of those "decrees" and blotted out in Jesus when He was nailed "to the cross." As both God and man, Jesus had the right to change the Covenant. He refused to live by an Old Covenant experience trusting in His human strength to obey. He declared: "the Father that dwelleth in me, he doeth the works." John 14:10. Every attempt to get Jesus to live for Himself and trust in His humanity failed. (See Matthew 27:40-44; Mark 15:30-32.) Therefore He confirmed a New Covenant based on faith in the creative power of God to bring humanity back to obedience to the divine Law.

The New Covenant was within Jesus and He declared: "I delight to do thy will, O my God: yea, thy law is within my heart." Psalms 40:8. Quoting the same Psalm the apostle Paul says of Jesus: "Then said he, Lo, I come to do thy will, O God. He taketh away the first, that he may establish the second." Hebrews 10:9. That is, He took away the Old Covenant and established the New. When He died upon the cross and cried out "it is finished" (John 19:30); the Old Covenant promises and all of the sacrifices and services used to ratify that Covenant were then done. The New Covenant was established, and Jesus publicly triumphed over his enemies: "And, behold, the veil of the temple was rent in twain from the top to the bottom." Matthew 27:51. Thus, with the death of Christ the earthly temple and all of its rituals were forever finished. Any attempt to place them at the center of the end time fulfillment of prophecy is wrong and will ultimately fail. Animal sacrifices can never avail, for the blood of Christ must be applied to all that are saved.

Satan abhors the New Covenant, for it brings men back to obedience to God and condemns his course of action. Consequently, he uses two methods to try to destroy it: First, he tempts men to place their hearts upon earthly things to draw their affections from the Lord, and second, he deceives men into thinking that God has changed His Law. He is successful on both accounts, but the last conflict revolves around the latter as we shall see.

Summary of Chapter Three

This chapter has brought us down through the life of Julius Caesar, the civil wars in Rome, the reign of Augustus and the establishment of the Principate, and then finally to the violent rule of Tiberius and the crucifixion of Jesus the "prince of the covenant." Well-established events in the life of these three Caesar's are given to lead us to Jesus and an understanding of His Covenant.

The covenant is spoken of often in the next chapter, and without a proper understanding of it we shall misplace the events of the prophecy. Therefore it is necessary for us to recognize the differences between the Old and the New Covenants and their promises. In the Old Covenant men promised God that they would obey His Law of Ten Commandments, but they did not have hearts that were softened and subdued by the Holy Spirit and therefore they could not obey Him. In the New Covenant the Spirit of God changes our hearts as we behold Jesus dying for our sins upon Calvary's cross. He places His Law within us in fulfillment of His promise in the New Covenant, and we are thus enabled to obey Him. This is known as the new birth. Thus the sacrifice of Jesus is central to understanding the vision that Daniel received by the Tigris River, for the covenant is the object of Satan's attack.

The next chapter reveals other important principles for our understanding of the final conflict, and we shall clearly comprehend the prophecy if we patiently move on developing point by point as we go. Before the cross the prophecy moved forward step by step, at times stopping and focusing for a couple of verses upon certain events to clarify points of importance. The events after the cross continue step by step in the same way that we have preceded thus far. These steps are needed to develop principles upon which the last conflict is based. Without them we cannot come to a right conclusion at the end. Many of the points, which are yet to be developed in the prophecy, may be difficult for us to accept. Thus it would do us well to stop at this point, pray, examine ourselves, and ask Jesus to fill us with His Spirit of understanding and to give us willing, obedient hearts.

Chapter 4: The Rise of the Papacy

This chapter begins with a discussion of the types. It then focuses upon the early Church and reveals its corruption by pagan philosophy. Next it discloses the exaltation of this corrupt system by the kings of the earth, and unfolds its fierce battles against paganism. Finally it proclaims the establishment of the Papacy.

Types and Antitypes in the Scriptures

Biblical types are spiritually significant; they are divinely drawn relationships between historical persons, events, or things and those of some subsequent period of time. Types are therefore prophetic in nature. The later persons, events, or things are called antitypes, and contain one or more details in common with the types that they fulfill. Types are generally worked out in Old Testament times through ancient Israel, and have their antitype fulfillment in New Testament times through Christ and His Church. Typology is the most significant inter-relationship between Old and New Testament time periods, and should therefore be clearly understood.

A few examples of some simple types will help to prove the significance of type and antitype relationships in the scriptures. In Romans 5:14 the apostle Paul tells us that Adam was a "figure of him that was to come." Adam, the type, brought sin into the world and through it death, but Christ, the antitype, in contrast brought righteousness and eternal life. (See Romans 5:12-19; 1 Corinthians 15:45-50.) Also, in type, Jonah "was three days and three nights in the whale's belly," so in the antitype, "shall the Son of man be three days and three nights in the heart of the earth." Matthew 12:40. Additionally, as Moses in the type "lifted up the serpent in the wilderness," even so in the antitype "must the Son of man be lifted up." John 3:14. Moreover, Noah's deliverance in the flood was a "figure," or type, "whereunto even baptism," the antitype, "doth also now save us." 1 Peter 3:20-21. Conversely, in type, "the flood came, and took them all away," therefore, in the antitype, the wicked are "taken" by death at Jesus' Second Coming. Matthew 24:38-41. (See also Luke 17:26-27, 34-37.) Thus it is easy to see that the scripture contains many simple types.

In addition, the Jewish sanctuary system is a complex type or "pattern," of the heavenly sanctuary, which was shown to Moses "in the mount." Hebrews 8:5. Every animal sacrifice is a type of the offering of Christ, the true "Lamb of

God." John 1:29. The annual feasts of the Jewish year are types of events in the Christian dispensation. Those feasts that were held in the springtime are typical of events in the days of Jesus and the early Church. The typical feast of the Passover took place on "the fourteenth day of the first month." Numbers 28:16. In the time of Christ it occurred on Friday, the very day that Jesus died upon the cross, and the apostle Paul testifies that "Christ our passover is sacrificed for us." 1 Corinthians 5:7. The typical feast of Unleavened Bread began the day after the Passover, it continued for seven days, and the first day was a ceremonial sabbath. (See Numbers 28:17-18.) This sabbath fell upon the weekly Sabbath of the Lord in Jesus' day, which John informs us was "an high day." John 19:31. The symbolic feast of the First Fruits came the next day, which was the very day that Jesus arose from the dead, and we are told that He has "become the firstfruits of them that slept," obviously fulfilling that type. 1 Corinthians 15:20. (See also Leviticus 23:5-11.) And finally, the typical feast of Pentecost took place 50 days later (see Leviticus 23:15-21), and in the book of Acts we are told that 50 days after Jesus' resurrection "the day of Pentecost was fully come…and there appeared unto them [the disciples of Christ] cloven tongues like as of fire," and they received the outpouring of the Holy Spirit. Acts 2:1-3. Thus the types in the Old Testament sanctuary services are prophecies of the experience of Christ and His Church in the New Testament dispensation.

Not only are the sacrifices and feasts types of events in the days of Jesus and the Church, but the priests of the earthly sanctuary also served "unto the example and shadow of heavenly things." Hebrews 8:5. Thus God's glory left the earthly temple (Matthew 23:38; 27:51), and now Christ ministers in "the true tabernacle, which the Lord pitched, and not man." Hebrews 8:2. For He "is not entered into the holy places made with hands, which are the figures of the true; but into heaven itself, now to appear in the presence of God for us." Hebrews 9:24. The articles of the earthly sanctuary (see the image on the next page), before which the Jewish priests ministered, are also types of the articles in the heavenly sanctuary where Christ is now ministering. (Note: the Court of the Tabernacle is typical of Christ's work on earth while the ministry in the Tent of the Tabernacle represents His work in heaven.) The earthly "candlestick of pure gold," the "altar of incense," and the "ark of the testimony" are clearly types of the heavenly "golden candlesticks," the "golden altar," and the "ark of his testament" found in the book of Revelation. Exodus 25:31-39; 30:1-7, 27; 25:10-22; Revelation 1:12; 8:3; 11:19. Thus it is clearly seen that the types are not only prophetic, but they are the most significant inter-relationship between Old and New Testament time periods.

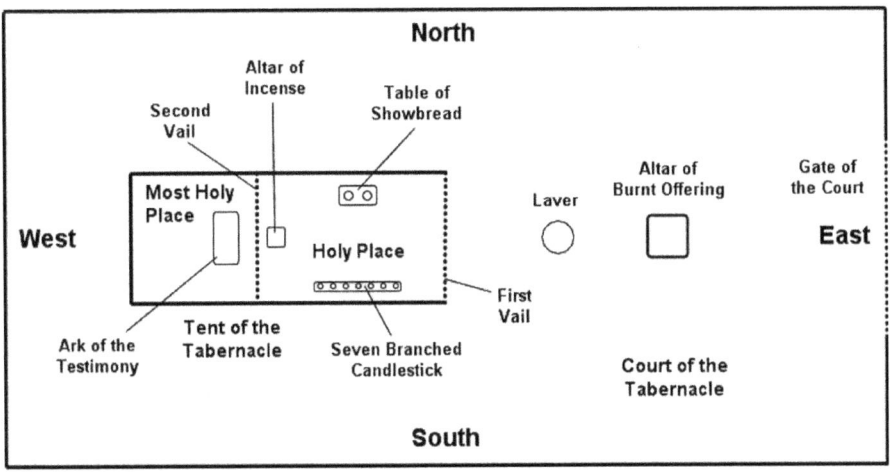

Types and the Book of Revelation

Three of the lines of prophecy in the book of Revelation start with a sanctuary scene, and they have seven divisions or periods of time associated with each of them. (See Revelation 1:10-3:22; 4:1-8:1; 8:2-11:18.) The seven time periods span the entire Christian era, as we shall see. The three sanctuary scenes also have an article from the holy place of the sanctuary linking them. The three lines of prophecy, their sanctuary imagery and articles, and their seven divisions are all descriptions of parallel events just as the prophecies of Daniel are parallel. They cannot be interpreted "privately" or independently. 2 Peter 1:20.

The first of these three lines of prophecy, the seven churches, opens with the vision of "one like unto the Son of man" that "had in his right hand seven stars," and "who walketh in the midst of the seven golden candlesticks." Revelation 1:13; 2:1. This first prophetic scene is the reality or antitype of the ministry of the high priest before the seven candlesticks in the Holy place of the typical, earthly sanctuary. John sees Jesus ministering in the Holy place of the heavenly temple, and the candlesticks, which are symbolic of His "seven churches" (Revelation 1:20), are the recipients of His blessings. Thus Jesus is shown walking among and ministering for His people that He declared to be "the light of the world." Matthew 5:14-16.

The third line of prophecy, the seven trumpets, likewise opens with the scene of an angel "having a golden censer; and there was given unto him much incense." Revelation 8:3. He was seen ministering before the "golden altar," which is the obvious antitype of the priest ministering before the altar of incense in the Holy place on earth. The angel that John sees is Jesus in the capacity of a divine messenger ministering the fragrant "incense" of His merits as the "prayers of the saints" ascend up before the Father's throne. Revelation 8:4. (That Jesus is often represented as an angel in Scripture see Genesis 22:11-18; Acts 3:25; Genesis 31:11-13; Exodus 3:2-4; Acts 7:30-32; Exodus 13:21; 14:19; Numbers 22:35; 23:4-5; Judges 6:11-16; 13:16-22; Zechariah 3:1-2; 1 Corinthians 10:1-4.) Thus events on the earth follow the sounding of the seven trumpets, and relate to the ministry of Jesus before the altar of incense in the Holy place in the heavenly temple.

In the second prophetic scene of the seven seals the apostle John sees "a door" that was standing open "in heaven," and within the door "a throne was set in heaven." Upon the throne he saw the "Lord God Almighty" and "a Lamb as it had been slain." Revelation 4:1-2, 8; 5:6. Jesus is seen sitting upon the throne with His Father and ministering His blood in behalf of His people. Many Bible scholars assume that since the throne of God is viewed here that it must be the Most Holy place of the heavenly sanctuary, but this is based upon the assumption that the throne of God is the Ark of the Covenant. However, the apostle clearly sees "seven lamps of fire burning before the throne," and a "golden altar which was before the throne." Revelation 4:5; 8:3. These are clearly articles in the Holy place as we have just described. The Most Holy place of "the temple of God" is not "opened" to view by the apostle until Revelation 11:19 where John then sees "the ark of his testament." Nevertheless, John does not see the throne of God there, or he would have certainly described it. (Additional information on the throne of God is given in chapter 6: The Judgment and the Woman.) Thus this second scene is also in the Holy place of the heavenly sanctuary, and, although its article is not explicitly mentioned, the throne of God must have been necessarily located on the "north side" of the apartment at the Table of Showbread with its twelve pierced "cakes." Exodus 26:35; Leviticus 24:5.

These three lines of prophecy began when Jesus ascended to heaven and started His ministry in the Holy place of the heavenly sanctuary. The Son of Man, the slain Lamb, and the Angel in the three sanctuary scenes are representations of our heavenly "mediator," Jesus Christ. 1 Timothy 2:5. All three lines of prophecy continue until Jesus' ministry ceases and He returns in power and glory at His Second Coming. They are also complimentary with Daniel's four prophecies after the time of the cross. (See the timeline on the top of the next page.) Thus we have more prophetic truth to draw from as we continue our study of the vision by the Tigris.

Jesus' Holy Place Ministry in the Revelation

Jesus Assends to Heaven	100 A.D. Philosophy Enters Church	538 A.D. Papal Rome Established	1560 A.D. Reformation Stagnates	1844 A.D. Judgment Begins
Revelation 1:9-3:22 - Candlesticks - The Seven Churches				

Lost Love	False Jews	In Satan's Seat	Jezebel Teaches Her False Doctrines	Living Dead	Open Door	Zealous Repentance
Revelation 4:1-8:1 - Table of Showbread - The Seven Seals						
Initial Conquest	Great Sword	False Balances	Killed by Sword, Hunger, & Beasts	Souls under the Altar Cry	Signs and Sealing	Silence in Heaven
Revelation 8:2-11:18 - Altar of Incense - The Seven Trumpets						
Hail & Fire on Earth	Bloody Sea	Bitter Waters	Sun, Moon, Stars Dark	Locusts Torment	Third of Men Slain	Christ's Kingdom

31 A.D. Church goes to the World	313 A.D. World Exalts a Corrupt Church	612 A.D. Rise of Islam	1449 A.D. Islam in Europe & Reformation	Heavenly Ministry Complete

Types and the Vision by the Tigris

A clear understanding of types and antitypes and how they relate to the geographical region of the Middle East is needed in order to understand the vision by the Tigris. The things that happened in Israel's history are "examples," or types, of the events in the Church, the antitype, "upon whom the ends of the world are come." 1 Corinthians 10:1-11. Therefore, the apostle Paul informs us that, "he is a Jew, which is one inwardly." Romans 2:28-29. In other words the true Jew is the person that has made a New Covenant with God, and is not necessarily of the bloodline of the Jewish race. The New Testament Church is not separate from Israel, but is a continuation and completion of the Old Testament "church in the wilderness." Acts 7:38. The Gentiles, according to Paul, "wert graffed in among" the Old Testament Church, so then "all Israel shall be saved," both Jews and Gentiles, "for ye are all one in Christ Jesus." Romans 11:16-32; Galatians 3:28-29. Thus any attempt to force a Jewish National fulfillment of prophecy at the end of time is a misapplication of scripture, for the Church is the antitypical "Israel of God." Galatians 6:16.

With the stoning of Stephen in A.D. 34 the Jews sealed their destiny as a nation. (See Acts 7:59-8:3. Note that the Jerusalem Council took place about A.D. 51, and Paul places the stoning of Stephen and persecution of the Church some 17 years earlier. See Galatians 1:13-2:10; Acts 15:1-29.) The end of the seventieth prophetic week of Daniel nine had come. The time "determined" upon the Jewish Nation was finished, and the true believing children of God were "scattered abroad" and they "went every where preaching the word." Daniel 9:24; Acts 8:4. The apostle Paul was also converted, and he began to take the gospel "far hence unto the Gentiles." Acts 22:21. Therefore, the Jews were "filled with envy" and Paul boldly declared: "It was necessary that the word of God should first have been spoken to you: but seeing ye put it from you, and judge yourselves unworthy of everlasting life, lo, we turn to the Gentiles." Acts 13:44-48. Accordingly, the apostle Peter, speaking to the Gentile believers, declared: "ye are a chosen generation, a royal priesthood, an holy nation…which in time past were not a people, but are now the people of God." 1 Peter 1:1-2; 2:9-10. God's covenant people are no longer limited to the geographical region of the Middle East. We must now look to the Church, the spiritual antitype of the Jewish Nation throughout the rest of the prophecy.

As we go through the cross, behold the establishment of spiritual Israel, and view the divine rejection of the Jewish nation at the end of the 490 years, we move from typical, geographical nations to antitypical, spiritual powers in the fulfillment of prophecy. Palestinian terms are still employed, but they are now applied spiritually. The glorious land, Israel, Jerusalem, mount Zion, Egypt, Babylon, Libya, Edom, Moab, Ammon, the Euphates, and Armageddon are some of the Palestinian terms used in the prophecies that must now be interpreted spiritually. Thus the cross and the types have significant implications to the vision by the Tigris. Since we are now concerned with spiritual, antitypical Israel then we must now also be concerned with spiritual, antitypical Babylon and Egypt when speaking of the kings of the North and of the South respectively. They cannot be geographical in nature since spiritual Israel is not located in the Middle East, and the focus upon that geographical location has no significance to the prophecy. Nevertheless, almost all modern interpreters focus upon the Middle East when interpreting prophecy! But we cannot pass by this principle too quickly, for a clear discernment of it will determine life or death in the last conflict.

Pagan Rome acquired the land of ancient Egypt, and technically it would then become the king of the South. However, the phrase "the king of the south" is not used until verse 25 of Daniel 11 and must be understood to refer to spiritual Egypt. The Kings of the North and South must be opposing ideologies or antitypical, spiritual powers within Rome, since all of the other prophecies of Daniel end with that kingdom. It is Rome that is now the empire under discussion in the vision by the Tigris, but after the cross it cannot be considered the king of the South because of its geographical conquests. It can only be regarded thus because of its spiritual nature. Though the Egyptians had many gods (see Exodus 12:12) it is nonetheless the denial of the divinity of the one true God, the Lord Jesus Christ (see 1 Corinthians 10:1-4), that is the most pronounced spiritual trait of Egypt's leadership. Pharaoh proclaimed, "Who is the LORD... I know not the LORD." Exodus 5:2. This is the same atheistic philosophy that God's Church had to contend with in the pagan rulers of Rome. Therefore, since Rome is the last kingdom in all of the prophecies of Daniel, and it was the pagan Roman Empire that was ruling the world when Jesus died upon the cross, and it was also the pagan rulers of Rome that denied the divinity of the Lord Jesus Christ, then the pagan powers within Rome must represent spiritual Egypt, the "king of the south," in the coming verses. This point will become more apparent as the application is made in the following sections. Thus we are now ready to deal with the rest of the vision by the Tigris.

Christian Philosophy

As Jesus commenced His ministry in the sanctuary above He took the "fire of the altar, and cast it into the earth...and there followed hail and fire mingled with blood." Revelation 8:5, 7. He sent the fire of the Holy Spirit upon the earth in power at Pentecost (see Acts 2:1-4), and all whose hearts, both Jews and Gentiles, who were prepared to receive Him caught fire: "and the third part of trees was burnt up, and all green grass was burnt up." (See also Psalms 1:1-3; 52:8; 92:12; Daniel 4; Isaiah 40:6-7.) The Church was then described in its purity as a "white horse" and its rider. It was strong and went forth to the world "conquering, and to conquer." Revelation 6:2 (See also Zechariah 10:3). Yet the Church in this state is declared to have left its "first love." Revelation 2:4. Man-made philosophies and heathen customs crept into the Church until Christians became steeped in error. It is here that the vision, which Daniel received by the Tigris River, continues its historical description, and reveals this union that the followers of "the prince of the covenant" would make with the world:

> **"And after the league made with him he shall work deceitfully: for he shall come up, and shall become strong with a small people."** Daniel 11:23.

The apostle Paul warned his fellow Christians to "beware lest any man spoil you through philosophy and vain deceit" (Colossians 2:8), of becoming "unequally yoked together with unbelievers." 2 Corinthians 6:14. This is the "league" or union into which peace loving Christians were deceived into making with the philosophers of Rome. It was during the second period of Church history, the second century A.D., according to the book of Revelation, that these philosophical teachers began to call themselves spiritual "Jews;"

that is, they claimed to be Christians. Revelation 2:9. Nevertheless, Jesus said that they were of "the synagogue of Satan." Of these teachers Justin Martyr is of particular interest to us because historians claim that he was the first of the line of the Christian philosophers:

> "The most eminent among the Greek Apologists of the second century is FLAVIUS JUSTINUS, surnamed 'Philosopher and Martyr.'... He is also the first Christian philosopher or the first philosophic theologian." Schaff, *History of the Christian Church*, vol. 2, chap. XIII, sec. 173, par. 1.

> "Justin Martyr is remarkable, as the first among these apologists whose writings have reached us, and as the first of those better known to us, who became a teacher of the Christian church, in whom we observe an approximation between Christianity and the Grecian, but especially the Platonic philosophy." *Rose's Neander*, p. 410.

Dr. Philip Schaff tells us in his *History of the Christian Church* that: "Justin forms the transition from the apostolic fathers to the church fathers properly so called... He belongs to orthodox Catholicism as modified by Greek philosophy." vol. 2, chap. XIII, sec. 173, par. 17. He also tells us that Justin continued to wear his philosopher's cloak "that he might the more readily discourse on the highest themes of thought." *Ibid*, par. 5. And Dr. Killen informs us that:

> "Justin, even after his conversion, still wore the philosopher's cloak, and continued to cherish an undue regard for the wisdom of the pagan sages. His mind never was completely emancipated from the influence of a system of false metaphysics; and thus it was that, whilst his views of various doctrines of the gospel remained confused, his allusions to them are equivocal, if not contradictory." *Ancient Church*, period 2, sec. 2, chap. 1, par. 6.

Justin was never really delivered from his pagan superstitions and used Platonic philosophy to interpret Christian theology. His teachings were like wine to those that desired salvation, but could not separate themselves from their pagan ways, and many followed in his footsteps:

> "From the time of Justin Martyr, the PLATONIC PHILOSOPHY continued to exercise a direct and indirect influence upon Christian theology, though not so unrestrainedly and naively as in his case. We can trace it especially in Clement of Alexandria and Origen, and even

in St. Augustin, who confessed that it kindled in him an incredible fire." Schaff, *History of the Christian Church*, vol. 2, chap. XIII, sec. 173, par. 23.

This statement by Dr. Schaff is a clear confession that Platonic philosophy is the "fire" upon which papal Christianity is built. It is this pagan philosophical teaching which "deceitfully" brought rise to the Roman Church. Although small at first, and with only a "small people," it took nearly 400 years for the Papacy to rise, as it gradually grew stronger and stronger. Pagan philosophy and its doctrines are the origin of the Roman Church, this "synagogue of Satan," not Peter or the apostles!

Philosophy Corrupts the Church

From the time of Justin we see a marked change in the way that the Christians related to the pagan world. Instead of showing the foolishness of pagan philosophy they began to embrace it, and incorporate it into their theology. This brought rise to new forms of worship, and doctrines foreign to scripture. Schools of Christian philosophy were opened, and streams of the unconverted were brought into the Church.

> "Unfortunately Justin was not the only heathen philosopher who came into the church bringing his heathen philosophy and customs with him, and very many common people would naturally follow the lead of such men, so that the few who 'continued steadfastly in the apostles' doctrine and practice' were lost to sight, and the church began to assume the color of paganism. This was the case whenever and wherever heathen philosophers accepted Christianity as merely another phase of their old-time philosophy." Waggoner, *Fathers of the Catholic Church*, p. 150.

The vision by the Tigris clearly reveals this change, which took place in the Christian world:

> **"He shall enter peaceably even upon the fattest places of the province; and he shall do that which his fathers have not done, nor his fathers' fathers; he shall scatter among them the prey, and spoil, and riches: yea, and he shall forecast his devices against the strong holds, even for a time."** Daniel 11:24.

Just prior to the year A.D. 150 Justin entered "peaceably" into Rome and started a school of Christian philosophy. He and his followers taught in other cities as well, even "the fattest places of the province." Justin did that which the other "fathers have not done." He brought his philosophical reasoning to bear upon Christian theology, and claimed that Greek philosophy was needed as a preparation for the truths of the Christian religion. With this understanding it can easily be seen why he taught that "Socrates was a Christian as well as Abraham, though he did not know it." Schaff, *History of the Christian Church*, vol. 2, chap. XIII, sec. 173, par. 19.

After Justin came a whole line of heretical Christian philosophers. Clement and his student, Origen, did more damage to Christianity than any of the other philosophers. First by continuing Justin's teaching that philosophy was necessary, and secondly by teaching that the meaning of the scripture was hidden from common men. Origen went to an even greater extreme by teaching that the scriptures contained many errors and impossibilities. It was through this that many philosophers, men who thought that they had true wisdom, men devoid of the Spirit of God, came over to Christianity.

> "Let it not be forgotten that these teachers to whom the people were thus led to leave the entire work of Bible instruction, were men who were insanely devoted to heathen philosophy and to its methods. As is clearly shown by the quotations from Clement and Origen, the two most noted teachers, they did not at all believe the Bible, but only the fancies of their own darkened and disordered mind. The fact that a thing was commanded in the Bible did not give it any weight with them, for they freely attributed falsehoods even to the law. Contrariwise, the prohibitions of the Bible would not stand in the way of their doing anything which their 'reason' should teach them was necessary. In short, the Bible, even as early as the third century, became only a plaything in the hands of these men. Its name only was used to give sanction to whatever theory or practice those professedly Christian philosophers devised out of their own hearts." Waggoner, *Sunday: The Origin of its Observance in the Christian Church*, p. 58.

Thus the Bible was effectually removed from the hands of the people. In some cases the scriptures were even changed or "corrected" by these men, which resulted in new and corrupt manuscripts. Eusebius tells us of one sect that "boldly perverted" the scriptures. They "fearlessly lay their hands upon the holy scriptures, saying that they have corrected them," and that their copies were "greatly at variance among themselves." *Ecclesiastical History*, book V, chap. XXVIII. Copies of some of these corrupt manuscripts exist even today. Gradually, men of learning replaced men of piety, self-exaltation replaced personal consecration, and philosophy and tradition replaced Bible doctrine.

> "In the interval between the days of the apostles and the conversion of Constantine, the Christian commonwealth changed its aspect. ... Rites and ceremonies, of which neither Paul nor Peter ever heard, crept silently into use, and then claimed the rank of divine institutions." Killen, *The Ancient Church*, preface, p. XVI.

A few of these institutions that were adopted at this time were: holy water, clinical baptism, the mass, the mysteries or sacraments, the sign of the cross and its display, bowing and genuflecting, the immortality of the soul, purgatory, prayers for the dead, martyr-worship, the worship of Mary, Christmas, and Easter. The last two institutions are based on the pagan sun festivals. They were substitutions made by the Church to facilitate the acceptance of the Christian faith by the common people. These and many other errors were introduced into the Christian Church during the two centuries after the apostles died.

> "It is not necessary to go into a subject which the diligence of Protestant writers has made familiar to most of us. The use of temples, and these dedicated to particular saints, ... holy water; asylums; holydays and seasons, use of calendars, processions, ... are all of pagan origin, and sancti-fied by their adoption into the Church." Newman, *An Essay on the Development of Christian Doctrine*, p. 373.

One of the great changes in Christian doctrine is that of the Sabbath institution. Some Christians began advocating Sunday sacredness shortly after the apostles died in an attempt to distance themselves from the Jews, for there was great anti-Jewish sentiment in Rome leading up to and following the destruction of Jerusalem in A.D. 70. They were therefore attempting to make their religion more agreeable to the heathen around them by separating themselves from any appearance of Judaism, and by modifying their doctrines and accepting pagan traditions into their worship. Consequently the Bible Sabbath became the first casualty of the Christian dispensation, and the following sums up the reason for the change:

> "The Church made a sacred day of Sunday ... largely because it was the weekly festival of the sun—for it was a definite Christian policy to take over the pagan festivals endeared to the people by tradi-

tion, and give them a Christian significance." Weigall, *The Paganism in Our Christianity*, 1928, p. 145.

Accordingly, Justin strongly denounced the Sabbath as a temporary Jewish custom, and exalted Sunday as: "the day on which we all hold our common assembly, because it is the first day on which God, having wrought a change in the darkness and matter, made the world; and Jesus Christ our Saviour on the same day rose from the dead." Apology 1:67. Justin's logic is unsound at best, since the reason that the Bible gives for the Sabbath rest being on the seventh day is that the work of creating "the heavens and the earth were finished," and not beginning. Genesis 2:1. (See also Exodus 20:8-11.) Jesus also, after His passion, rested in the grave over the hours of the Sabbath and rose after it had passed. (See Luke 23:52-24:1.) The Sunday institution is in direct conflict with the Sabbath of the scriptures, and despite the effort of these corrupt Christian teachers it took hundreds of years for it to become an almost universal institution.

The application of the prophecy to history is obvious. The "he" refers to the pagan philosophers of Rome that would enter in and corrupt the Church. "And he shall do that which his fathers have not done, nor his fathers' fathers." He would do things that the apostles and the other apostolic Church leaders would never consider: "he shall scatter among them the prey, and spoil, and riches." That is, he would scatter the false doctrines, rites, and superstitions of the pagans among the Christians. The "strong holds" against which he was to "forcast his devices" are the cities as well as the political and military powers of the king of the South — pagan Rome. "Even for a time." A "time" or year is equal to 360 days with 30 days to a month and 12 months to a year. (See Daniel 11:13, margin; Genesis 7:11; 8:2-4.) A day in symbolic prophecy is equal to one literal year. (See Ezekiel 4:4-6; Numbers 14:34.) Therefore this prophetic "time" is equal to 360 literal years. If we begin the 360-year period when Justin "entered peaceably" into Rome as the starting point, just before the year A.D. 150, then we will end with the fall of the pagan power, the King of the South, in the Roman Empire just prior to the year A.D. 510. (See the section The Establishment of the Papacy for the fulfillment of this time period.)

Constantine and Christian Warfare

During the second period of Church history God's people not only had to deal with apostasy and the inroads of pagan philosophy from among themselves, but they were greatly persecuted as well: "And there went out another horse that was red: and power was given to him that sat thereon to take peace from the earth, and that they should kill one another: and there was given unto him a great sword." Revelation 6:4. (See also Matthew 10:34; Revelation 8:8-9.) The "ten days" of tribulation that the "church of Smyrna" was called to endure are the ten years, from A.D. 303 to 313, that Diocletian lead a bloody persecution against them after which the second period ends. Revelation 2:8, 10. These persecutions tended to keep the Church from degenerating very quickly. However, "the third century saw the completion of the transformation of the principate of Augustus into an undisguised autocracy that received its definitive form under Diocletion and Constantine I." Boak and Sinnigen, *A History of Rome to A.D. 565*, p. 448. Thus the Roman Empire once again changed its system of government, and with this the Church became exalted and united itself closely to the kings of the earth; thereby accelerating its degeneration.

The third period of Church history begins with the nominal conversion of Constantine. The scripture says, "there fell a great star from heaven, burning as it were a lamp." Revelation 8:10. Stars represent the leaders of God's people (see Revelation 1:20-2:1), and fallen stars represent corrupt leaders. Satan was at one time an "anointed cherub" standing next to the throne of God, and was the highest representative of the heavenly host. Ezekiel 28:14 He was given the name "Lucifer," which means "day star," because of his great beauty, knowledge, and leadership ability. Isaiah 14:12, margin. Yet, Jesus said of him after his rebellion: "I beheld Satan as lightning fall from heaven." Luke 10:18. Likewise, the fallen star under discussion is in reference to Constantine, who Eusebius speaks of as a "mighty luminary," "diffusing the effulgence of his holy light to the ends of the whole world." *Life of Constantine*, book 1, chaps IV, VIII. Constantine claimed to be a follower of the true God, but the scripture refers to him as "Wormword," or bitterness. He fell upon "the rivers, and upon the fountains of waters," representing His corruption of the gospel ministry through whom truth was to flow. Those that believe in Jesus are said to have "rivers of living water" flowing from within them, and the Lord says of Himself that He is the "fountain of living waters." John 7:38; Jeremiah 2:13. Consequently, through Constantine's corrupting works, "many men died of the waters, because they were made bitter." Revelation 8:9-11. His conversion was a political maneuver to gain power over his rivals, and history proves that he was nothing but pagan:

> "Eusebius tells us in his 'Life of Constantine,' book 1, chapter 27, that it was when Constantine was in Gaul, meditating an attack upon Maxentius, that he first decided to recognize the God of the Christians. His motive was purely a selfish one. Attributing magical power to his

opponent, he concluded that it would not do for him to depend on his military forces alone; he also must have supernatural assistance in his battles." *Sunday: The Origin of its Observance in the Christian Church*, p. 89.

The wars that followed were the first to be fought in the name of the meek and lowly Christ, and the vision by the Tigris focuses upon these same events:

> **"And he shall stir up his power and his courage against the king of the south with a great army; and the king of the south shall be stirred up to battle with a very great and mighty army; but he shall not stand: for they shall forecast devices against him. Yea, they that feed of the portion of his meat shall destroy him, and his army shall overflow: and many shall fall down slain."** Daniel 11:25-26.

Early in the forth century a change came to the Roman Empire. Because the Church was greatly persecuted the bishops of the city of Rome appealed to Constantine, emperor of Gaul, to deliver them from the hand of Maxentius, a cruel and contemptible pagan emperor:

> "In A.D. 312, an embassy from Rome went to Constantine at Arles, and in the name of the Senate and people requested him to deliver the city from the despotism of the tyrant. Constantine gladly embraced the opportunity thus offered, and quickly set out toward Rome." Jones, *The Two Republics*, p. 180.

Constantine, whose only desire was for power, gave himself over as the military leader of an apostate Christianity. The passage says that he was to "stir up his power and his courage against the king of the south," the pagan Maxentius. On his way to Italy with about 98,000 men, "a great army," he claims to have seen a vision of the cross and was instructed to paint it on the shields of his soldiers. By doing this Constantine was appealing to the Christians in Maxentius' army to recognize their "true friend" and change sides, thus he "forecast devices against him." Nevertheless, Maxentius had "a very great and mighty army" numbering 170,000 infantry and 8,000 horsemen situated in the city of Verona in northern Italy while he remained at Rome with a massive reserve greater than that in the north.

Constantine first stormed Susa and took it. He next marched upon Turin, Brescia and finally Verona, where, beginning in the afternoon and continuing through the night he crushed the northern forces. From there he went on to Aquileia and Modena where he fought against great resistance but was victorious. After this the road was open to Rome, and the prophetic significance of the next battle is clearly expressed with the following:

> "Thus, when the battle was joined, both commanders were assured of victory by their protecting gods, and at least in as much as they were both acutely aware of the fact, the chroniclers were right to see the battle in retrospect as one of the decisive clashes between Christianity and paganism." Smith, *Constantine the Great*, p. 110.

On the 28th of October, A.D. 312, the battle of Milvian Bridge was fought. Constantine divided his army into two groups, and when Maxentius came out to meet him on the Via Flaminia, he was surprised by an attack at his left flank when the rest of Constantine's army came down the Via Cassia. The problem for Maxentius lay in the fact that his intelligence officers had failed to inform him of the division of Constantine's army, and herein is the passage fulfilled that says, "they that feed of the portion of his meat shall destroy him." In the midst of the confusion Maxentius and his army tried to retreat, multitudes crowded onto the Milvian Bridge, and thousands ran into the Tiber River and drowned. Maxentius himself lost his life in the conflict. So the pagan army, "the king of the south," was to "overflow: and many shall fall down slain." The word "overflow" in the original means to drowned; thus the prophecy is again confirmed by the history of the events.

The Edict of Milan

Just as the "king of the south" referred to more than one of the Ptolemies in the early part of the vision by the Tigris, so the "king of the south" here refers to more than one of the pagan leaders of the Roman Empire. Constantine overthrew Maxentius and became ruler of much of the Western half of the empire, but there were two other pagan rulers left in the kingdom, Licinius and Maximin Daia. The events that transpired between Constantine, Licinius, and the Church are spoken of in the next few verses of the vision:

> **"And both these kings' hearts shall be to do mischief, and they shall speak lies at one table; but it shall not prosper: for yet the end shall be at the time appointed."** *Daniel 11:27.*

In January and February of A.D. 313, Constantine met with Licinius, the pagan emperor in the East, at Milan to finish an alliance between them. It was at this time that the famous Edict of Milan was written, giving freedom to all Christians throughout the Roman Empire:

"When I, Constantine Augustus, and I, Licinius Augustus, came under favourable auspices to Milan… We have resolved among the first things to ordain, those matters by which reverence and worship to the Deity might be exhibited. That is how we may grant likewise to the Christians, and to all, the free choice to follow that mode of worship which they may wish…" Eusebius, *Ecclesiastical History*, book X, chap. V.

"And both these kings hearts shall be to do mischief, and they shall speak lies at one table." Although peace was made between Constantine and Licinius, both intended to rule the world themselves. Licinius was not a persecutor of the Christians but had no special love for them, and he agreed to the edict only at the prompting of Constantine. Moreover, at Milan, Constantine and Licinius agreed to appoint a new Caesar in Rome, a man by the name of Bassianus, a relative of Licinius, and also married to Anastasia, Constantine's stepsister. Through Bassianus, Licinius had planned the overthrow of Constantine, but at Milan his plot was not detected. Before the talks were complete, news came to Licinius that Maximin Daia had crossed into Europe with his army and took Byzantium. Licinius immediately left Milan, and on April 30, with a small force of only 30,000 men, he surprised and quickly overthrew Maximin. His success left Constantine and himself joint rulers of the Roman Empire.

After his victory Licinius soon initiated his plot in the late summer of A.D. 313 while Constantine was still in Italy. Bassianus and his brother Senecio were planning to murder Constantine at the instigation of Licinius. This would leave Licinius as Augustus Maximus. "But," as the scripture says, "it shall not prosper." Constantine detected the plot, and Bassianus was executed. Then, in the summer of A.D. 314, at the instigation of Constantine, a skirmish broke out between them, at which Constantine came out victorious over Licinius. The following year peace was concluded between them once again for a number of years. "For yet the end shall be at the time appointed" is in reference to the war between Constantine and Licinius and shall be discussed in the section: The Overthrow of Licinius.

The Original Sunday Law

We have already mentioned that Constantine brought corruption into the Church by uniting himself closely with its leaders. After the Edict of Milan Constantine became increasingly involved with them. Those who had gone through many years of persecution were suddenly catered to by the state. They were sitting in "Satan's seat," and did not know it. Revelation 2:13. They had helped Constantine gain power, and in exchange he officially recognized the exaltation of Sunday that the Bishops thought to perpetuate. Daniel 7:25, where the "little horn" power would "think to change times and laws," is primarily speaking of the change of the Bible Sabbath from Saturday to Sunday by the Bishops of the corrupt Church. This is obvious, because the Sabbath is the only commandment that refers to time. Directly related to this is the original law for the enforcement of Sunday, and the vision by the Tigris now directs us to this event:

> **"Then shall he return into his land with great riches; and his heart shall be against the holy covenant; and he shall do exploits, and return to his own land."** *Daniel 11:28.*

Constantine returned "into his land" in possession of "great riches" (Hebrew: a large estate), which, after his brief engagement with Licinius, added Upper Moesia, the Pannonias, Macedonia, and the Greek peninsula to his possessions along with the rest of Europe and Northern Africa that he already possessed. Licinius continued to hold Thrace, Asia Minor, Roman possessions in the East, Egypt, and Libya. For eight years peace lasted between Constantine and Licinius. During this time they both strengthened themselves for war, and Constantine spent much of it in religious affairs: "And his heart shall be against the holy covenant," that is, he would set his heart against the Commandments of God, the foundation of His everlasting covenant. (See Exodus 34:28; Hebrews 8:10.) The change that the bishops had made to the Sabbath of God, by longs years of philosophical reasoning, was now enforced by the establishment of the first Sunday law in recorded history on March 7, A.D. 321:

> "On the venerable Day of the Sun let the magistrates and people residing in cities rest, and let all workshops be closed. In the country, however, persons engaged in agriculture may freely and lawfully continue their pursuits; because it often happens that another day is not so suitable for grain-sowing or for vine-planting; lest by neglecting the proper moment for such operations the bounty of heaven should be lost." Schaff, *History of the Christian Church*, vol. 3, chap. VII, sec. 75, par. 5, note 1.

Constantine's words do not immediately appear to be religious. Nevertheless Eusebius, a bishop of the Catholic Church and a personal friend and advisor of Constantine, commenting upon this decree declared:

"All things whatsoever that it was duty to do on the Sabbath, these we have transferred to the Lord's day." Eusebius, *Commentary on the Psalms*, chap. XCII; quoted in *The Sabbath Manual* by Justin Edwards, pp. 125-127.

And again:

"He commanded, too, that one day should be regarded as a special occasion for religious worship." Eusebius, *Oration in Praise of Constantine*, chap. IX.

Thus Constantine, in enforcing an apostate Christian institution of the bishops, set his heart "against the holy covenant," for to impose a change to any of God's laws, which are to be placed into the heart of the believer and worked out in the life, is to pervert God's covenant. God's Law must be obeyed through freedom of conscience and love to Him. Nevertheless, the Sabbath command is especially given the designation: "perpetual covenant." Exodus 31:16. Constantine had no concept of the purpose of the Sabbath, or of the holiness of God's Law, for he was pagan to the core. His only purpose was to unite his empire, and the exaltation of Sunday did its work in merging the pagans and the apostate Christians into one body. "Of all his blending and melting together of Christianity and heathenism, none is more easy to see through than this making of his Sunday law: The Christians worshipped their Christ, the heathen their sungod." Heggtveit, *Illustrated Church History*, p. 202. Thus Constantine and the bishops fulfilled the prophecy unknowingly!

Additionally, the political power given to the Catholic Bishops by Constantine had the most devastating results. In this blending of church and state we see the first glimpses of religious persecution that always follows such unions and clearly characterized the Roman Church for 1260 years. For some years there had been contention between the Catholic Church and the Donatists, a group of African Christians that refused to have a Catholic Bishop over them. The armies of Constantine were given to the Catholics to suppress the religious strife, and a massacre ensued in the spring A.D. 321. Nevertheless, within three months Constantine accepted an appeal from the Donatists, and he issued an edict permitting the exiled to return to their homes. The fulfillment of the passage before us can easily be seen in the life of Constantine. "He shall do exploits, and return to his own land;" the "exploits" being those of his armies against the Donatists after which he saw his error, was obliged to "return," withdraw his armies from Africa, and issue another edict of religious toleration. Constantine continued to remain neutral in the Donatist question the rest of his reign, but he did not hesitate to meddle in other religious affairs.

The Overthrow of Licinius

Licinius became increasingly hostile toward the Christians in his realm. "He re-kindled the persecution of the Christians, like a long-extinguished fire, and fanned the unhallowed flame to a fiercer height than any who had gone before him." Eusebius, *Life of Constantine*, book II, chap. I. The persecutions increased the agitation with Constantine and the bishops of Rome, and at length Constantine instigated war. The vision by the Tigris now brings us to the final conflict between Constantine and Licinius, "the king of the south."

> **"At the time appointed he shall return, and come toward the south; but it shall not be as the former, or as the latter. For the ships of Chittim shall come against him: therefore he shall be grieved, and return, and have indignation against the holy covenant: so shall he do; he shall even return, and have intelligence with them that forsake the holy covenant."** *Daniel 11:29-30.*

At the appointed time Constantine was to make war with the pagans. "But it shall not be as the former," as when Justin and his followers entered "peaceably even upon the fattest places of the province," Rome and Alexandria, spreading their philosophical ideas among the pagans as verse 24 brings out. Nor would it be "as the latter," when Constantine came against Maxentius in the invasion of Italy with his "great army," as verses 25 and 26 reveal. "For the ships of Chittim shall come against him;" that is, ships from Constantine shall come against Licinius. The Strong's Hebrew dictionary on the word Chittim, number 3794, reads: "an islander in general, i.e. the Greeks or Romans on the shores opposite Palestine." Constantine's war with Licinius was not only a military expedition; both men had assembled navies.

By the summer of A.D. 323, Constantine had amassed 200 warships, and Licinius also constructed 350 of them. Moreover, they both recruited large armies and they met in battle on the third day of July at Hadrianopolis. Licinius lost 34,000 men and many thousands more deserted him. He then retreated to Byzantium. Constantine followed him there and waited for his son Crispus whom he had put in charge of his fleet. Licinius' officers and sailors were inexperienced and when the battle was engaged Abantus committed too many vessels for them to move freely. His losses to Crispus were great, and to make matters worse, "during the second night a storm swept over his constricted anchorages, piling up ships on the shore." Smith, *Constantine the Great*, p. 174. This was the end of Licinius' fleet:

> "Then his [Constantine's] fleet under Crispus defeated Licinius' under Abantus (Amandus) not far from the entrance to the Hellespont, and a storm then destroyed Licinius' fleet utterly." Burckhardt, *The Age of Constantine the Great*, p. 281.

With the ruin of 130 ships and the loss of nearly 5,000 sailors Licinius quickly fled to Chrysopolis. Constantine pursued him there and when the battle was finally engaged he again fought and defeated Licinius. After loosing another 25,000 men, Licinius fled to Nicomedia, was persuaded to surrender by his wife Constantia, and was finally murdered by the hand of Constantine in A.D. 324. Thus the king of the South was here overthrown, and the entire Roman Empire was for the first time placed into the hands of a Christian emperor. Nevertheless, paganism still remained strong in the Roman Empire, and its destruction will be more fully discussed in the section: The Establishment of the Papacy.

The Council of Nicaea

The last part of verse 30 is now before us: "therefore he shall be grieved, and return, and have indignation against the holy covenant: so shall he do; he shall even return, and have intelligence with them that forsake the holy covenant." This is in reference to the council of Nicaea, in A.D. 325, over which Constantine himself presided. After his victory over Licinius he found the church divided over the Arian controversy, and in an attempt to unite it he called together 300 Bishops throughout the empire to the city of Nicaea. Eusebius states of Constantine that he "proceeded through the midst of the assembly, like some heavenly messenger of God, clothed in raiment which glittered as it were with rays of light, reflecting the glowing radiance of a purple robe, and adorned with the brilliant splendor of gold and precious stones." *Life of Constantine*, book III, chap. X. Constantine was obviously exalted by the bishops of Rome as Dr. Schaff also relates:

> "What a revolution of opinion in bishops who had once feared the Roman emperor as the worst enemy of the church, and who now greeted the same emperor in his half barbarous attire as an angel of God from heaven, and gave him, though not yet even baptized, the honorary presidency of the highest assembly of the church!" *History of the Christian Church*, vol. 3, chap. IX, sec. 120, par. 6.

The fallen messenger was doing his work of corruption, and the apostate Bishops readily yielded truth for power and money. During the council, and for the first time in the history of Christianity, canons were formed regulating forms and practices of worship. The commandments and traditions of men were replacing God's Holy Law, and since truth was set aside and men were no longer controlled by conscience the arm of the state was used to enforce false doctrines and the requirements of the bishops. In a letter written by Constantine to the churches of the Alexandrians about the council, he declared:

> "Beloved brethren, hail! We have received from Divine Providence the inestimable blessing of being relieved from all error, and united in the acknowledgment of one and the same faith... For that which has commended itself to the judgment of three hundred bishops cannot be other than the doctrine of God; seeing that the Holy Spirit dwelling in the minds of so many dignified persons has effectually enlightened them respecting the Divine will." Socrates, *Ecclesiastical History*, book I, chap. IX.

Constantine's words of exaltation toward the Bishops were obviously meant to pacify and unify the various factions in Christendom. On the other hand, in his letter to the rest of the churches of Rome, Constantine reflects the hatred of the Bishops toward the Jews and anything Jewish. Additionally, he was instrumental in establishing the exact day upon which Easter was to be celebrated making sure that there was no connection to the Jewish Passover. He then again exalts the Bishops to the place of God:

> "In the first place, it seemed very unworthy of this most sacred feast, that we should keep it following the custom of the Jews; a people who having imbrued their hands in a most heinous outrage, have thus polluted their souls, and are deservedly blind... But to sum up matters briefly, it was determined by common consent that the most holy festival of Easter should be solemnized on one and the same day... These things therefore being thus consistent, do you gladly receive this heavenly and truly divine command: for whatever is done in the sacred assemblies of the bishops is referable to the Divine will..." *Ibid*.

In the council Constantine had "intelligence with them," the bishops, "that forsake the holy covenant." The section in reference to the feast of Easter begins this way, "We have also gratifying intelligence to communicate to you..." *Ibid*. The testimony of history is clear that if there was anything that served to lower the influence of the Sabbath of the fourth Commandment it was the hatred of the Jews and the establishment of the feast of Easter. (It is interesting to note that the Sabbath was given at creation, two millenniums before the existence of a Jew. Nevertheless, the association is made to the Jews anyway.) For centuries the councils of the Church continued to make laws suppressing the Sabbath of the fourth Commandment and exalting Sunday. The council of Laodicea, in A.D. 364, decreed that: "Christians shall not Judaize and be idle on Saturday, but shall work on that day... If, however, they are found Judaizing, they shall be shut out from Christ." Hefele, *History of the Councils of the Church*, vol. II, p. 316. Consequently, when the Commandments and Laws of God are replaced by tradition then it is obvious that the "holy covenant" cannot be made, for God's Law must be written into the heart. Thus it is clear also that Constantine was associating with those who were forsaking the "holy covenant," since they were the ones who provoked Him in making laws against it.

Additionally, it was during this time, while the Bishops were uniting themselves closely to Constantine that he wrote the following letter, in part, to Eusebius of Caesarea:

> "I have thought fit to intimate this to your prudence, that you should order to be transcribed on well-prepared parchment, by competent writers accurately acquainted with their art, fifty copies of the Sacred Scriptures, both legibly described, and of a portable size, the provision and use of which you know to be needful for the instruction of the Church." Socrates, *Ecclesiastical History*, Book I, chap IX.

Eusebius was conformed to the doctrines and writings of the philosophical Origen. The fifty copies "of the Sacred Scriptures" that Constantine asked him to make came from the manipulated, corrupt manuscripts of Origen:

> "Eusebius was a great admirer of Origen and a deep student of his philosophy. He had just edited the fifth column of the Hexapla which was Origen's Bible. Constantine chose this, and asked Eusebius to prepare fifty copies for him." Wilkinson, *Our Authorized Bible Vindicated*, p. 20.

Copies of these manuscripts are believed to have made it to our day. Two of them are known as the Vaticanus and the Siniaticus, which are used almost exclusively when translating bibles today. Jerome used similar corruptions in his translation of the Latin Vulgate in A.D. 380, which became the authorized Catholic Bible for all time. The problem with theses manuscripts is that they downplay the importance of obedience to God's Law and have made Christianity merely a relational institution. (Compare Revelation 22:14 in any version translated primarily from the Vaticanus. This corruption reads: "Blessed are they that wash their robes," while versions translated from the Received Text read: "Blessed are they that do His commandments." The former leaves men to determine their own standard while the later is definitive.) Those who have accepted the pure and holy manuscripts of God in opposition to the corrupt have endured fierce persecution. Consequently, the association of the Church with Constantine resulted in a further degrading of its purity by the production of these apostate manuscripts of the scriptures. Thus it can clearly be said that Constantine had "indignation against the holy covenant."

The Establishment of the Papacy

If the prophecy spent a lot of time on Antiochus the Great so that we can understand the importance of the land of Babylon to the phrase "the king of the north," then we can be sure that when the prophecy spends seven verses upon the events in the life of Constantine it is for a reason. Constantine became the first leader of a corrupt Christian-political union. The wars fought by him in the name of Christ were literal, physical wars. They were fought with real weapons, and real blood was shed and people died. This is an extremely significant principle to the prophecy and to the final conflict at the end. The fact that spiritual powers fight real, literal wars will come into play in verse 40, for it is spiritual Babylon and Egypt that are in conflict there. Nevertheless, the verse under discussion finalizes the events in the life of Constantine, moves onto the complete overthrow of paganism in the Roman Empire, and then to the establishment of the Papacy:

> "And arms shall stand on his part, and they shall pollute the sanctuary of strength, and shall take away the daily sacrifice, and they shall place the abomination that maketh desolate." *Daniel 11:31.*

The first part of the verse before us would be more accurately translated: "And arms from him shall stand, and they will pollute the sanctuary, the fortress." This is clearly referring to the removal of the glory and capital of the pagan Roman Empire from Rome, "the sanctuary, the fortress" (see verses 7, 10, 19 and 39 on the word "fortress"), to Constantinople by Constantine in the year A.D. 330. Constantine did much for his new city to take the glory from Rome. He surrounded it with high walls, built wonderful palaces in the southern districts, peopled it with noblemen and their households from the old city, beautified it with a hippodrome, fountains, porticoes, and other buildings, built a new Senate

House and placed the same honors upon it as the former Senate, and brought the pagan images from their temples into the common light of day to adorn it. Thus the fortress was polluted and a new capital established in the Eastern Roman Empire.

The wars against the pagans, which Constantine started, would take nearly 180 more years of struggle before paganism finally collapsed. However, the pagans not only had the corrupt Church to contend with, they had the barbarian tribes from the north pressing upon them, and by the year A.D. 476 the Western Roman Empire had fractured into ten divisions. The ten tribes and the date of their accessions are well documented by Jones in his work *The Great Empires of Prophecy*. Here are the ten: the Heruli, the Vandals, the Ostrogoths, the Alamanni, the Visigoths, the Franks, the Suevi, the Burgundians, the Anglo-Saxons, and the Lombards. These ten barbarian tribes are symbolized by the ten "toes" in Daniel chapter two, and by the "ten horns" upon the fourth beast, which represents Rome, in Daniel seven: "And the ten horns out of this kingdom are ten kings that shall arise." Daniel 7:24.

The second part of the verse under discussion, "and shall take away the daily" (the word "sacrifice" is not in the original and has no significance to the text), next jumps to the time when the pagan power would be completely overthrown. This "daily," which is also translated "continual" or "continually" in 80 places in the Old Testament, is the same as the "daily" of Daniel chapter eight. There the angel explains that it was "by reason of transgression" that "a host was given" to the Roman "little horn" to oppose the "daily," the pagan power, which was also to be "taken away" from him. Daniel 8:11-12. The apostle Paul gives us a divine commentary upon this "daily" that was taken away. He says that it would restrain the rise of "the mystery of iniquity…until he be taken out of the way." The "mystery of iniquity" was understood for centuries by Protestantism to be the Roman Papacy, and is also called "that Wicked." 2 Thessalonians 2:7-8. This phrase links us back to Daniel eight, for the word "Wicked" in this passage could also be translated as "transgression" like it is in 1 John 3:4. Thus the "daily" that is taken away, so that the papal "transgression" could arise, in Daniel eight is the pagan powers in the Roman Empire. Matthew Henry gives a similar thought on the restraining power in 2 Thessalonians 2:6-8:

> "This is supposed to be the power of the Roman empire [pagan of course], which the apostle did not think fit to mention more plainly at that time; and it is notorious that, while this power continued, it prevented the advances of the bishops of Rome to that height of tyranny to which soon afterwards they arrived." *A Commentary on the Whole Bible*, vol. 6.

Paul did not state directly that the "he" that was restraining was the pagan Roman powers that were controlling the empire, because it would have caused much opposition to his letter and his ministry. Nevertheless, he tells us in his letter to the Romans that the "he," the "daily," or the "continual" did then represent the reigning powers of pagan Rome:

> "The powers that be [pagan Roman rulers] are ordained of God. Whosoever therefore resisteth the power, resisteth the ordinance of God: and they that resist shall receive to themselves damnation. For rulers are not a terror to good works, but to the evil. Wilt thou then not be afraid of the power? do that which is good, and thou shalt have praise of the same: For he is the minister of God to thee for good. But if thou do that which is evil, be afraid; for he beareth not the sword in vain: for he is the minister of God, a revenger to execute wrath upon him that doeth evil. Wherefore ye must needs be subject, not only for wrath, but also for conscience sake. For for this cause pay ye tribute also: for they are God's ministers, attending continually upon this very thing." *Romans 13:3-6.*

Thus, it was "he," the "rulers" of pagan Rome, that "continually" restrained the rise of "evil" until the Papacy received the "arms" that it needed to ascend to power. In the year A.D. 496, Clovis, king of the Franks, was converted to the Catholic faith, and immediately went to war for the Church. In 507 he overthrew the Visigoths in southern France and "The following year [A.D. 508], Clovis received the honorary title of consul from the Eastern emperor, Anastasius I, and entered Tours wearing a purple tunic and scattering gold to the crowd, who acclaimed him consul or emperor." *Encyclopedia Britannica*, article "European History and Culture," 2003 ed., vol. 18, p. 610. Theodoric, ruler of the barbarians in Italy, promptly made peace with Clovis, and after this the Catholic power continued to expand. Hence this year, A.D. 508, marks the end of paganism in the Roman Empire, and thus it was during the reign of Clovis that the "daily" was "taken away" from Rome. The king of the South is not mentioned again until verse forty. Notice this statement about Clovis:

> "He had on all occasions shown himself the heartless ruffian, the greedy conqueror, the bloodthirsty tyrant; but by his conversion he had led the way to the triumph of Catholicism; he had saved the Roman Church from the Scylla and Charybdis of heresy and paganism." *Historian's History of the World*, Vol. VII, p. 477.

The cessation of the barbarian invasions and the removal of paganism from Rome in the days of Clovis mark the demise of the daily or the king of the South. If A.D. 508 is the proper date of its removal then the beginning of the "time" or 360 year period of Daniel 11:24 must of necessity begin in the year A.D. 148. (See the section: Philosophy Corrupts the Church.) The exact date of the entrance of Justin Martyr into the city of Rome is not established, but various sources testify of his entrance there just prior to the year A.D. 150:

> "Justin came to Rome around A.D. 150 or slightly earlier — a date fixed by the date of the first Apology — where he founded his school of philosophical instruction and engaged in active controversy with other philosophers and 'Christian' teachers." Barnard, *Justin Martyr: His Life and Thought*, p. 13.

Hence, the war against paganism in the Roman Empire began with Justin Martyr in A.D. 148 and ended with Clovis in 508. This prepared the way for the establishment of the Papacy. The first three prophecies of Daniel have both a pagan and a papal phase of Rome: The "legs of iron" in chapter two, the beast with "great iron teeth" and "ten horns" in chapter seven, and the "daily" desolation in chapter eight are all symbolic of the Roman Empire under its pagan phase. (See Daniel 2:33, 40; 7:7, 17; 8:9, 11, 13, 23-25.) The feet of "iron and clay," the "little horn" that grows up on the ten-horned beast in Daniel seven, and the "transgression of desolation" in chapter eight all represent papal Rome. (See Daniel 2:31, 41-43; 7:8, 24-25; 8:10, 12-13.) Thus, the first three prophecies of Daniel are clearly parallel, and his vision by the Tigris is no exception and also speaks of the Papacy: "And they shall place the abomination that maketh desolate." The Abomination, or papal Rome, was set up after pagan Rome, the king of the South, was "taken away."

In Daniel chapter seven we are told that the papal "little horn" could not be set up until it first subdued "three kings" of the original "ten horns." Daniel 7:24. These three kingdoms were the Heruli in A.D. 493, the Vandals in A.D. 534, and the Ostrogoths in March, A.D. 538. They were all Arian powers that were opposed to the establishment of the Papacy, and therefore had to be removed before the Papacy could exercise its civil power over the kings of Europe. With the destruction of the Ostrogothic army, the last of the three Arian kingdoms was finally subdued. Papal Rome could then wield its political power over the entire Western Roman Empire. This year must therefore be taken as the beginning date of the "abomination," and marks the rise of the fifth government system of Rome — the Papacy.

Summary of Chapter Four

In this chapter we have seen a change in the principles used to interpret the geographical language of the Middle East. The types and the history of the events support the change from the geographical to the spiritual. The experience of Adam, Jonah, Noah, and others prefigured events of Jesus and His Church. The sanctuary system as well is a type of the greater ministry of Christ and His relationship with His people. Israel and the nations that surrounded them in ancient times are also types of nations, powers, and events that transpire after the cross of Jesus. The types are therefore prophetic in nature. Consequently, the sanctuary, Israel, Egypt, and Babylon are symbols that are used much in the prophecies of Daniel and the Revelation, and unless we view them as antitypical we will not understand prophecy.

The introduction of pagan philosophical principles through teachers such as Justin Martyr, Clement, and Origen brought corrupt doctrines and traditions into the Church. Eventually these teachers gained the ascendancy and their teachings took the place of divine truth. In the forth century the leaders of the Church became closely united with the state, and Constantine used his armies to support and advance its cause against paganism. Pagan Rome is referred to as spiritual "Egypt" or "the king of the south" by the vision. A principle that becomes apparent, when speaking of the battles of Constantine, is that these spiritual powers are still literal powers that make literal war. We cannot spiritualize away the wars that have transpired, and make them wars of words or doctrinal controversies.

Laws were also made to support the false teachings of the Bishops, and in particular Sunday worship was established throughout the empire. The Sabbath of the fourth commandment is called "a perpetual covenant" (Exodus 31:16), and it is referred to in the prophecy when it says that Constantine's "heart shall be against the holy covenant" when he established the first Sunday law in recorded history in A.D. 321. This is the clear meaning of the passage, for God gave three full verses of events in the life of Constantine the Great leading up to this one event. He also gave three verses of events in the life of Constantine after his Sunday legislation, so that we could be sure of its meaning.

Ultimately, through tradition and legislation and the overthrow of paganism and Aryanism in the Roman Empire the Papacy was officially established in A.D. 538.

Chapter 5: The Papal Dominion

In this chapter we shall discuss the long years of Papal rule. The Papacy's main characteristics in the prophecies are its religio-political union and its persecuting acts. It began its rule in the "dark ages," which lasted until the light of Bible truth sprouted in the Reformation and blossomed in the New World.

The Papal Church-State Union

The Papacy is called the "abomination that maketh desolate" because of the acts that it performs by uniting itself with the state. Through the state the Papacy controls men and persecutes those who disagree with her agenda. This union is spoken of in all four of Daniel's prophecies. The "great image" has feet of iron mingled with "brittle" clay. Daniel 2:41-43, margin. Clay is at times used in the Bible to represent God's people when it is soft and pliable, but when it is hard and unchangeable it represents an apostate and corrupt people. (See Isaiah 64:8; Jeremiah 18:1-6; Romans 9:17-26.) Thus, the iron represents the Roman Empire and the brittle clay that mingles with it symbolizes the apostate Roman Church.

The fourth beast with "great iron teeth" in the vision of Daniel seven is the Roman Empire, and the "little horn," which was different from the other ten horns and that "came up" among them, represents a religio-political system. Its works identify it: "And he shall speak great words against the most High, and shall wear out the saints of the most High, and think to change times and laws." Daniel 7:25. This horn that speaks against God, persecutes His people, and thinks to change His Law is obviously religious in nature, and wields the power of the state. The protestant reformers from the days of Wycliffe understood the "little horn" to be the papal Antichrist. George Joye, who was a contemporary of Tyndale, stated it clearly and accurately when he wrote: "This little horne was, & is the Antichristes kingdom of the popes of Rome, with al their unclene clargye." Froom, *The Prophetic Faith of Our Fathers*, vol. 2, p. 362. (In modern English Joye said: "This little horn was and is the Antichrist's kingdom of the popes of Rome with all their unclean clergy.") The great Protestant reformer, Martin Luther, also declared:

> When Daniel "saw the terrible wild beast which had ten horns, which, by the consent of all is the Roman Empire, he also beheld an-

other small horn come up in the middle of them. This is the Papal power, which rose up in the middle of the Roman Empire." *Works*, vol. II, p. 386.

This papal little horn "came up among" the ten divisions of the Roman Empire, but it rose to power "after them" in A.D. 538. It subdued "three kings," the Heruli, Vandals, and the Ostrogoths, and it thinks that it can change the "times and laws" of God. The most obvious of these changes being the Sabbath commandment, since it primarily deals with time. The papal little horn also became "more stout than his fellows," that is, it became more powerful than the other horns. (See Daniel 7:8, 24-25.) To these points most will agree that they clearly fit the Church of Rome. Thus Daniel's "little horn" in chapter seven is shown to be a corrupt religio-political system.

Additionally, in the scriptures God's people are often represented as a woman. The Lord speaking through Jeremiah says: "I have likened the daughter of Zion to a comely and delicate woman." Jeremiah 6:2. The apostle Paul speaking of the Church adds: "For I am jealous over you with godly jealousy: for I have espoused you to one husband, that I may present you as a chaste virgin to Christ." 2 Corinthians 11:2. The apostle in Ephesians chapter five describes the relationship between a man and a woman and then finishes his explanation by saying: "This is a great mystery: but I speak concerning Christ and the church." Ephesians 5:22-32. Thus the Church is described as a beautiful woman united to Christ in marriage.

When God's people unite themselves with the various nations around them they are likened to a woman playing the part of a harlot. The Lord declared of Israel as she united with the heathen: "Thou hast also committed fornication with the Egyptians… Thou hast played the whore also with the Assyrians… Thou hast moreover multiplied thy fornication in the land of Canaan unto Chaldea… How weak is thine heart, saith the Lord GOD, seeing thou doest all these things, the work of an imperious whorish woman." Ezekiel 16:26-30. The prophecy in Daniel eight uses male and female symbolism to represent the religio-political union of papal Rome. The following passage from the King James Bible is given with the tenses as they are in the original:

> "And out of one of them came forth a little horn [feminine], which waxed exceeding great, toward the south, and toward the east, and toward the pleasant land. And she waxed great, even to the host of heaven; and she cast down some of the host and of the stars to the ground, and stamped upon them. Yea, he magnified himself even against the prince of the host, and from him the daily was taken away,

and the place of his sanctuary was cast down. And an host was given her against the daily by reason of transgression, and she cast down the truth to the ground; and she practised, and prospered." *Daniel 8:9-12*, margin.

The female characteristics of the "little horn" in chapter eight obviously represent the actions of the corrupt Church, while the masculine signifies the actions perpetuated by the state. Therefore, the Roman state crucified the "prince of the host," had the "daily," pagan powers "taken away," and had the "place" of its pagan "sanctuary" removed from Rome to Constantinople. The apostate Church on the other hand persecutes God's people, the "host of heaven," receives an army to oppose the "daily by reason of transgression," "cast down the truth to the ground" by its corruption of the various doctrines and commandments of the Bible, and "prospered" while doing it.

The little horn of the beast of Daniel seven represents the Roman Church as it grew up and wielded the power of the state against the true Church of God, and the little horn in Daniel eight describes both the church and the state united. These little horn powers both persecute God's people, they both act against the Law of God, and consequently they both represent the Papacy. Invariably, whenever the Church controls the state there is always persecution of those that rebel against its authority, as happened to the Lollards and the Puritans in England and the Reformers and Evangelicals in Europe during the Reformation. This occurs because tradition and force are the controlling powers, which seek to shape the consciences of men, and not the conviction of the Holy Spirit by means of the scriptures. Thus it is easy to see why God calls the Papacy the "abomination that maketh desolate."

The Dark Ages

The early years of papal rule became known as the Dark Ages, which lasted until the middle of the 15th century and the beginning of the Renaissance. During the Dark Ages all learning was repressed with the exception of that sanctioned by the Papacy. Art, science, and the philosophical and cultural works of the previous thousand years were prohibited, and possession of these works would earn the holder the title of witch, necromancer, or some other appropriate designation to condemn him. The unfortunate result was often burning at the stake. The Bible, which is "a lamp…and a light" (Psalms 119:105), was also regarded with disdain, and the circulation of it was prohibited. Darkness beyond all human understanding had begun to grip the world, and the scripture relates it in the most graphic language in the forth trumpet:

"And the fourth angel sounded, and the third part of the sun was smitten, and the third part of the moon, and the third part of the stars; so as the third part of them was darkened, and the day shone not for a third part of it, and the night likewise." *Revelation 8:12*.

It is truly said that the noontime of the Papacy is the midnight of the world. Without the knowledge of the Bible, men were completely at the mercy of papal traditions and its superstitious teachings. Unfortunately, many scoffers believe that it was the Bible that brought the darkness, but the scripture says of itself: "if they speak not according to this word, it is because there is no light in them." Isaiah 8:20. It was those who were rejecting the Bible and God's Laws that brought the darkness, and the vision now focuses upon this period:

"And such as do wickedly against the covenant shall he corrupt by flatteries: but the people that do know their God shall be strong, and do exploits." *Daniel 11:32*.

The leaders of the papal religio-political "abomination" corrupted "by flatteries" those who were exalting human laws and traditions. These people were doing "wickedly against the covenant" by obeying the traditions of the Roman Church, taught by the bishops, rather than obeying God's Commandments. Thus the voice of truth was suppressed, and ultimately God's people, who were in the minority, were forced into desolate and solitary places. Jesus condemned the Jews for doing this very thing saying:

"This people draweth nigh unto me with their mouth, and honoureth me with their lips; but their heart is far from me. But in vain they do worship me, teaching for doctrines the commandments of men." *Matthew 15:8-9*.

Despite the darkness that was then prevailing throughout the western world, God still had those who were "strong" and determined to work for Him by doing "exploits." Through great sacrifice to themselves these Christians kept pure religion alive during all of the ages of darkness. A few among these people were the Albigenses, the Huguenots, and the Waldenses. The Waldenses could trace their origin back to the days of the apostle Paul, and they possessed unadulterated copies of the scriptures in the original languages of Greek and Hebrew as well as their native tongue. Disguised as humble laborers they proselytized throughout Europe, and they scattered portions of the scriptures wherever they went. The expanse of their missionary journeys is given in the following:

> "There was no kingdom of Southern and Central Europe to which these missionaries did not find their way, and where they did not leave traces of their visit in the disciples whom they made... Even the Seven-hilled City they feared not to enter, scattering the seed on ungenial soil, if perchance some of it might take root and grow." Wylie, *History of the Waldenses*, pp. 22-23.

Despite the forced repression of the scriptures, they gradually made their way throughout the land. The Old and New Testament "witnesses," according to the apostle John, prophesied, "clothed in sackcloth," during the long years of papal darkness. Revelation 11:3. Many were the converts of these humble laborers, and their efforts were slowly undermining the foundations of the Roman apostasy.

The Long Ages of Persecution

The fragments of the scriptures scattered throughout Europe did their work to illuminate the hearts of many, and those that accepted them rejoiced to find their Lord. "The entrance of thy words giveth light; it giveth understanding unto the simple." Psalms 119:130. As truth spread the papal rulers sought out the perpetrators. Many of the humble missionaries were arrested, and their lights were extinguished by the hatred of the power loving clergy. Wylie continues:

> "Their naked feet and coarse woolen garments made them somewhat marked figures in the streets of a city that clothed itself in purple and fine linen; and when their real errand was discovered, as sometimes chanced, the rulers of Christendom took care to further, in their own way, the springing of the seed, by watering it with the blood of the men who had sowed it." *History of the Waldenses*, p. 23.

Their lives were not sacrificed in vain. The scattering of the Word and the blood of these missionaries produced the fruit that later ripened into the Protestant Reformation. Nevertheless, the persecution of these humble laborers is clearly revealed by the prophecies. The opening of the fourth seal is simultaneous with the sounding of the fourth trumpet in the Revelation, which reveals the Dark Ages. This seal declares that power was given to the Papacy "to kill with sword, and with hunger, and with death, and with the beasts of the earth." Revelation 6:8. This passage is also parallel to Daniel 7:25 where it says that the "little horn" would "wear out the saints of the most High," and to chapter eight which declares that God's people would be "trodden under foot" by the papal "transgression of desolation." Daniel 8:13. The vision by the Tigris also corresponds perfectly with the other prophecies:

"And they that understand among the people shall instruct many: yet they shall fall by the sword, and by flame, by captivity, and by spoil, many days." Daniel 11:33.

In His message to the fourth Church God rebuked His people for allowing the Roman Church, "that woman Jezebel, which calleth herself a prophetess, to teach." Revelation 2:20. Nevertheless, there were some among the people then living throughout the empire that studied and understood Bible truth, and He used these people to "instruct many." When the light of truth, started by the Waldenses and other missionaries, began to break it was supplemented by the teachings of Wycliffe, "the Morning Star of the Reformation," early in the 14th century. Then came Huss and Jerome, and in A.D. 1517 Luther posted his 95 Thesis against the abuses of the Roman Church upon the Church door at Wittenberg signaling the beginning of the Protestant Reformation. Simultaneously, other reformers, including Zwingle and Calvin, began to spring up across Europe. Then came William Tyndale and his translation of the "Received Text" of Erasmus, which was intended to give the "plowboy" a clear knowledge of the scriptures. And later, in the 18th century John Wesley became a powerful teacher and instituted the "class meetings" to instruct his followers.

During this long period Rome sought to destroy those that she could not corrupt: "yet they shall fall by the sword, and by flame, by captivity, and by spoil, many days." Consider the following historical statement:

"That the Church of Rome has shed more innocent blood than any other institution that has ever existed among mankind, will be questioned by no Protestant who has a competent knowledge of history." Lecky, *History of the Rise and Influence of the Spirit of Rationalism in Europe*, vol. 2, p. 40.

Over 50 million people lost their lives by the hand of this religio-politial system throughout its 1260-year rule. It would take volumes to touch upon all of the different forms of cruelty and instances of persecution that happened during papal Rome's rule, but one device of the papal death machine stands above the rest — the Inquisition that began under pope Innocent III in the 13th century. It quickly became an extremely cruel weapon against those who were following the scriptures. It mattered not to the Papacy the age, sex, or rank of an individual. If anyone refused to accept its dictates they were considered heretics and were brought before the inquisitor and tried in the following manner:

> "The procedure, therefore, resolved itself mainly into a questioning of the accused by the inquisitor in order to determine if he really were a heretic. If he refused to answer or made statements that the inquisitor believed to be false, torture was employed to force the truth from him. He was then brought back into the courtroom and asked to sign, as a freely made confession, the words which had been wrung from him on the rack. But if he refused to sign, he often was put to the torture again." Thorndike, *The History of Medieval Europe*, pp. 446-447.

With the invention of the Inquisition a flood of terror was opened for God's people. Men had their property seized, and they were persecuted, tortured, and murdered. They were stretched, dismembered, flayed alive, fed to animals, beheaded, and drowned. Their children were stolen and forced into the Roman religion, and many of the women were raped and defiled by the wicked devices of their captors, and the popes of Rome sanctioned all of these atrocities under the fanciful cry of heresy! These horrors were committed for no other reason than for refusing to accept the false doctrines of the Papacy such as purgatory, image worship, the mass, and the papal Sunday institution. The persecution lasted for "many days" according to the prophecy, and, after the Papacy came to power, it continued with greater or lesser fury for centuries. Thus the prophecy is clearly fulfilled by the facts of history.

Help from the Comforter

The greatest need of man today is the presence of the Spirit of God. Jesus dwelt much upon the endowment of the Holy Spirit, and our acceptance of His Spirit is the best response that we can possibly give to God. With that gift come all of the resources of heaven. The Holy Spirit is not a power, but a divine person, and the Bible speaks of Him as having divine characteristics and emotions. He can be grieved, pleased, and vexed. (See Ephesians 4:30; Acts 15:28; Isaiah 63:10.) The Holy Spirit also speaks, comforts, teaches, testifies, reproves or convicts, guides, and imparts the love of God. (See also Acts 13:2; 9:31; John 14:26; 15:26; 16:8, 13; Romans 5:5.) When Jesus was about to part from this world He declared: "And I will pray the Father, and he shall give you another Comforter, that he may abide with you for ever." John 14:16. Thus God's people were promised continued help for the future by the impartation of the Holy Spirit, and it is this help from God's Spirit that the vision by the Tigris next speaks of:

> "**Now when they shall fall, they shall be holpen with a little help: but many shall cleave to them with flatteries.**" *Daniel 11:34.*

Jesus promised His followers that the Father would send to them the Holy Spirit. He was to be with them, to stand by their side and to comfort them, to teach them the things that they needed to know, and to speak through them when they stood before the kings of the earth: "And when they bring you unto the synagogues, and unto magistrates, and powers, take ye no thought how or what thing ye shall answer, or what ye shall say: For the Holy Ghost shall teach you in the same hour what ye ought to say." Luke 12:11-12. (See also Matthew 10:19-20.) Thus when God's people fell into the hands of the Roman abomination they were guaranteed a "little help." It was only in this way that they could sing praises as they were fed to lions, burned at the stake, and stretched on the rack.

The Holy Spirit will be with God's people if they are obedient to His will. Satan on the other hand uses anything, no matter how vile, to compel men to do his bidding. Thus God's cause during the papal persecution was not free from "flatteries." Many joined with them from selfish motives just as Judas associated himself with the disciples of Jesus. Satan was attempting to get God's people to trust in themselves and to exalt themselves, and therefore to destroy them, for the scripture says, "Pride goeth before destruction, and an haughty spirit before a fall." Proverbs 16:18. There is only safety in humility for the child of God: "The sacrifices of God are a broken spirit: a broken and a contrite heart, O God, thou wilt not despise." Psalms 51:17. Consequently, there will always be the unconverted in the church until the final shaking at which the Lord will separate His true children from the false, "the wheat" from "the tares." Matt 13:24-30.

Purification by Trial

God's children are not to shun trials and difficulties. It is through them that they are purified, for the Lord "shall sit as a refiner and purifier of silver: and he shall purify the sons of Levi, and purge them as gold and silver." Malachi 3:2-3. Trials must be expected, as the apostle declares: "all that will live godly in Christ Jesus shall suffer persecution." 2 Timothy 3:12. John the Baptist was beheaded, and Jesus was crucified. Shall we therefore expect to enter the city of God without trial?

"Beloved, think it not strange concerning the fiery trial which is to try you, as though some strange thing happened unto you: But rejoice, inasmuch as ye are partakers of Christ's sufferings; that, when his glory shall be revealed, ye may be glad also with exceeding joy." *1 Peter 4:12-13.*

"Blessed are they which are persecuted for righteousness' sake: for theirs is the kingdom of heaven. Blessed are ye, when men shall revile you, and persecute you, and shall say all manner of evil against you falsely, for my sake. Rejoice, and be exceeding glad: for great is your reward in heaven: for so persecuted they the prophets which were before you." *Matthew 5:10-12.*

No one likes trials and troubles, but the scripture does not promise a life of ease to the Christian. Rather, the scripture clearly promises persecution as revealed in the passages above, and the prophecy under discussion shows that the purpose of this persecution is meant to purify God's people:

"And some of them of understanding shall fall, to try them, and to purge, and to make them white, even to the time of the end: because it is yet for a time appointed." Daniel 11:35.

From the long list of believers that lost their lives by the Papacy there were those that had clear "understanding" of the scriptures and taught them. These Christians were at times weak and doubting, yet they found strength through the conviction of the Holy Spirit, prayer, and the study of the scriptures to seal their testimony with their blood. The persecution that came upon them was "to purge, and to make them white," so that they could testify to the power and glory of God in their lives.

The trials and persecutions were to last "even to the time of the end," or until the end of the 1260 years. (See chapter 7: The 1260 Years.) When the fifth seal was opened it described the anguish of God's children that were "slain for the word of God," and they cried out: "How long, O Lord, holy and true, dost thou not judge and avenge our blood on them that dwell on the earth?" The answer is given that, "they should rest yet for a little season, until their fellowservants also and their brethren, that should be killed as they were, should be fulfilled." Revelation 6:9-11. It seems strange to many that God would sit back and allow these things to happen to His children, but His purpose is to purify and prepare them for His kingdom as well as to reveal the true character of the papal system.

The Popes Blaspheme God

In Daniel chapter seven the papal little horn has "a mouth speaking great things," and these great things are spoken, "against the most High." Daniel 7:8, 25. In the book of Revelation the papal beast also has "a mouth speaking great things and blasphemies," and they are likewise spoken "against God." Revelation 13:5-6. These are obvious references to the same power and Revelation 13 will be discussed in more detail in chapter six. Additionally, the apostle Paul was also speaking of the Papacy when he said that the man of sin, "opposeth and exalteth himself above all that is called God, or that is worshipped; so that he as God sitteth in the temple of God, shewing himself that he is God." 2 Thessalonians 2:4. This statement by the apostle is his inspired interpretation of the vision by the Tigris:

> **"And the king shall do according to his will; and he shall exalt himself, and magnify himself above every god, and shall speak marvellous things against the God of gods, and shall prosper till the indignation be accomplished: for that that is determined shall be done."** *Daniel 11:36.*

In verse three the prophecy tells us that the mighty king, Alexander did "according to his will," and in verse 16 pagan Rome did the same and there were none that could "stand before him." The "king" mentioned here is the pope of Rome that also "shall do according to his will." The popes had universal sway over the nations of Europe for centuries. That the popes have had power to do their will is clear from history; one need only study Medieval Europe to know that these things are true. Consider the following quote about pope Gregory VII:

> "He also regarded the pope [himself] as entrusted by God with supreme oversight and control of all human society; he believed himself to be above kings, and empowered to issue orders to them and to punish them if they did not obey. He thought the State a worldly institution built up by sinful men who often were violent and unjust, whereas the Church was a divine foundation. Consequently the pope should correct erring or incompetent monarchs. Gregory was not content to try to free the Church from the control of feudal lords; he also attempted to bring various European states into feudal subjection to the Papacy… Gregory endeavored to make the rulers of Spain, England, Hungary, and Denmark his vassals." *The History of Medieval Europe*, p. 287.

The arrogance of the popes is disgusting to a pure and holy God, yet He allowed them to develop their pride for our sakes, so that we can see the character of this corrupt institution. He shall even "exalt himself, and magnify himself above every god, and shall speak marvellous things against the God of gods." Here in the verse under discussion the king speaks marvelous things, or blasphemies against God just as the other prophecies reveal. What is blasphemy? The Bible gives two definitions: First, the Jews speaking to Jesus said, "For a good work we stone thee not; but for blasphemy; and because that thou, being a man, makest thyself God." John 10:33. Jesus was God in human flesh, and therefore He had the right to claim divinity. Nevertheless, the Jews' definition, that man claiming to be God is blasphemy, is correct. The Pharisees likewise give us a second definition; when speaking about Jesus they said: "Who is this which speaketh blasphemies? Who can forgive sins, but God alone?" Luke 5:21. The second definition of blasphemy is man claiming the power to forgive sins. Jesus had the power to forgive sins being God in human flesh, but no other man can claim such a prerogative.

Do these two definitions fit papal Rome? Do the popes claim to be Gods on earth? Consider the following statement by pope John XXII:

> "He [the pope] alone promulgates law; he alone is absolved from all law. He alone sits in the chair of the blessed St. Peter, not as mere man, but as man and God." Milman, *History of Latin Christianity*, second edition, 1857, vol. 5, p. 278.

By claiming the right and power to create laws, to change the Commandments of God, and to free themselves from the obligation of the Law the popes set themselves in God's place, for the scripture says that, "the LORD is our lawgiver." Isaiah 33:22. Not only though do the popes claim that they have the right to change God's Laws, but the quote above is clearly a blasphemous claim by pope John XXII to be God on earth. This is not an isolated statement. Consider another: "All the names which in the Scriptures are applied to Christ, by virtue of which it is established that He is over the church, all the same names are applied to the Pope." Bellarmine, *On the Authority of the Councils*, chap. 17, 1628 ed., vol. 1, p. 266. Can we possibly call the pope Savior, Messiah, Prince of Peace, Creator, or Lord? I think not. Here is another similar statement by pope Leo XIII:

> "We [the popes] hold upon this earth the place of God Almighty." *The Great Encyclical Letters of Leo XIII*, 1894, p. 304.

And another statement by Pope Pius XI:

> "You know that I am the Holy Father, the representative of God on the earth, the Vicar of Christ, which means I am God on the earth." *The Bulwark*, October 1922, p. 104.

Can anyone deny the blasphemous character of such statements? These are not just a few isolated examples, but they reveal the character of a corrupt and detestable system of religion that has existed for many centuries. Nevertheless, does the Papacy claim the right and power to forgive sins, our second identification of blasphemy? The following statements speak for themselves:

> "The priest holds the place of the Saviour Himself, when, by saying, 'Ego te absolvo,' he absolves from sin ... To pardon a single sin requires all the omnipotence of God." Alphonsus de Liguori, *Dignity and Duties of the Priest*, pp. 34-36, 1888.

> "Does the Priest truly forgive the sins, or does he only declare that they are remitted? The Priest does really and truly forgive the sins in virtue of the power given to him by Christ." Deharbe, *A Complete Catechism of the Catholic Religion*, p. 279, 1924.

> "Yes, beloved brethren, the [Catholic] priest not only declares that the sinner is forgiven, but he really forgives him." Fr. Michael Mueller C.SS.R, *The Catholic Priest*, Baltimore, Maryland: 1872, Kreuzer Brothers, pp. 78-79.

These are clear statements from the Roman Church itself. That the popes have spoken marvelous things and blasphemies is obvious to all that will take the time to consider. Many more statements could be produced, but these few have been given for brevity. Consequently, this blasphemous power was to "prosper till the indignation be accomplished: for that that is determined shall be done." The indignation is in reference to the hatred propagated towards God's people, which continued until the Papacy lost its civil power. All those who refused to accept such blasphemous claims were persecuted, tortured, or killed. In three verses we have been told that this long period of persecution would come to an end. God obviously intended to comfort his afflicted people with these words.

The Pope Enforces Celibacy

The institution of Celibacy is an incredible invention of man. For centuries the Roman Church debated the issue of celibacy, and many believed that sexual intercourse was impure and must be restricted or eliminated from the clergy. The higher offices were the first to become celibate while the lower offices, under certain circumstances, required abstinence, but through time the lower offices were added to the restriction. In the tenth and eleventh centuries many were joining the Roman priesthood simply to gain control of the lands of Europe without any regard for spiritual things: "Feudal nobles, however, looked covetously upon the richly endowed monasteries and often sought the office of abbot for the sake of the lands." *The History of Medieval Europe*, p. 281. Simony was common, and the practice, by powerful priests, of transferring the Church office and lands from father to son also became widespread. Therefore: "To insure further that the clergy should not become worldly, it was felt that the rules against the marriage of the clergy must be strictly enforced, as is the case today in the Roman Catholic priesthood." *ibid.*, p. 282. Pope Gregory VII in A.D. 1075 prohibited by decree any married clergy from performing their priestly functions, and in 1139 the second Lateran Council declared existing marriages invalid and banned the marriage of priests completely. Thus over time the human institution of celibacy became canonized. The next verse under discussion points as well to the papal doctrine of celibacy:

"Neither shall he regard the God of his fathers, nor the desire of women, nor regard any god: for he shall magnify himself above all." Daniel 11:37.

Some have made the mistake of assuming that the prophecy is speaking of an atheistic power here. "Neither shall he regard the God of his fathers," does not mean, "neither shall he believe in the existence of God." This verse speaks rather of a corrupt religious organization. When the Israelites became corrupted by their traditions Isaiah declared that: "they regard not the work of the LORD, neither consider the operation of his hands." Isaiah 5:12. However, they still claimed at least a superficial belief in God. Thus the king that does not "regard the God of his fathers" is a religious power, and the prophecy is still speaking of the Papacy. The Papacy is an entirely human made religion based upon human traditions. It has exalted itself above all of the gods of the nations, and has magnified itself "above all" as we have already seen.

Man's "desire of women" was disregarded and the institution of celibacy was strictly enforced. The apostle Paul clearly speaks of this phenomenon in his first epistle to Timothy: "Now the Spirit speaketh expressly, that in the latter times some shall depart from the faith... forbidding to marry." 1 Timothy 4:1-3. However the apostle gave clear counsel on the institution of marriage:

> "For I would that all men were even as I myself. But every man hath his proper gift of God, one after this manner, and another after that. I say therefore to the unmarried and widows, it is good for them if they abide even as I. But if they cannot contain, let them marry: for it is better to marry than to burn." *1 Corinthians 7:7-9*.

The institution of celibacy has proved to do just the opposite of that for which it was intended. Many of the priests who were forced to leave their wives committed adultery because they could not "contain" themselves. Some took mistresses and others embraced homosexuality and indulged in the grossest of perversions. These perversions carried over into the society of the common people, and corruption multiplied. God had declared: "It is not good that the man should be alone… Therefore shall a man leave his father and his mother, and shall cleave unto his wife: and they shall be one flesh." Genesis 2:18-24. Today's pedophilia and homosexual problems in the Roman priesthood stem directly from disobedience to this institution of God. It is simply impossible to disregard God's commands without suffering consequences.

Death and the Immortal Soul

Two of the greatest falsehoods of Rome are the ideas that the soul of man lives on in consciousness after death and that the soul itself is immortal. These doctrines, which are closely related to each other, open the door to many other falsehoods, and are also directly connected to the worship of saints and relics. Few realize that these doctrines can have eternal consequences. However, with them Satan can impersonate the dead friends and relatives of God's people and through these impersonations he can convince the living to follow his lies and falsehoods. A good example of this is found in 1 Samuel. The prophet Samuel had died, so king Saul, being in a serious military situation, sought out a woman that had a "familiar spirit." 1 Samuel 28:7. In the séance that followed the woman said that she "saw gods ascending out of the earth. And he said unto her, What form is he of? And she said, An old man cometh up; and he is covered with a mantle. And Saul perceived that it was Samuel, and he stooped with his face to the ground, and bowed himself." 1 Samuel 28:13-14. The spirit then spoke to Saul and declared: "for the LORD hath rent the kingdom out of thine hand, and given it to thy neighbour, even to David." 1 Samuel 28:17. Saul believed the spirit and lost his life in the battle that followed, and the Bible says:

> "So Saul died for his transgression which he committed against the LORD, even against the word of the LORD, which he kept not,

and also for asking counsel of one that had a familiar spirit, to enquire of it." *1 Chronicles 10:13-14.*

A sad fate for a man that once served God because he disobeyed and enquired of "a familiar spirit" and not of the Lord. The Lord told the children of Israel to kill anyone with a familiar spirit. (See Leviticus 20:27; Deuteronomy 18:10-12.) At one time even "Saul had put away those that had familiar spirits, and the wizards, out of the land." 1 Samuel 28:3. His disobedience to God had led him to inquire of the spirit because the Lord would not answer him in his unrepentant state. Nevertheless, the spirits are obviously demons disguised as people returned from the dead or as angels. Thus Saul deceived himself in believing "it," for he was not talking to Samuel, but with a demon!

The state of man in death is clearly described in the Bible so that none need be deceived. According to the book of Job the dead man does not know and "perceiveth it not" when "his sons come to honour" him at his grave. Job 14:21. Solomon also tells us that "the living know that they shall die: but the dead know not any thing," and, he continues, "whatsoever thy hand findeth to do, do it with thy might; for there is no work, nor device, nor knowledge, nor wisdom, in the grave, whither thou goest." Ecclesiastes 9:5-6, 10. The Psalmist says that, "the dead praise not the LORD, neither any that go down into silence." "For in death there is no remembrance of thee." Psalm 115:17; 6:5. Moreover, the dead man's "breath goeth forth, he returneth to his earth; in that very day his thoughts perish." Psalm 146:4. Hence, this state or condition of man in death is described as an unconscious sleep. (See 2 Samuel 7:12; Psalm 13:3; Matthew 27:52; John 11:11-14; Acts 7:59-60; 1 Thessalonians 4:14.)

The idea that the soul of man is immortal does not come from the Bible, for man in his present existence is "mortal," and the Bible says that God "only hath immortality." Job 4:17; 1 Timothy 6:15-16. Man's soul is not a separate entity from his body that lives on after death. At man's creation the Bible declares that the Lord "breathed" into him "the breath of life; and man became a living soul." Genesis 2:7. The word "soul" typically just means a living person in the Bible (see Acts 2:41; 7:14; 27:37; Romans 13:1; 1 Peter 3:20), but it is sometimes used to mean the life of a believer in his incorruptible, immortal body received in the resurrection in contrast to his corruptible, mortal, earthly state that he currently possesses. (See Matthew 10:28; 1 Corinthians 15:51-53; Revelation 22:12.) The soul does not have life of itself, for "the soul that sinneth, it shall die." Ezekiel 18:4. Therefore, no one has immortality until they are resurrected or translated. (Moses, Elijah, and the 24 elders have already been translated and have received immortality; see Jude 9; 2 Kings 2:11; Matthew 17:1-3; 27:50-53; Ephesians 4:8; Revelation 4:4.) When Satan spoke to Eve in the Garden of Eden he presented the first instance of this falsehood recorded in the Bible:

> "And the serpent said unto the woman, Ye shall not surely die: For God doth know that in the day ye eat thereof, then your eyes shall be opened, and ye shall be as gods, knowing good and evil." *Genesis 3:4-5.*

Eve accepted Satan's lie, was deceived into thinking that she would not die, and then ate the forbidden fruit. In this instance Satan used the medium of a snake, but it serves his purpose well to impersonate our dead relatives and friends. Therefore the false doctrine that man's soul returns directly to heaven at death supports the idea that the dead are immortal. The notion that our dead relatives and friends are in heaven and can look down upon us, speak to us, and give us instruction is false. It opens the door for Satan to speak directly to us in the guise of a heavenly messenger. This concept has also facilitated the adoption of the idea that we can pray to saints and their relics. But it is Satan that answers such prayers. The theory of the immortal soul has also produced other falsehoods as well. Purgatory and an eternally burning hell can be traced directly to this unbiblical doctrine. (See chapter 7: The End of Sin and Sinners.) Only a clear scriptural understanding of death and immortality, and a strong denunciation of these false teachings and the spiritual manifestations that accompany them, will protect us in the last great conflict that this earth will see, for Satan will deceive the world through his wonder working power.

The Worship of Patron Saints

The worship of patron saints is an important part of the religious life of Roman Catholics. They are highly regarded, and are believed to bring special blessings to the worshipper. The act of canonization today of an individual is a lengthy process by Rome, and includes gathering proof of at least two supposed miracles that have taken place in the life of his followers after his death. The first official canonization of a saint took place in A.D. 993, but many saints were on the list long before that time. Of the saints Mary and Joseph seem to have taken the highest honors, and they are often invoked for protection from various evils.

The scripture directly condemns the worship of anyone or anything except God alone. (See Exodus 34:14; Deuteronomy 8:19-20; Matthew 4:10.) To worship saints is to break the first commandment where God says: "Thou shalt have no other gods before me." Exodus 20:3. The apostle Peter rebuked Cornelius for bowing to worship him: "And as Peter was coming in, Cornelius met him, and fell down at his feet, and worshipped him. But Peter took him up, saying, Stand up; I myself also am a man." Acts 10:25-26. Even an angel refused worship from the apostle John when he "fell at his feet to worship him." The angel said to him, "See thou do it not: I am thy fellowservant, and of thy brethren that have the testimony of Jesus: worship God." Revelation 19:10. The popes would never say such things! They have always commanded worship from their subjects, for themselves, and for their patron saints. The prophecy next speaks of the honor that Rome places upon these saints:

> **"But in his estate shall he honour the God of forces: and a god whom his fathers knew not shall he honour with gold, and silver, and with precious stones, and pleasant things."** Daniel 11:38.

The word "forces" here means a "place or means of safety, protection, stronghold, [or] fortress." *Theological Wordbook of the Old Testament*, No. 1578a. This is clear from the following passages where the word is translated strength in the King James, but clearly means safety or protection: Psalms 27:1; 28:8; 31:4; Proverbs 10:29; Isaiah 25:4; 30:2-3; Ezekiel 30:15; Nahum 3:11. Therefore the popes and the believers of the Roman religion would "honour" or worship different gods for protection from various evils. The term "patron" signifies one who is honored as a special guardian or protector, hence the term patron saints. In the Middle Ages there were patron saints for various trades, churches, cities, and nations. Each of these patrons had a special day that "was celebrated both by religious services and by banquets and social gatherings." *The History of Medieval Europe*, p. 335. Thus the patron saints were closely integrated with society, and their superstitious worship multiplied:

> "The number of saints and their festivals multiplied very rapidly. Each nation, country, province or city chose its patron saint, as Peter and Paul in Rome, St. Ambrose in Milan, St. Martin, St. Denys (Dionysius) and St. Germain in France, St. George in England, St. Patrick in Ireland, St. Boniface in Germany, and especially the Virgin Mary, who has innumerable localities and churches under her care and protection." Schaff, *History of the Christian Church*, vol. IV, chap. X, sec. 99, par. 2.

The masses of people had become steeped in superstition by the corrupt religious system that usurped authority over them, and because of their superstitions it was common for them to give gifts of money, property, or other precious things to the saints for protection from disease, loss, or illness:

> "Saints could make a marriage fertile or cure illness, and their friendship had to be won by gift at their shrine or the foundation of a church in their honour, which was probably the main reason for the proliferation of churches in the eleventh century." *The Oxford Illustrated History of Medieval Europe*, p. 134.

The Papacy was the beneficiary of these gifts, and therefore the superstitious beliefs of the people helped to aggrandize the Roman Church and the power of the bishops. Keeping men in ignorance is key to Rome's power and authority. Men were taught that they could remedy their corrupt lives with God and win eternal life by giving gifts to the saints. Thus they honored them "with gold, and silver, and with precious stones, and pleasant things."

This corrupt system of saint worship is kindred to another Papal institution called indulgences. Through indulgences a man could buy forgiveness and gain salvation for himself, or he could rescue a friend or relative from the fires of purgatory with his gifts. Indulgences were one of the means of enriching Rome, and are still acknowledged as valid by the Papacy today. This wicked system was firmly opposed by the Protestant Reformation, and it is amazing that the Protestants are now so conducive to Rome. Such institutions, as the worship of patron saints and the purchasing of indulgences, can never bring a person to a saving knowledge of God or to eternal life.

Idolatry and Land Distribution

Bowing before an image was unheard-of for the first 300 years of the Christian Church, but slowly the practice entered as the pagans became associated with the Church in the days of Constantine. The Church degenerated from the worship of Christ to martyr and saint worship and finally to image worship in the eighth and ninth centuries. The second council of Nicaea in A.D. 787, called for this special purpose, "unanimously pronounced that the worship of images is agreeable to Scripture and reason, to the Fathers and councils of the Church." Gibbon, *The Decline and Fall of the Roman Empire*, chap. XLIX, par. 17. The veneration of these included more than just images as Dr. Schaff relates:

> "Under images were understood the sign of the cross, and pictures of Christ, of the Virgin Mary, of angels and saints. They may be drawn in color or composed of Mosaic or formed of other suitable materials, and placed in churches, in houses, and in the street, or made on walls and tables, sacred vessels and vestments. Homage may be paid to them by kissing, bowing, strewing of incense, burning of lights,

saying prayers before them; such honor to be intended for the living objects in heaven which the images represented. The Gospel book and the relics of martyrs were also mentioned among the objects of veneration." *History of the Christian Church*, vol. IV, chap. X, sec. 102, par. 5.

This use of the sacred images made idolatry common among the people of the Roman Church. To support this institution they removed the second commandment from the Decalogue, which forbids making images and bowing before them. (Exodus 20:4-6.) The tenth commandment was then divided into two so as to maintain the number. This species of idolatry is connected with the worship of the patron saints of the previous verse and is the theme of the passage now under discussion:

"Thus shall he do in the most strong holds with a strange god, whom he shall acknowledge and increase with glory: and he shall cause them to rule over many, and shall divide the land for gain." Daniel 11:39.

The "most strong holds" are the great cities of the Empire. They all, without a doubt, had their patron saints. That the patron of these cities is connected to image worship is clearly seen in this verse where it is called a "strange god." This phrase is often used in the Bible when speaking of the various gods of the pagan nations that surrounded Israel and commonly links them with their idols. (See 1 Samuel 7:3-5; 2 Chronicles 14:3; 33:15.) Rome does not hesitate to command worship of these relics. The *Tridentine Profession of Faith* of 1564, which was "issued to be recited publicly by all bishops and beneficed clergy," says that the saints, "are to be venerated and invoked; that they offer prayers to God for us and that their relics are to be venerated." *Documents of the Christian Church*, p. 266-267. It is general knowledge that the Roman Church develops idols of the various patron saints for the use of worship, and they are commonly on display within and in front of their churches and homes. Thus the connection is clear.

Pepin III and his son Charles the Great, better known as Charlemagne, donated many of the lands that they conquered directly to the Roman Church in honor of the various saints. Through these and other donations, made as well to the saints and relics, the Papacy possessed much of the land of Europe. "The Church was the greatest landholder in existence; in the Carolingian period one third of all Gaul belonged to the Church." *The History of Medieval Europe*, p. 283. We read also that in Germany: "In the eleventh century a full half of the land and wealth of the country, and no small part of its military strength, was in the hands of churchmen." Bryce, *The Holy Roman Empire*, chap. VIII, par. 6. In 1493, after Christopher Columbus discovered the new world, the Spanish pope Alexander VI issued two bulls granting Spain the exclusive right to all newly discovered and undiscovered lands lying west of a meridian 320 miles west of the Cape Verde Islands. All new lands discovered east of that demarcation were assigned to Portugal. The line was later moved to 1185 miles west of the Cape Verde Islands and sanctioned by pope Julius II in another bull in 1506.

The popes claim to have the right to divide the world among the different nations of the earth. The various rulers of the nations were given permission by the popes to conquer other lands to extend the dominions of the Roman Church. Even the Indians in America were to be forced into the Roman Church:

> "As Peter's successor, the pope claimed the right to give away the Western continent, a gift that involved an unending right of tenure. Alexander's donation… directed barbarous nations to be subdued, and no pains to be spared in reducing the Indians to Christianity." Froom, *The Prophetic Faith of Our Fathers*, vol. II, p. 169.

Thus the popes have divided "the land for gain," even claiming the right to distribute America to whomsoever they please. They believe that all of the world should be in subjection to them and bow to them. However, their authority and control over people is based upon superstition and suppression of scriptural truth. How disgusting this must be to a pure and holy God who requires only faith in Jesus and His promises that lead men to obey His will. (See Romans 4; Galatians 3; Ephesians 2:8-10.)

America and Freedom

When the Reformation broke in Germany the light that had been suppressed for centuries began to shine forth in greater power. The scriptures slowly made their entrance into the hearts and minds of the people of Europe; various doctrines were discovered, and many sects appeared throughout the land. Yet, in spite of the numerous truths that were uncovered at that time, there was still light to be revealed. Many of the errors of Rome continued their hold upon the people. One such error was the *Corpus Christianum*; the idea that the church and society were an indivisible entity. Luther, Zwingli, and other reformers held onto this falsehood while the Anabaptists and the various evangelical groups were opposed to any union of church and state.

The evangelicals saw the Church as a community of experiential believers —those who professed a certain set of teachings — scattered throughout society. These two ideals, being mutually exclusive, obviously brought strife.

With the acceptance of the *Corpus Christianum* by the Reformers the advancement of truth became stagnate, and those who came out of oppression became the oppressors. As early as A.D. 1527 Zwingli had the Anabaptist preacher Felix Mantz drowned in Lake Constance for teaching opposing doctrines within his realm. Moreover, as the Reformation spread to England so did the persecution of the various evangelical sects that sprang up there. Many of those that desired a place to worship God according to the dictates of their own consciences made their way to America. Freedom however was not brought from Europe to America on the Mayflower or any other ship. As the pilgrims landed upon the shores of the vast North American continent they brought with them the seeds of intolerance from Europe. They created cities and states that reflected their beliefs and enforced their ideals with fanatical zeal:

> "According to the records, the first American law of this nature was placed on the statute books of Virginia in 1610. It required Sunday attendance at church under penalty of death for persistent violation." Blakely, *American State Papers*, p. 17.

Idolatry, witchcraft, blasphemy, Sunday desecration, and heresy were at the top of the list, and the punishment was often a heavy fine, imprisonment, banishment, or death. "The New England Way, as it was called, envisaged a static society, within each unit of which would be the church, sitting tight on its covenant and guarding the gates against promiscuous admission...but the theology of the covenant inevitably bred contempt for lesser breeds outside the covenant." Miller, *Roger Williams*, p. 53. One may wonder that freedom could survive at all in the societies that existed in the colonies. Jesus declared of His Church at this time: "I know thy works, that thou hast a name that thou livest, and art dead...for I have not found thy works perfect before God." Revelation 3:1-2. Nevertheless, God was working on the minds of His people, and the truth of religious freedom and the separation of church and state were ultimately to take hold in America.

When the Puritans, who were convinced that they alone had Bible truth, first established the Massachusetts Bay Colony in A.D. 1628, they immediately legislated their brand of religious fanaticism and persecuted any who did not bow to their dictates. In 1631 a young British preacher named Roger Williams arrived in this totalitarian prison. Being persecuted in England and searching for freedom of conscience in the New World he took a stand against this church-state regime. He contended that the first four commandments of the Decalogue were requirements that man owed to God and not to the state, and he declared that men were to "Render therefore unto Caesar the things which are Caesar's; and unto God the things that are God's." Matthew 22:21. He also proclaimed that the settlers should pay the Indians for their land; an ideal that they did not appreciate. Thus he became very unpopular.

In A.D. 1635 he fled into the wilderness in the middle of a New England winter and found refuge with the Narragansett Indians among whom he made many converts. He later bought land from the Indians, founded the state of Rhode Island, and established the first democratic colony in the new world with a charter of religious liberty. Williams declared in his book, *The Bloudy Tenet of Persecution*, in 1644: "An enforced uniformity of religion throughout a nation or civil state, confounds the civil and religious, denies the principles of Christianity and civility, and that Jesus Christ is come in the flesh." He also maintained that there should be a "wall of separation between the garden of the church and the wilderness of the world." *The Complete Writings of Roger Williams*, vol. 1, p. 108. Bancroft further writes of Roger Williams:

> "He was the first person in modern Christendom to assert in its plentitude the doctrine of liberty of conscience, the equality of opinion before the law... Williams would permit persecution of no opinion, no religion, leaving heresy unharmed by law, and orthodoxy unprotected by the terrors of penal statutes." *History of the United States*, 1888 ed., vol. I, part 1, p. 255.

Multitudes of the oppressed such as Quakers, Baptists, and Sabbath keepers flocked to Rhode Island to escape persecution. Furthermore, it was the principles that Roger Williams set down, and which were later espoused by Madison and Jefferson, that ultimately became the foundation for the freedoms declared by the Constitution and the Bill of Rights in the United States of America. In his work entitled *Memorial and Remonstrance* written in 1785 Madison declared:

> "The religion then of every man must be left to the conviction and conscience of every man; and it is the right of every man to exercise it as these may dictate. This right is in its nature an unalienable right. It is unalienable, because the opinions of men, depending only on the evidence contemplated in their own minds, cannot follow the dictates

of other men: it is unalienable also because what is here a right toward men is a duty toward the Creator."

The ratification of the Bill of Rights on December 15, 1791 gave minorities the privilege to practice their various religions without forced conformity or persecution by the majority. George Washington declared in a letter of 1793 to the New Church in Baltimore:

> "We have abundant reason to rejoice that in this Land the light of truth and reason has triumphed over the power of bigotry and superstition, and that every person may here worship God according to the dictates of his own heart."

The desire for religious liberty is the reason that the Bill of Rights was established, and the First Amendment declares in part: "Congress shall make no law respecting an establishment of religion, or prohibiting the free exercise thereof." This Amendment prohibits Congress from making any kind of religious laws; thus freeing the minorities from persecution by majority religions. Hence, President Jefferson declared in his inaugural address in 1801:

> "All, too, will bear in mind this sacred principle, that though the will of the majority is in all cases to prevail, that will to be rightful must be reasonable; that the minority possesses their equal rights, which equal law must protect, and to violate would be oppression... And let us reflect that, having banished from our land that religious intolerance under which mankind so long bled and suffered, we have yet gained little if we countenance a political intolerance as despotic, as wicked, and capable of as bitter and bloody persecutions."

One year later Jefferson also wrote to the Danbury Baptists: "I contemplate with sovereign reverence that act of the whole American people which declared that their legislature should 'make no law respecting an establishment of religion, or prohibiting the free exercise thereof,' thus building a wall of separation between church and state." Hence, church and state were clearly understood to be separate institutions; thus protecting the minority religions and opening the door for the oppressed from every land to flee to America.

James Madison further declared in his inaugural address in 1809 that the responsibility of the government was, "to avoid the slightest interference with the right of conscience or the functions of religion, so wisely exempted from civil jurisdiction." In 1819 he also observed that "the morality of the priesthood, and the devotion of the people, have been manifestly increased by the total separation of the Church from the State." Hunt, *The Writings of James Madison*, vol. 8, p. 132. Thus after centuries of trial and persecution God's people had a country where they could worship Him in freedom, and it wasn't long after the establishment of the United States of America that the Papacy lost its civil, persecuting power as we shall see in the next chapter.

Summary of Chapter Five

We have seen that the papacy is a religio-political system that began its reign officially in A.D. 538. Its power was absolute, and the height of its reign is called the Dark Ages. The Bible was prohibited, and anyone possessing it would necessarily pay by the sacrifice of his life. All who opposed papal rule were persecuted or destroyed. Yet during the height of its power God had people that followed Him, and witnessed for Him. These brave people kept alive true religion for centuries. They held onto the scriptures and scattered these pure manuscripts throughout Europe as humble missionaries. Multitudes were stretched on the rack or burned at the stack because of Rome's hatred of scripture truth, and the Bible plainly says that they "were slain for the word of God, and for the testimony which they held." Revelation 6:9. Nevertheless, the Lord did not leave His people without help. Whatever trials they endured were brought upon them for their benefit, and they were comforted and purified by the Holy Spirit.

The Roman Church exalted itself to the place of God, and claimed the power to change the Laws of God. It spoke magnificent things against the God of heaven, commanded celibacy of its clergy, perpetuated the immortality of the soul doctrine, demanded saint and image worship, and divided the lands of the earth to benefit itself. Nevertheless, the Lord in His mercy, working through His tried and troubled people, brought about freedom in America with the establishment of the Constitution and Bill of Rights, which prohibit the creation and enforcement of any religious laws in the United States. Thus we are now prepared to discuss the events at "the time of the end."

Chapter 6: The Final Conflict

This chapter begins with a discussion of the Moslems, the wounding of the papal religio-political system by France, and then moves through the present time into the future. The final conflict is the focus, and all of the previous chapters converge here to give us insight into the climactic events of the prophecy.

The Moslems in Bible Prophecy

Since there is much agitation with the Moslems at the present time many have wondered if the Bible reveals anything. It would, therefore, do us well to take a look at what prophetic truth has to say about the Moslems, and, although a full discussion of Mohammedanism as portrayed in the prophecy of Revelation nine is beyond the scope of this work, I shall give a brief outline. When the fourth trumpet, found in Revelation eight, sounded the Dark Ages began, and the Papacy commenced its rule of the Western Roman Empire. The fifth and part of the sixth trumpets in the book of Revelation describe the rise and development of Islam, and its conflicts with the Church in Eastern Rome, or as it is more commonly called the Byzantine Empire, and the Papacy in the West respectively.

> "And I beheld, and heard an angel flying through the midst of heaven, saying with a loud voice, Woe, woe, woe, to the inhabiters of the earth by reason of the other voices of the trumpet of the three angels, which are yet to sound!" *Revelation 8:13.*

The first woe, or fifth trumpet, refers to Mohammed as "a star fallen from heaven unto the earth." Revelation 9:1. We have already seen that a fallen star represents an apostate religious leader, as in the life of Constantine the Great, and here we have a description of Mohammed and the rise and work of the Moslems as they made war upon the Eastern Empire. Early in the seventh century the Romans and the Persians were embroiled in a bitter conflict. Heraclius, emperor and leader of the Roman armies, at length gained the victory over Chosroes, the Great King of Persia, but it was not without cost. Both kingdoms were exhausted from the conflict, and the way was thus prepared for the expansion of Islam. The historian Edward Gibbon describes its introduction:

"The loss of two hundred thousand soldiers, who had fallen by the sword, was of less fatal importance than the decay of arts, agriculture, and population in this long and destructive war; and although a victorious army had been formed under the standard of Heraclius, the unnatural effort appears to have exhausted rather than exercised their strength. While the emperor triumphed at Constantinople or Jerusalem, an obscure town on the confines of Syria was pillaged by the Saracens, and they cut in pieces some troops who advanced to its relief; an ordinary and trifling occurrence, had it not been the prelude of a mighty revolution. These robbers were the apostles of Mohammed; their fanatic valour had emerged from the desert; and in the last eight years of his reign Heraclius lost to the Arabs the same provinces which he had rescued from the Persians." *The Decline and Fall of the Roman Empire*, chap. XLVI, last paragraph.

Despite the loss that Heraclius suffered at the hands of the Arabs he did manage to save Constantinople, "which might not have held out had he abandoned it in the depths of its adversity. As it was, that great city was to endure for centuries to come, [and] was to serve as a protection to Western Europe from attacks from the east..." Thorndike, *The History of Medieval Europe*, p. 152. The Arabian Desert, being a desolate wilderness, is called "the bottomless pit," and the "key" is the religion of Islam. Revelation 9:1. "Islam inspired the Arabs to leave the deserts of Arabia and embark on world conquest." *Compton's Encyclopedia*, article "Persian History," 1972 ed., vol. 16, p. 213. Like the "smoke" rising from "a great furnace," within 100 years of Mohammed, the Moslems spread the aggressive, hostile influence of Islam from India to the Atlantic Ocean and into the Pyrenees in Spain, further obscuring the light of the pure gospel of Jesus Christ. (See the map on page 140.) Nevertheless, "...the warlike Franks, with their superior physique, set a limit to the westward expansion of Islam, just as in eastern Europe Constantinople was a barrier which they could not break down." *The History of Medieval Europe*, p. 179. As the hordes of the Mohammedans swept through the various kingdoms they are symbolized as a swarm of "locusts" with "power, as the scorpions of the earth have power." Their attacks were directed against "those men which have not the seal of God in their foreheads," that is, against an apostate Christianity. Revelation 9:2-4. (See also Ephesians 4:30.) The prophecy tells us that "in those days shall men seek death, and shall not find it; and shall desire to die, and death shall flee from them." Revelation 9:6. Their constant attacks upon the Eastern Empire were an unceasing torment to the apostate Christians; yet the Moslems were unable to conquer them.

The description of the Mohammedans as they made war is given symbolically in Revelation 9:7-9: "And the shapes of the locusts were like unto horses prepared unto battle." The Arabian's were skilled horsemen, and their use of the animal made them as swift and powerful as a plague of locusts. "On their heads were as it were crowns like gold, and their faces were as the faces of men. And they had hair as the hair of women." One clear mark of the Mohammedan warrior was his turban or miter. And the description of their physical appearance by the prophecy is accurate. They always wore beards, and their hair was uncut, yet they were as fierce as any men could be, for "their teeth were as the teeth of lions." "And they had breastplates, as it were breastplates of iron." The breastplate was used among them as far back as the days of Mohammed's battle of Ohud in A.D. 624. "And the sound of their wings was as the sound of chariots of many horses running to battle." Their military was primarily cavalry and archers.

For centuries the Mohammedans did not have a civil government that extended over all of their various tribes, but near the close of the thirteenth century they consolidated into a great monarchy called the Ottoman Empire. "They had a king over them" according to the prophecy, and the name of the first was Othman, its founder. Revelation 9:11. The prophecy also says that they were given power "to hurt men five months." Revelation 9:5, 10. This period, twice mentioned, is obviously symbolic, as are the many other prophetic time periods. Using again our principle of "each day for a year" in prophecy we easily conclude that the Ottoman Turks would "hurt men" for 150 years. (For an example of the calculation of prophetic time, see chapter 4: Philosophy Corrupts the Church.) The beginning of this period is reckoned from the time that the Moslems in the form of the Ottoman Empire first began to "hurt men," and Gibbon gives us the date of this event:

> "It was on the twenty-seventh of July, in the year twelve hundred and ninety-nine of the Christian Era, that Othman first invaded the territory of Nicomedia; and the singular accuracy of the date seems to disclose some foresight of the rapid and destructive growth of the monster." *The Decline and Fall of the Roman Empire*, chap. LXIV, par. 14.

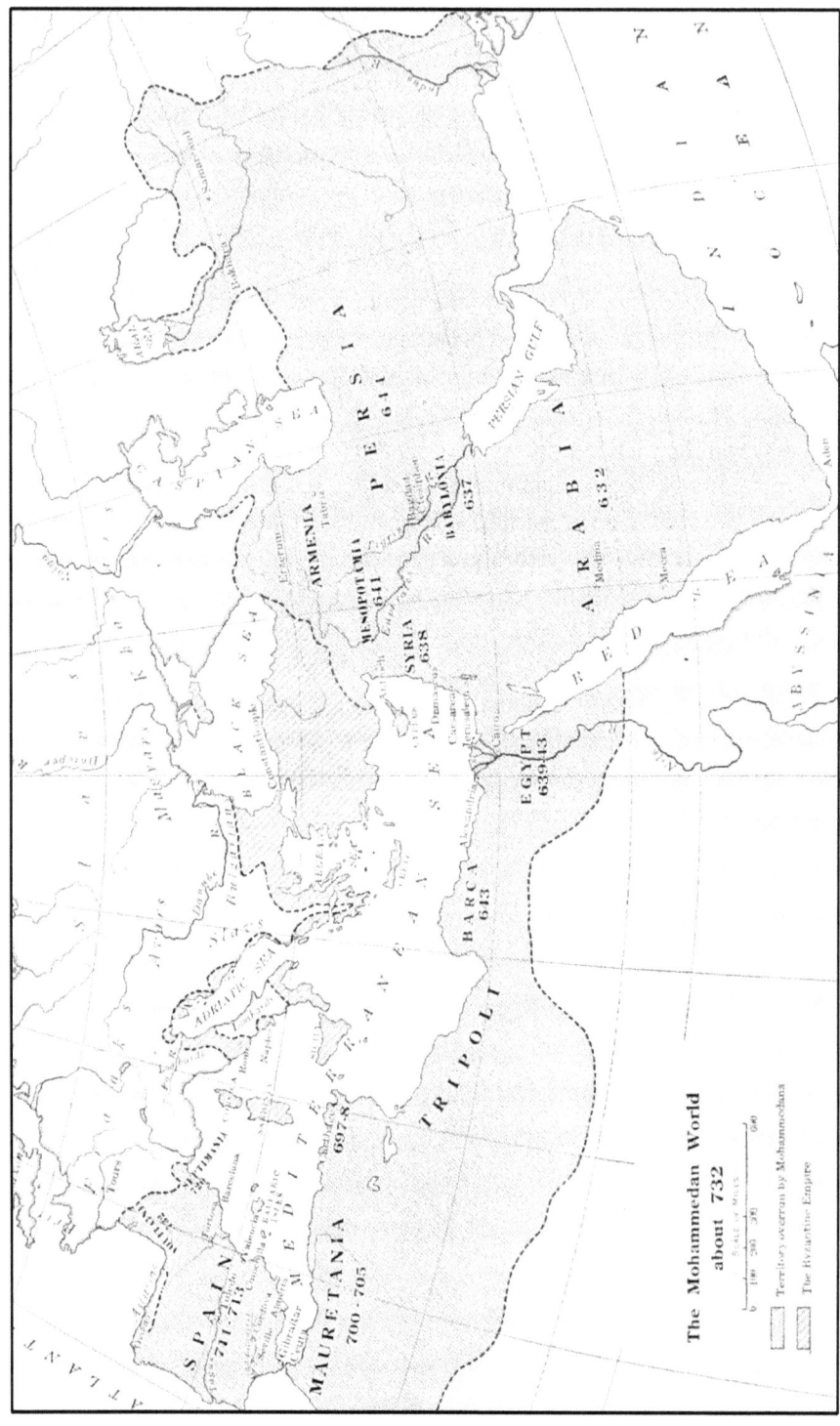

The character of the Ottoman government is given in Hebrew and Greek, respectively "Abaddon" and "Apollyon," which means destroyer in both languages. Revelation 9:11. During the 150 years they were engaged in perpetual war with the Eastern Empire, and seized and held several Greek provinces, but were never able to conquer it. At the termination of the 150-year period, in A.D. 1449, a change came and the last Byzantine emperor, Constantine Deacozes, was enthroned in Constantinople, but it was not until he had sent an ambassador to Adrianople to obtain permission of the Turkish Sultan that he received the throne! "Amurath received him with honour, and dismissed him with gifts; but the gracious approbation of the Turkish sultan announced his supremacy, and the approaching downfall of the Eastern Empire." *The Decline and Fall of the Roman Empire*, chap. LXVII, par. 13. Constantine had acknowledged his submission to the Sultan. The Eastern Empire was then completely at the mercy of the Moslem power; its independence was forever gone and the first woe ended: "One woe is past; and, behold, there come two woes more hereafter." Revelation 9:12. The angel that was ministering before the golden altar then spoke:

> "Saying to the sixth angel which had the trumpet, Loose the four angels which are bound in the great river Euphrates. And the four angels were loosed, which were prepared for an hour, and a day, and a month, and a year, for to slay the third part of men." *Revelation 9:14-15.*

When the sixth trumpet sounded the second woe, which was to "slay the third part of men," began, and the "four angels" that were restraining the advancement of the Moslems from European conquest "were loosed." The waters of "the great river Euphrates" are the "peoples, and multitudes, and nations, and tongues" (Revelation 17:15) of the Christian West. (This will become more apparent when we speak of Mystical Babylon in the section: The European Beast.) The Turks besieged and finally overthrew Constantinople in 1453, and after that they had greater success in Europe and threatened the very existence of the Papacy:

> "This solemn event — the fall of Constantinople — accomplished, there was no need of any reconciliation of the Greek and Latin Churches. The sword of Mohammed had settled their dispute. Constantinople had submitted to the fate of Antioch, Jerusalem, Alexandria, Carthage. Christendom was struck with consternation. The advance of the Turks in Europe was now very rapid. Corinth and Athens fell, and the reduc-

tion of Greece was completed. The confines of Italy were approached A.D. 1461. The Mohammedan flag confronted that peninsula along the Adriatic coast. In twenty years more Italy was invaded. Otranto was taken; its bishop killed at the door of his church. At this period, it was admitted that the Turkish infantry, cavalry, and artillery were the best in the world. Soliman the Magnificent took Belgrade A.D. 1520. Nine years afterwards the Turks besieged Vienna, but were repulsed. Soliman now prepared for the subjugation of Italy, and was only diverted from it by an accident which turned him upon the Venetians. It was not until the battle of Lepanto that the Turkish advance was fairly checked." Draper, *History of the Intellectual Development of Europe*, vol. II, chap. IV, part I, par 9.

A description of the Turkish army under the sixth trumpet is given in the prophecy: "And the number of the army of the horsemen were two hundred thousand thousand." This number is supposed to be the total number of Turkish cavalry over the entire period of time that they were "to slay the third part of men." Such a number is believed to be correct, but would be impossible to tally, and is not required to understand the rest of the prophecy. "And thus I saw the horses in the vision, and them that sat on them, having breastplates of fire, and of jacinth, and brimstone." Red, blue, and yellow were common colors of the Turkish warriors. "And the heads of the horses were as the heads of lions; and out of their mouths issued fire and smoke and brimstone. By these three was the third part of men killed, by the fire, and by the smoke, and by the brimstone, which issued out of their mouths. For their power is in their mouth, and in their tails: for their tails were like unto serpents, and had heads, and with them they do hurt." Revelation 9:16-19. The Turks with great advantage used firearms, which had been recently introduced into warfare, and it was their artillery that largely gave them victory over Constantinople; they used cannons to breach its walls. The discharging of the small weapons by the riders looked to the prophet as if fire was proceeding from the horses' mouths. He is here describing the beginnings of modern warfare 1400 years in advance!

At that time God raised up the Protestant reformers, and the troubles brought upon the Papacy by the Moslem Turks gave them the needed freedom to spread their message throughout Western Europe. Thus God used their entrance into Europe to aid the Reformation! The Turks remained strong in Europe until 1718 when the Austrians drove them from Hungary. They then, through internal strife and division, began their long descent and their final submission to the Christian powers of Europe. The time period that the Turks would "slay" men is here given by the prophecy to the very day when using

The Final Conflict

our principle of "each day for a year." A "year" of 360 days equals 360 literal years, a "month" of 30 days gives us 30 years, and the single "day" represents a year. The hour that is mentioned is $1/24^{th}$ of a day and is calculated to be $1/24^{th}$ of a literal year or 15 days. Adding the four periods together gives us 391 years and 15 days. Appending this period to the 150 years already given in the first woe gives us a total of 541 years and 15 days. This period then extends from July 27, 1299 to August 11, 1840.

In the year A.D. 1839 hostilities broke out between two Moslem powers: the Sultan of the Ottoman Empire and Mehemet Ali, pasha of Egypt. Ultimately, the Sultan's army was destroyed and his fleet taken by Mehemet to Egypt. The Sultan had little recourse but to seek help from the powers of Europe. On July 15, 1840, the four great Christian powers, England, Prussia, Austria, and Russia, unanimously agreed to intervene in an official document drawn up in a conference held in London. Relevant extracts of the event as found in the *Moniteur Ottoman*, August 22, 1840, are here quoted: "Subsequent to the occurrence of the disputes alluded to, and after the reverses experienced, as known to all the world, the ambassadors of the great powers at Constantinople, in a collective official note declared that their governments were unanimously agreed upon taking measures to arrange the said differences. The Sublime Porte, with a view of putting a stop to the effusion of Mussulman blood, and to the various evils which would arise from a renewal of hostilities, accepted the intervention of the great powers." The Pasha was to vacate portions of the Ottoman Empire and return the Sultan's fleet that he had captured. In return he was to receive the hereditary government of Egypt and portions of Syria. Once the ultimatum was delivered to the Pasha, it should be obvious that the Ottoman supremacy at Constantinople would be at an end being then yielded to the Christian powers. As to the delivery of the ultimatum: "His Excellency, Rifat Bey, Muslesar for foreign affairs, has been dispatched in a government steamer to Alexandria, to communicate the ultimatum to the Pacha." Was the ultimatum delivered to the Pasha, and was the Sultan's authority therefore yielded to the powers of Europe on August 11, 1840, as the prophecy demands? The following is an extract from a letter dated Constantinople, August 27, 1840, and found in the *London Morning Chronicle* of September 18, 1840:

> "Immediately on the arrival of the Cyclops steamer with the news of the convention of the four powers, Mehemet Ali, it is stated, had quitted Alexandria… During the interval of his absence, the Turkish government steamer, which had reach Alexandria on the 11th, with the envoy Rifat Bey on board, had been by his orders placed in quarantine, and she was not released from it till the 16th. Previous, however, to the

Porte's leaving, and on the very day on which he had been admitted to pratique, the above named functionary had had an audience of the Pacha, and had communicated to him the command of the Sultan, with respect to the evacuation of the Syrian provinces, appointing another audience for the next day, when, in the presence of the consuls of the European powers, he would receive from him his definite answer, and inform him of the alternative of his refusing to obey; giving him the ten days which have been allotted him by the convention to decide on the course he should think to adopt."

The steamer, which left Constantinople on August 5, arrived in Alexandria on August 11 and the ultimatum communicated to the Pasha that same day, but do we have evidence that the Sultan's authority was then yielded to the powers of Europe that day? Consider the following extract from the same writer of the article in the *London Morning Chronicle* above, and dated Constantinople, August 12, 1840, just one day after the termination date:

"I can add but little to my last letter, on the subject of the plans of the four powers; and I believe the details I then gave you comprise everything that is yet decided on…

"The manner, however, of applying the force, should he [the Pasha] refuse to comply with these terms — whether a simple blockade is to be established on the coast, or whether his capital is to be bambarded, and his armies attacked in the Syrian provinces — is the point which still remains to be learned; nor does a note delivered yesterday by the four ambassadors, in answer to a question put to them by the Porte, as to the plan to be adopted in such an event, throw the least light on this subject. It simply states that provision has been made, and there is no necessity for the Divan alarming itself about any contingency that might afterwards arise."

On August 11 the Pasha received the ultimatum sent from Constantinople at the Sultan's own request. The above quote tells us that the Sultan also *yesterday*, August 11, received an answer to a question that he put to the four ambassadors, which could have remarkable consequences upon his empire, "as to the plan to be adopted" if the Pasha refused to comply. They replied only that "provision has been made," but he was not told what the plan was. It was completely out of his hands once the ultimatum was delivered. The Sultan, who had looked to Europe for help, was then yielded to the Christians; they thereafter controlled the destiny of his empire. The Moslem power in Constantinople thus surrendered its authority in the same way that it received it!

Since 1840 the Moslems are never again mentioned directly in the prophecies. However, this does not mean that they will not play a part in the last conflict, for the entire world will be engaged. The prophecies do not mention any of the wars of the 20th century or the destruction of the World Trade Center on September 11, 2001, but they focus rather upon those conflicts that directly affect the people of God or that are critical to the continuity of prophetic interpretation. Obviously then the current problem with the Moslems will be eclipsed by a greater crisis that will confront the world and affect God's children. The second woe describes yet another power, a "beast that ascendeth out of the bottomless pit" (Revelation 11:7), which we shall look at in the next section. Consequently, the prophecies focus upon other powers, and they clearly give insight into the events behind the coming crisis.

The Atheist Beast

Paganism, atheism, and the theory of evolution are all related and depend upon each other for their existence. The theory of evolution and the atheist ideology existed in the ancient philosophies of Greece and Rome. They went underground during the long years of papal rule, but were not buried very deep. They still remained in subtle forms in the false doctrines of papal Rome. These theories arose to the surface again in the Renaissance and then gained dominance in France in the 18th century. The result in France was a revolution and a violent de-Christianization in the 1790s. Pagan and atheistic ideas continued to make their way from France into our modern thinking through the evolutionary writings of Darwin and others. That evolution is ancient pagan philosophy transformed into modern atheism is clearly seen from the following statements:

> "The theory of evolution is built on the age-old philosophy of uniformity of natural forces… This viewpoint …was the very essence of all ancient pagan philosophical systems." Clark, *Creation Speaks*, p. 14.

> "Evolutionism then came to the surface again…first in the revival of pantheism, then in deism, and finally in full-fledged atheism." Morris, *The Long War Against God*, p. 206.

It was Clovis, king of the Franks, that had brought an end to pagan rule in the Roman Empire in A.D. 508, and at that time the king of the South passed from the scene of prophecy clearing the way for the establishment of the Papacy. As we come to the end of the 1260-year period of papal rule we find a revolution taking place in France, and the revolutionary leaders, who were deists and atheists, began the process of de-Christianization. A new calendar was introduced on October 5, 1793, with a ten day weekly cycle; thus abolishing the Bible seven day, creation week. This served to eliminate the Sabbath as well as the various traditional festivals and Sunday observance. "On November 6 the Convention accorded the communes of France the right to officially renounce the Christian Church." Durant, *The Age of Napoleon*, p. 73. On the 17th the Bible was rejected and a week later they made a decree:

> "… 'that all the churches and chapels of every religion and sect which exist in Paris shall be closed forthwith now,' and anyone who asked for their reopening should be arrested as a suspicious person." Aulard, *Christianity and the French Revolution*, p. 109.

When atheism returned in France it was given the designation: "the beast that ascendeth out of the bottomless pit." Revelation 11:7. The bottomless pit, being a place of emptiness and desolation, describes the condition of the nation where atheism germinated and revived. This atheist beast first made "war" upon the Bible, God's "two witnesses." Revelation 11:3-8. Jesus said of the Old Testament: "they are they which testify [or witness] of me." John 5:39. And of the Gospel of the New Testament He declared: "And this gospel of the kingdom shall be preached in all the world for a witness unto all nations." Matthew 24:14. Thus the two witnesses referred to are the Old and New Testaments of the Bible, which the French openly burned in the streets. Symbolically they were "overcome" and killed by this atheist beast and lay dead "in the street." Without the Bible corruption multiplied and fornication was actually legalized. An English visitor in 1796 wrote of the French:

> "Everyone plunges into the mud pool of vice as soon as he or she is strong enough to paddle in it without fear of parental or political control." Sydenham, *The French Revolution*, p. 231.

France is "the great city, which spiritually is called Sodom and Egypt, where also our Lord was crucified." Revelation 11:8. The body of our Lord is declared in scripture to be His Church (see 1 Corinthians 12:12-27), and it was in France that the members of Christ's body were put to death in large numbers. In one instance, the St. Bartholomew Massacre in 1572, 70,000 Protestants living in France were murdered in a two-month period. The slaughter began in Paris and quickly spread throughout the nation, and in the end the pious

Huguenots were literally extinguished from the earth. Christ was symbolically "crucified" in the body of His Church. At the time of the revolution the watchword of the infidels in France in reference to our Lord was: "Crush the Wretch!" They did everything that they could to remove Christianity from the nation and hence in another sense "crucified" our Lord. "Sodom" describes the licentious and corrupt nature and "Egypt" the atheistic character of the French nation at that time. (See Genesis 19:4-5; Exodus 5:2.)

The attack upon the Bible, and Christianity in general, lasted for "three days and a half." Revelation 11:9-11. Using our principle for determining time in symbolic prophecy, "each day for a year," we find that France was to make war upon them for three and one half years. This period, which began in the fall of 1793, culminated in the spring of 1797. The Constitutionalists party gained a majority in both Chambers of the French legislature in March and April, 1797, and the extreme members in the "Council of Five Hundred" soon demanded "the immediate repeal of all revolutionary laws." After that, "A commission was appointed to consider the question of religious freedom." *The Cambridge Modern History*, vol. 8, chap. XVI, pp. 506-507. Not all of the revolutionary laws were immediately repealed. However, in April of that year, Protestants and Jews alike were given legal freedom to practice their worship without fear:

> "Both protestants and Jews submitted to the laws and silently enjoyed the liberty accorded them after centuries of persecution." *Christianity and the French Revolution*, p. 151.

Three and one half years after they were enacted the laws prohibiting worship were repealed, and the Bible was obviously openly tolerated again. However, the problems for the Roman Church were not yet over. The French government allowed worship, but for a time retained its atheistic spirit and vented its wrath upon the Papacy. The Directory appealed to Napoleon "to destroy, if possible, the center of the unity of the Roman Church..." *Ibid.*, p. 151. The Papacy must be attacked at Rome! Daniel's greatest prophecy now brings us to the time when the king of the South, France, did indeed attack the Papacy:

> **"And at the time of the end shall the king of the south push at him: and the king of the north shall come against him like a whirlwind, with chariots, and with horsemen, and with many ships; and he shall enter into the countries, and shall overflow and pass over."** *Daniel 11:40.*

The French government denied the Lord Jesus Christ just as surely as Pharaoh or the Caesars. Therefore France "at the time of the end," in A.D.

1798, clearly fits the designation of spiritual Egypt, and is "the king of the south" in the verse under discussion. Pagan atheism, which lost its power to the Papacy in A.D. 508, reemerged as an atheistic or anti-Christian power in France and made war against the Bible and Christianity for three and one half years but ultimately turned its wrath upon the Papacy. The words "push at" in our passage are translated "gore" in Exodus 21:28, and mean to strike with the horns. The nation represented by spiritual Egypt, France, would therefore "gore" or "wound" the Papacy. In 1798 the French army under general Berthier marched into Rome, proclaimed a republic, and took Pope Pius VI captive to Valence, France where he died on August 29, 1799:

> "The object of the French Directory was the destruction of the pontifical government, as the irreconcilable enemy of the republic... The aged pope was summoned to surrender the temporal government; on his refusal, he was dragged from the altar... His rings were torn from his fingers, and finally, after declaring the temporal power abolished, the victors carried the pope prisoner into Tuscany, whence he never returned (1798)." Trevor, *Rome: From the Fall of the Western Empire*, pp. 439-440.

Rome was again forced to change its government system by the hand of the French military. The nations of Western Europe at length became divided and free to govern themselves. The Papacy lost its political power in 1798 and thus it received a deadly wound. This wounding of the papal religio-political system is also referred to in the book of Revelation:

> "And I stood upon the sand of the sea, and saw a beast rise up out of the sea, having seven heads and ten horns... And I saw one of his heads as it were wounded to death." *Revelation 13:1-3*.

The book of Revelation gives us a clear description of this papal, European Beast and it will be discussed in more detail in the section: The European Beast. The vision by the Tigris tells us that it was wounded "at the time of the end," in 1798, by the king of the South, or atheism. Hence, the Atheist Beast arose in France and made war upon the Papacy, and, although France no longer retains its atheistic character, modern atheism continues in the form of socialism and communism. The significance of this will be further discussed in the section: The Final Powers Identified.

The Second Advent Movement

Once the Papacy lost its political authority, the Bible could then be printed and distributed without hindrance. The Old and New Testament witnesses "stood upon their feet; and great fear fell upon them which saw them. And they heard a great voice from heaven saying unto them, Come up hither. And they ascended up to heaven in a cloud; and their enemies beheld them." Revelation 11:11-12. In 1804 the British Bible Society was organized, in 1817 the American Bible Society followed, and since then many organizations have been busy printing and distributing the scriptures. This explosive distribution of Bibles quickly brought men to search the scriptures, and fueled the religious revivals of the 19th century.

The greatest revival during that period began in the 1830s when several prophetic expositors from around the globe concluded that the 2300-day prophecy of Daniel eight would soon reach its fulfillment. There was Joseph Wolff who proclaimed the message in over 20 countries in Asia and Europe, Bengel in Germany whose movement spread to Russia, Hentzepeter in Holland, Hutchinson in Canada who sent a paper called the *Voice of Elijah* to many places around the globe, multitudes too numerous to mention in England, and in 1833 a man named William Miller initiated the movement in America. It would be impossible to trace the movement in every country, but I shall present the Millerite movement as it happened in America. Through the study of the 2300-day prophecy Miller came to the conclusion that the judgment of the nations, the purification of the Church, and the Second Coming of Jesus would culminate between March 21, 1843 and March 21, 1844. Upon his first presentation of the subject:

> "Miller found himself engaged in a revival. He had not planned it that way, but the preaching of prophecy, he discovered, produced a profound effect upon the listeners… This experience was to be repeated many times." Nichol, *The Midnight Cry*, p. 43.

In Daniel eight is found the longest time prophecy in the Bible. Daniel is told that at the end of "two thousand and three hundred days; then shall the sanctuary be cleansed." Daniel 8:14. Using the day for a year principle Miller understood there to be 2300 years covered by the prophecy. He also understood that additional information was given to Daniel in chapter nine where he is told that 70 weeks, or 490 years, were "determined" specifically for the Jewish nation. Daniel 9:24. The word translated "determined" means literally to "cut off" in the original language. Hence he understood that the 490 years were to be cut off from the 2300 years of the previous vision of which Daniel was praying for understanding. (See Daniel 9:1-2.) The angel revealed to Daniel the starting point of the 490 years to be "from the going forth of the commandment to restore and to build Jerusalem." Daniel 9:25. Miller then calculated the termination of the 490 years to be in A.D. 34 with the stoning of Stephen and the beginning of the proclamation of the gospel to the gentile world. (See chapter 3: The Time of the Prince.) He understood that there was then 1810 years remaining of the 2300 years after the 490-year period ended. This brought him to the conclusion that the closing of the 2300-day prophecy would be sometime between the spring of 1843 and the spring of 1844. At the completion of the 2300 days the angel said that the sanctuary would be "cleansed," and Miller and his associates believed that this event was the coming of Christ to purify the Church and to judge the earth by fire. In 1818 when Miller first discovered these time prophecies he declared:

> "I need not speak of the joy that filled my heart in view of the delightful prospect, nor of the ardent longings of my soul, for a participation in the joys of the redeemed. The Bible was now to me a new book. It was indeed a feast of reason: all that was dark, mystical, or obscure to me in its teachings, had been dissipated from my mind, before the clear light that now dawned from its sacred pages; and O how bright and glorious that truth appeared." *Apology and Defence*, p. 12.

With the fall of papal Rome in 1798 and the clear prophetic signs that were recently fulfilled the Millerite movement quickly gained momentum. (The Lisbon earthquake in 1755 shook much of Europe, Africa, and America, and was felt in many other countries of the world. The dark day of May 19, 1780 was followed by the appearance of a blood colored moon that same evening, and then came the meteoric shower of November 13, 1833. All these signs indicated that the Second Coming of Jesus was near. See Matthew 24:29; Revelation 6:12-13.) Greater impetus came to the movement when an associate of Miller, Josiah Litch, boldly proclaimed in 1838 that the time prophecy in Revelation nine was about to be fulfilled and that the power of the Moslem Turks, the Ottoman Empire, would be broken in August 1840. He was ridiculed for his prediction, nevertheless just a few days before the culmination he declared that the Ottoman Empire would come to a close on August 11, and that the "hour, and a day, and a month, and a year" of the Turkish power would be ended. Revelation 9:15. (See the section: The Moslems in Bible Prophecy.) When the ultimatum, which surrendered the Ottoman Empire into the control of the allied nations of Europe, was delivered to the Pasha of Egypt on that very day, multitudes were convinced that Miller's principles of prophetic interpretation were correct, and it greatly extended his influence:

> "This striking fulfillment of the prophecy had a tremendous effect upon the public mind. It intensified the interest of the people to hear upon the subject of fulfilled and fulfilling prophecy. Dr. Litch said that within a few months after August 11, 1840, he had received letters from more than one thousand prominent infidels, some of them leaders of infidel clubs, in which they stated that they had given up the battle against the Bible, and had accepted it as God's revelation to man. Some of these were fully converted to God, and a number of them became able speakers in the great second advent movement." Loughborough, *The Great Second Advent Movement*, p. 132.

Initially Miller and his associates believed that the termination of the 2300-day prophecy would come sometime in 1843 or early in 1844, and they loudly sounded the cry known as the first angels message: "Fear God, and give glory to him; for the hour of his judgment is come." Revelation 14:6-7. However, when Jesus did not come they were for a time disappointed in their expectation. A new impetus came in the summer of 1844 when it was demonstrated that the prophecy must extend to the tenth day of the seventh month of the Jewish calendar. This time a specific day was given for the coming of Jesus to judge the earth — October 22, 1844. This date was chosen as the most accurate reckoning of the typical cleansing of the earthly sanctuary and corresponds to the "tenth day of the seventh month...day of atonement" of the Jewish sacred calendar as determined by the Karaite Jews for that year. Leviticus 23:27. The preaching of time had a tremendously powerful effect upon the people. The Millerites went forth proclaiming the message with energy and in a few short months warned the people in America of the soon coming of Jesus in judgment upon the earth. To a lesser degree similar events took place in Europe and in other countries of the earth.

The Millerites and the other Adventists around the world were disappointed in their expectations of the Second Coming of Jesus to the earth. They had interpreted the *time* when the prophecy would terminate correctly, but they misunderstood the *application* of the cleansing of the antitypical sanctuary. They believed the sanctuary to be this sinful earth, which was to be cleansed by fire, and the Church, which was then to be completely redeemed by the Second Coming of Jesus. They did not realize it then, but the Bible had prophesied of their movement. The proclamation and disappointment of the 2300-year vision of Daniel eight was prophesied in Revelation chapter 10, during the second "woe," or sixth trumpet, where an "angel" is seen with the "little book" of Daniel opened in his hand:

> "And I saw another mighty angel come down from heaven… And he had in his hand a little book open… And the voice which I heard from heaven spake unto me again, and said, Go and take the little book which is open in the hand of the angel which standeth upon the sea and upon the earth… And I took the little book out of the angel's hand, and ate it up; and it was in my mouth sweet as honey: and as soon as I had eaten it, my belly was bitter." *Revelation 10:1-10.*

The "little book" of Daniel was declared by the heavenly Messenger to be sealed until "the time of the end," which began in 1798. Daniel 12:9. The eighth chapter of Daniel was then laid "open" by the Great Second Advent Movement. The Second Coming of Jesus was a "sweet" expectation, but resulted in a "bitter" disappointment for the believers. They had unknowingly fulfilled the prophecy in the Revelation! After their bitter experience a small band of the Millerite believers met and prayed together for light to understand the *application* of the 2300-day prophecy and the antitype of the cleansing of the sanctuary there revealed. "As this people carefully looked over their reckoning of the period, they found no defect; but the Lord did not come, neither was the earth cleansed by fire. What did it mean? Of a surety they knew that the Lord had been with them in the great movement; but now they were in suspense. Their confidence in the Lord was unshaken. They knew He would not forsake them. The light would come from some source." *The Great Second Advent Movement*, p. 192. Through study of the scriptures and the witness of the Spirit they began to see more fully the purpose of the sanctuary and its type and antitype relationship to the work in heaven. They discovered that Jesus' ministry in the sanctuary above had moved. His coming was to the Most Holy place in heaven and not to the earth as they had thought, and they followed Him there by faith. (See the section: The Judgment and the Woman.) They then understood their disappointment, and that they "must prophesy again before many peoples, and nations, and tongues, and kings." Revelation 10:11. Hence they realized that God was calling them to a greater task.

Just prior to the great disappointment in 1844 the various denominational churches began to persecute those who accepted the message of the soon coming of Jesus and the judgment: "Heavy opposition developed, and much antagonistic literature was published...designed to contravene the positions of the Adventists." Froom, *Movement of Destiny*, p. 69. The advent believers had no choice but to separate themselves from those churches: "Increasing separation, voluntary and involuntary, followed." Ibid., p. 70. During this separation another message, known as the second angel, began to go forward and it declared that the denominational churches, Evangelical, Protestant, and Catholic alike, by their rejection of the proclamation, had "fallen" and become a part of spiritual "Babylon." Revelation 14:8. They understood from scripture that Babylon means confusion (Genesis 10:10, margin; 11:9, margin), and spiritual Babylon is thus symbolic of confusion of religious doctrine. The first person to give this message was a man by the name of Charles Fitch in 1843. An extract of his sermon transcript clearly gives the tone of the message:

"I do say, if you are a Christian, come out of Babylon. If you intend to be found a Christian when Christ appears, come out of Babylon, and come out now. Throw away that miserable medley of ridiculous spiritualizing nonsense, with which multitudes have so long been making the Word of God of none effect, and dare to believe the Bible." *Come Out of Her, My People*, p. 19.

Another Second Advent leader, L. D. Mansfield, in a letter written from Oneida, N.Y., March 21, 1844, said:

"God is moving upon the minds of his dear children who are waiting for the Lord from heaven, and leading them not only to heed the angel 'having the everlasting gospel to preach, saying, The hour of his judgment is come,' but to obey the subsequent command, 'Come out of her, my people!' I am more fully persuaded than ever before, that the religious organizations of the present day constitute no small portion of that Babylon which is to be thrown down with violence, and found no more at all." *The Great Second Advent Movement*, p. 176.

Those churches that rejected the message of the judgment and the soon coming of Christ continued their round of ceremonies. They had accepted traditions rather then yield to the word of God, and Satan, impersonating the work of Jesus, began to answer their prayers after 1844. The false manifestation of tongues and various miracles and wonders seen today are the direct result of this apostasy. They failed to continue with the advancing light from the prophecies and had changed leaders unaware!

The Historicist method of interpretation, which God's people accepted for centuries, and which Miller used, began to be discarded by the various denominations at that time. In 1887 Doctor H. Grattan Guinness describes the apostasy in Protestantism as being nearly universal:

> "Never was there a time in the Church's history when she more needed the barriers which prophecy has erected for her protection. And now when they are so sorely needed, they are not to be found. Futurism has crept into the Protestant Church, and broken down these sacred walls." *Romanism and the Reformation*, p. 140.

The Protestants have ignored Rome's role in the prophecies and are now courting the very power that they once abhorred. They are intoxicated with her "wine." Revelation 17:2. They have clung to her spurious Sabbath, propagated her eternal hell fire doctrine, and coddled the immortality of the soul falsehood. They have also accepted the corrupt Alexandrian manuscripts of Rome, and since 1881, when the *Revised New Testament* was released, the Protestants have produced a multitude of new translations reflecting their common positions. Almost all of these new versions, with the exception of the *New King James Bible*, are based upon those corrupt manuscripts. Accordingly, the fallen churches are now uniting more closely with the Papacy and they will ultimately persecute the children of God. Thus a global crisis is developing for those who cling to His pure Word.

The Judgment and the Woman

The cleansing of the sanctuary, brought to view in Daniel eight, is typified by the work of the high priest in the Most Holy place of the earthly sanctuary. In the ancient system accounts were made of the deeds, both good and bad, of God's people, and placed within books. (See 1 Kings 11:41; 14:19, 29; 15:7, 23, 31.) They were documented by the "recorder," "remembrancer," or "writer of chronicles," and stored within the Most Holy place following the pattern that Moses had set up. (See 2 Samuel 8:16 margin; 2 Kings 18:18; Deuteronomy 31:24-26; Joshua 24:26; 1 Samuel 10:25; 1 Chronicles 16:4.) Additionally, throughout the ancient daily service the repentant sinner would bring an offering to the sanctuary, place his hands upon the victim's head, confess his sins over it, and slay the animal with his own hands. The officiating priest then took some of the blood, sprinkled it either in the Holy place or in the court, ate part of the flesh, and finally burned the remainder of the animal. (See Leviticus 4; 6:24-30.) These sin offerings symbolized the transfer of the guilt of sin from the penitent through the sacrifice, by the priest, and into the sanctuary. Therefore the sanctuary became defiled and needed cleansing. On a special day at the end of the year, called the Day of Atonement, the officiating high priest entered the Most Holy place with blood to blot out the record of sins recorded there, and then cleansed the Holy place and the Court of the actual defilement. (See Leviticus 16:1-19.)

The earthly sanctuary had long since disappeared by A.D. 1844, and the sanctuary of Daniel eight is the antitypical one in heaven within which Jesus is now ministering. (See Hebrews 3:1; 7:24-8:2.) The intercession of the priest throughout the year in the first apartment of the earthly temple, "within the veil," typifies the work of ministration upon which Christ entered at His ascension. Hebrews 6:19-20. Throughout the centuries an "account" or record of the deeds of God's people had been accumulating in the Most Holy place of the heavenly temple and was stored there until the judgment. Matthew 12:36-37. (See also Job 16:19; Ecclesiastes 12:14.) Their guilt, having been remitted and forgiven by the blood of Christ, was "borne" or "carried" away by Jesus, their high priest, and was collecting in the first compartment, the Holy place in heaven, as they confessed their sins to Him. Isaiah 53:4-6. (See Jeremiah 17:1; 1 John 1:9; Romans 3:24-25.) The heavenly sanctuary had therefore become defiled and was in need of cleansing. (See also Hebrews 9:23.)

On the antitypical Day of Atonement in 1844 Jesus declared to His Church: "behold I have set before thee an open door, and no man can shut it." Revelation 3:8. The "door" of the Most Holy place was then opened. Jesus entered upon the second phase of His ministry, within the "second veil" (Hebrews 9:3) of the heavenly temple, to examine and purge the record of the sins of His people with His blood. (See Hebrews 9:22-26; 10:17.) Everything that they have ever done is recorded there (see Ecclesiastes 12:14) and is even now being examined, and Jesus is standing as advocate for His people. (See 1 John 2:1; Zechariah 3:1-4.) This work of investigation takes a period of time after which He returns to the Holy place and removes the defilement from there, thus cleansing His temple in heaven.

The movement of the throne of the Ancient of days with its "wheels as burning fire" in Daniel seven is the antitype of the moveable chariot throne in the ancient sanctuary system, and is symbolic of a movement or change in ministry. Daniel 7:9. (See Isaiah 6:1-2; Ezekiel 1, 10; 1 Chronicles 28:18; 2 Chronicles 3:10 margin, 11-13; 5:7-8.) The judgment before which the "Ancient of days" presided, and before whom the "books were opened" is clearly the object of this motion. Daniel 7:10. This movement of the Ancient of days into the judgment is parallel with the cleansing of the sanctuary in the Most Holy place in heaven where the books of record are kept. (See Daniel 8:14.) Thus the two prophecies of Daniel are closely related, and these events are also connected with the scenes of the Most Holy place and the judgment in the book of Revelation. In Revelation 11:19 the door to the Most Holy place was opened in the heavenly temple and "there was seen in his temple the ark of his testament." The events that transpire on earth while Jesus is ministering in the Most Holy place in heaven are then brought to view. Therefore another section of the book of Revelation is opened to reveal insights into the events that transpire upon this earth after 1844. It was at that time that the scripture could say that, "the hour of His judgement is come." Revelation 14:6-7. This part of the book of Revelation does not have seven consecutive divisions as the first three sections of the book do, but it contains many simultaneous subsections, which I have termed *The Final Conflict* section of the book. Hence all of the prophecies converge at the end as shown in the following image:

Outline of the Prophecies

605 B.C. Babylon	331 B.C. Greece	✝	538 A.D. Papal Rome	Kingdom of God Setup
	Daniel 2, 7, 8-9, 10-12			
539 B.C. Medo-Persia	201 B.C. Rome			Judgment Begins
		Revelation 1:9-11:18		
	31 A.D. Jesus in Holy Place			1844 A.D. in Most Holy
			The Final Conflict:	11:19-19:21

After John the Revelator sees the Most Holy place opened he next beholds "a woman clothed with the sun, and the moon under her feet, and upon her head a crown of twelve stars." Revelation 12:1. A woman in prophecy represents a religious organization. (See 2 Corinthians 11:2; Jeremiah 6:2.) A pure woman symbolizes God's true church. (See Ephesians 5:22-32.) Hence, this virtuous woman, representing God's people throughout the Old and New Testaments, is seen in 1844 clothed with the glorious light of the gospel, and standing on the moon. (See Song 6:10; Acts 7:38; 2 Corinthians 4:4.) Just as in the natural world the moon has no light of its own, but reflects the light of the sun, so the types reflect the light and glory of the gospel. The moon therefore is symbolic of the types and shadows of the Old Testament dispensation while the sun, with which the woman is clothed, represents the full light of the New Testament gospel. Thus God's children, at the time of the judgment, are seen planted firmly on the gospel as it is presented in the types and shadows of the Old Testament and in the radiant light of the New.

This glorious woman through much pain and labor brings forth "the remnant of her seed, which keep the commandments of God, and have the testimony of Jesus Christ." Revelation 12:17. These characteristics thus give us a description of God's true people at the end of time, so that we can know where He wants us to be, and that we can escape the deceptions of Satan. This people do not follow the traditions of men, but all of the "commandments of God" that are found in the Decalogue in Exodus chapter 20. This identification eliminates the majority of the Christian organizations upon the earth today, for only a few obey the Sabbath Commandment. The second identification, "the testimony of Jesus Christ," is, according to the angel, "the spirit of prophecy." Revelation 19:10. Which means that they would not only understand the prophecies, but that they would have the gift of prophecy manifested among them. (See Acts 2:14-18; Revelation 1:9-10; 22:9.)

One other identification, which is mentioned in Revelation 14:12, is that these people are also declared to have "the faith of Jesus." It is a faith that depends entirely upon the Word of God and enables them to live above the corruptions of the world as Jesus did. (See Romans 3:31; 10:17; 1 John 5:4.) This identification, "the faith of Jesus," will be fully demonstrated in the last conflict. Therefore the scripture gives us undeniable evidence as to those who constitute God's children, spiritual Israel, just prior to Christ's return. (See Revelation 14:14-15; Acts 1:9-11.)

The European Beast

In the book of Revelation we have presented a hideous red colored creature that has "seven heads and ten horns." Revelation 12:3; 13:1; 17:3. It is described in chapter 12 as a "great red dragon" with "seven crowns upon his heads," and is clearly declared to be "that old serpent called the Devil and Satan." Revelation 12:9. Heads represent rulers or governing bodies in the Bible. (See Exodus 18:25; Numbers 10:4; 1 Chronicles 5:24; Psalms 110:6.) The seven crowned heads symbolize the seven consecutive governments of Rome through which Satan has and will work to suppress and destroy God's people. (See Revelation 17:10.) The ten horns are the ten nations to which Rome was originally divided. (See Daniel 7:24; and chapter 4: The Establishment of the Papacy.) In Revelation 13 this same creature, like a chameleon, changes its appearance to that of a "beast" rising from the "sea" of humanity (see Revelation 17:15) on the European continent:

> "And I stood upon the sand of the sea, and saw a beast rise up out of the sea, having seven heads and ten horns, and upon his horns ten crowns, and upon his heads the name of blasphemy. And the beast which I saw was like unto a leopard, and his feet were as the feet of a

bear, and his mouth as the mouth of a lion: and the dragon gave him his power, and his seat, and great authority." *Revelation 13:1-2.*

This ten-horned beast is made-up of the characteristics of the four beasts of Daniel seven given in reverse order, and has many of the same identifying marks as the little horn power. It blasphemes God, persecutes His children, and reigns for the same 1260 years as the little horn and the abomination of desolation. (See Revelation 13:5-7; and chapter 7: The 1260 Years.) One point should be clarified when talking about the reign of the beast. Characteristics like the ten horns and the 1260 years are identifying marks that connect the beast of Revelation to the little horn and the abomination of Daniel. They are, however, not intended to point us backward in time to the past reign of the Papacy, but they are intended to point us forward in time to its restored reign after 1844. The ten crowns on its horns indicate that this beast comes to power when the kings that rule over the original ten divisions of Rome are again united, and the prophecy clearly says of the beast: "And I saw one of his heads as it were wounded to death; and his deadly wound was healed." Revelation 13:3. Thus the prophecy points us to a time when the Papacy is restored to its former glory after 1844.

In Revelation 17 is found a description of the "great whore," Mystical Babylon, riding upon the same seven-headed, ten-horned Beast. Since a woman in prophecy represents a religious organization (see the section: The Judgment and the Woman), then the "great whore" that rides this "scarlet-colored beast" represents a corrupt religious system. Revelation 17:1-5. (See also Hosea; Ezekiel 16:1-34.) This "MOTHER OF HARLOTS AND ABOMINATIONS OF THE EARTH" is likened to the female characteristics of the little horn of Daniel eight and "the abomination that maketh desolate" of Daniel 11, and the ten horns are again the nations that reign over the territory to which Western Rome was originally divided and are the same as the ten horns of Daniel seven. These nations will yet unite themselves more closely to the apostate Church. This Beast is therefore a union of the nations of Western Europe and the Roman Church, and is the same creature as the first Beast of Revelation 13. This change of appearance by the Dragon into the Beast is needed so that it can make effective war with the last day remnant Church. Its anger will yet be displayed in a dramatic way:

> "And the dragon was wroth with the woman, and went to make war with the remnant of her seed, which keep the commandments of God, and have the testimony of Jesus Christ." *Revelation 12:17.*

"And it was given unto him to make war with the saints, and to overcome them: and power was given him over all kindreds, and tongues, and nations." *Revelation 13:7.*

"And I saw the woman drunken with the blood of the saints, and with the blood of the martyrs of Jesus: and when I saw her, I wondered with great admiration." *Revelation 17:6.*

The Bible says that this Beast "was, and is not; and shall ascend" or "yet is," and the seven heads of the Beast are "seven mountains, on which the woman sitteth;" an obvious reference to the seven hilled city — Rome. Revelation 17:8-9. The seven heads are also said to be "seven kings" representing its seven government systems in sequence: "five are fallen, and one is, and the other is not yet come." Revelation 17:10. The head that "is" exists at the same time that the Beast "is not." The present tense "is not" period of the Beast existed in 1844, because this section of the Revelation is brought to view when the apostle John looks into the Most Holy place of the heavenly sanctuary as discussed in the last section. The wounding of the papal Beast in 1798 ended the "was" period, the Beast "is not" in 1844, and the passage predicts that it "shall ascend" and that its "deadly wound" will be "healed." Revelation 13:3; 17:8. The healed wound of the Beast is said to be "the eighth" head or government of Rome, but that it "is of the seven." Revelation 17:11. The seven heads are not separate empires, but they are the seven consecutive government systems of Rome that are clearly defined in history as: (1) the Monarchy, (2) the Republic, (3) the Principate, (4) the Autocracy, (5) the Papacy, (6) the divided, free nations of Western Europe, and (7) the European Union which has recently emerged.

In A.D. 1844 the Bible could say that the seventh head "is not yet come; and when he cometh, he must continue a short space," but the seventh head has now risen. Revelation 17:10. It has "ten horns which…are ten kings… These have one mind, and shall give their power and strength unto the beast." Revelation 17:12-13. The ten horns represent those nations that occupy the dominion of the original ten divisions of Rome — Western Europe. For rulers of Western Europe to "have one mind" means that they think and work together, thus they have one government system that unites them — the European Union. This seventh period began on November 1, 1993 when the treaty of Maastricht that formed the EU went into force, and at the end of a short period of time in the near future they will give their power and strength back to the Papacy: "For God hath put in their hearts to fulfill his will, and to agree, and give their kingdom unto the beast." Revelation 17:17. The Papacy will again receive political power from all of the nations of Europe, its deadly wound will be healed, the church-state union will be realized, and the Beast will come from the "wilderness" and "shall ascend out of the bottomless pit." Revelation 13:3; 17:3, 8. The "beast that was, and is not, even he is the eighth, and is of the seven." Revelation 17:11. The eighth is really the fifth head, the Papacy, with its wound healed and restored to power. It comes out of the wilderness of which it was forced to go into by Berthier in 1798. (See the timeline below.)

The Protestant churches must of necessity support this union in Europe, and some are even advocating today that the pope be declared their spiritual leader. These same organizations along with the Papacy are also insisting that the new EU Constitution proclaim Christianity as the national religion. When the EU becomes a Christian nation by law it will mark the rise of the Beast from the abyss and the healing of the deadly wound. Thus the Beast, although led by the Papacy, is not limited to the Papacy alone, but includes the multitudes in Europe professing Protestant beliefs as well. Nevertheless, if the Beast is restricted to Europe, the symbols of Babylon and the Euphrates are not. Babylon is a conglomerate kingdom (see Revelation 16:12-13, 19), and just as the Euphrates River flowed through the ancient city of Babylon supporting it, so the Euphrates is symbolic of the various peoples that support antitypical Babylon. (See Revelation 16:12; 17:15.) Babylon encompasses more than just Western Europe, and has expanded to include the apostate Protestants that have immigrated to America, and it must therefore have a part to play in the final conflict.

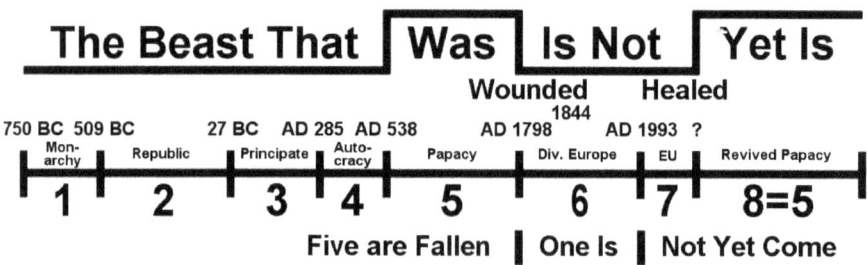

The American Beast

The woman of Revelation 17 is called the "MOTHER OF HARLOTS," therefore the daughters, of necessity, have the same occupation. The Roman Church claims to be the "mother and mistress of all churches." *Documents of the Christian Church*, p. 267. Her daughters are obviously churches that sacrifice their connection with God and unite themselves with the state in a similar manner. The works of the daughters are not mentioned in connection with the beast, but are portrayed in Revelation 13:11-17 where the apostle gives a description of "another beast." In chapter 14 we have depicted God's last day remnant "which were not defiled with women." Revelation 14:4. The word "women" is in the plural indicating many and, since the first beast is connected primarily with the papal, mother of harlots, the second beast must also of necessity be connected with her protestant, harlot daughters, for it rises after the first and forces the world to worship the first beast that the mother harlot is riding.

Notice the identifying marks of this second beast at its beginning: (1) It rises from the "earth" in contrast to the first beast that rose from the "sea," and upon which "the four winds of the heaven strove." Revelation 13:11, 1; Daniel 7:2. The seas or waters in prophecy are symbolic of "peoples, and multitudes, and nations, and tongues," and the winds represent destruction and warfare. Revelation 17:15 (see also Jeremiah 4:6-13; 25:31-33.) Therefore the "earth," which is declared in Genesis 1:10 to be "dry land," must portray a sparsely populated region upon which there was no previous kingdom to overthrow and subdue. (2) It is seen "coming up" about the time that the first beast is going into "captivity" into the wilderness in 1798. Revelation 13:10-11. (3) This beast is first represented by the mildness of a "lamb" with "two horns," and is a clear reference to Jesus the Lamb with "seven horns." Revelation 13:11; 5:6. Thus it is a nation professing Christian principles. (4) It is a republican power because it appeals to the people and says to "*them* that dwell on the earth, that *they* should make an image to the beast, which had the wound." Revelation 13:14. (5) It also clearly becomes a super-power at some point since it "exerciseth all the power of the first beast before him, and causeth the earth and them which dwell therein to worship the first beast, whose deadly wound was healed." Revelation 13:12.

The only kingdom on earth that meets the criteria above is the United States of America. It rose from the unpopulated areas of the earth, and began its rise into a nation about the time that the first beast was going into captivity in 1798. It was founded upon Christian principles, has a republican form of government, and today the United States has become the only super-power upon the earth. Hence, the United States clearly fits the identification given in the prophecy, and it is obvious that America is the land to where the Protestant daughters of the Papacy have fled.

The works of the American beast, after the European beast ascends from the bottomless pit, have the most devastating consequences associated with them: (1) It "maketh fire come down from heaven on the earth in the sight of men." Revelation 13:13. Fire from heaven in the scripture is symbolic of the outpouring of the Holy Spirit. (See Luke 3:16; Acts 2:1-4.) The prophecy is referring to the outpouring of a false Holy Spirit, which will not only be attended by the specious gift of tongues that is now flooding the Christian world, but it will "deceive" men, "by the means of those miracles which he had power to do in the sight of the beast." Revelation 13:14. (Note: some interpreters see the fire from heaven by the second beast as symbolic of the bombs dropped by the United States to bring the world into submission.) (2) These deceived people will then "make an image to the beast, which had the wound by a sword, and did live." That is, they will cause church and state to unite. The constitution, which guarantees freedom of worship and speech, is now being brought into question, and it shall be completely set aside to make a likeness to the European Beast, which is soon to arise. The voice of the majority will press the legislators in America to unite with religious institutions to control and force "worship." Despite the clear statement of the First Amendment the government will enforce Church traditions, and this enactment will form the "image of the beast" in America. (3) The United States will then be in a position to play its part in the last great conflict. It will cause those who dwell upon the earth to receive a "mark in their right hand, or in their foreheads." Revelation 13:15-17. This mark is the impress of sin (Job 10:14; Jeremiah 2:22), and is shown to be in opposition to the seal of God's Law, which is placed into the foreheads of His people. (See Isaiah 8:16; Revelation 7:1-3; 12:17; 14:1, 12.) Hence, these three works are devastating to the Church and carry the gravest warning message from God:

"And the third angel followed them, saying with a loud voice, If any man worship the beast and his image, and receive his mark in his forehead, or in his hand, The same shall drink of the wine of the wrath of God, which is poured out without mixture into the cup of his indignation; and he shall be tormented with fire and brimstone in the presence of the holy angels, and in the presence of the Lamb: And the smoke of their torment ascendeth up for ever and ever: and they have no rest day nor night, who worship the beast and his image, and whosoever receiveth the mark of his name." *Revelation 14:9-11.*

The cause of the wickedness in America today rests squarely upon the backs of the Protestant preachers because they have shunned the Word of God, and have followed the traditions and the Futurist theories of Rome. They have continued to exalt the worship of Sunday and kindred errors thus advocating transgression of God's Law. Nevertheless, those who disobey His Law and exalt the traditions of man cannot worship Him. (See Matthew 15:9.) Cain disobeyed God's requirements and then killed his brother because Abel's obedience enraged him. (See Genesis 4:1-15.) He hardened his heart against God, and God placed a mark, the sign of eternal disobedience, upon him. Thus, Cain is a type of those that receive the "mark of the beast" at the end of time. This mark of sin is an institution of Papal authority and worship. It is in opposition to the Commandments of God (1 John 3:4), and is enforced by the America Beast upon the world. This mark is the establishment of Sunday by law. Notice that the Papacy claims the change from Sabbath to Sunday as the mark of its authority:

> "Of course the Catholic Church claims that the change [from Saturday to Sunday] was her act. It could not have been otherwise, as none in those days would have dreamed of doing anything in matters spiritual and religious without her, and the act is a *mark* of her ecclesiastical power and authority in religious matters." Letter by the Chancellor of Cardinal Gibbons, November 11, 1895. (Italics supplied.)

> "Sunday is our *mark* of authority... The Church is above the Bible, and this transference of Sabbath observance is proof of that fact." *Catholic Record*, London, Ontario, September 1, 1923. (Italics again supplied.)

Many more statements could be produced, but these should suffice. Sunday is obviously the mark of papal authority and is not an impression that can be seen. The mark is to be received in their "foreheads" symbolizing belief, or in the "right hand" denoting works. Revelation 13:16. Those who believe the Sunday institution will obviously follow it and they will receive the mark in their "foreheads." However, many will keep Sunday from fear of the ruling authorities at that time and they will receive the mark in their "right hand." God's people on the other hand can only receive His seal in their "foreheads." (See Ezekiel 9:4; Revelation 7:3; 14:1; 22:4.) That is, they believe and keep God's whole Law because they love Him. No man can truly keep His Law from fear of punishment. Nevertheless, none have yet received the mark, and no one will receive it until a national law in America is passed enforcing Sunday and the light of truth has been presented warning men against it. Thus the message will of necessity go forth with a "loud voice." Revelation 14:9.

The daughters of the harlot are at work in America. The Protestants, which came from the heart of Rome and fled to America to escape persecution, have themselves become corrupt since 1844. They have not advanced in the light, and they continue to propagate many of the same falsehoods and traditions that come from their mother. This is why the Bible calls this second Beast the "false prophet." Revelation 19:20. They are Christian in name and claim that they accept the Bible as the Word of God and "prophesy" from it their falsehoods.

They are accepting Satan's deceptions and are being led by him. Thus the United States will do that which its constitution forbids. It will exalt an institution of the Papacy causing the world "to worship the first beast, whose deadly wound was healed."

The First Amendment has become the arena around which the great controversy now revolves. Satan is enraged with the freedom that God's children have to worship Him, and he is even now working to break down the wall separating the church from the state that protects the religious minority from persecution by the majority. In 1985 Chief Justice of the United States, William Rehnquist, declared in his dissent: "The 'wall of separation between church and state' is a metaphor based on bad history, a metaphor which has proved useless as a guide to judging. It should be frankly and explicitly abandoned." *Wallace v. Jeffree*, 472 U.S. 38. He argued that the only purpose of the First Amendment was to keep the federal government from establishing a national religion. Since that time many books and other documents have been written with the purpose of undermining the First Amendment, and it is now the object of the most violent attacks.

David Barton, in his book *The Myth of Separation*, argues that the First Amendment was never intended to separate "orthodox Christianity" from the state, and that it only guarantees "freedom of worship and conscience" within "traditional Christianity." p. 29. Likewise, the popular author David Limbaugh, following the lead of David Barton, declared: "You'll note there is no language in either — or anywhere else in the Constitution — mandating a wall of separation between church and state." *Persecution*, p. xi. This book documents the various instances in America where Christians are mistreated. The inferred solution to the "persecution" is to unite church and state in America. In order to support his illusion he has even attempted to rewrite history declaring: "it was the Puritans, with their biblically based governments modeled on their church covenants, who laid the primary foundation for our constitutional government." *Ibid*, p. 303. Thus he is calling Christians in America back to the totalitarian days of the Puritans.

Anyone who understands American history knows that the Puritans were violent persecutors of the minorities among them. Ironically Mr. Limbaugh fails to document their hatred of freedom, their persecution of minorities, and the real foundation of the United States Constitution that came through Roger Williams. Unfortunately, the majority of Americans today are ignorant of their past history, and they will easily capitulate to the popular deception. Justice William Rehnquist and author David Barton have supplied the apostate movement with its twisted logic, and David Limbaugh and others are providing it with its emotional energy. The First Amendment will simply be discarded or revised by the vote of the majority when the proper stimulus is applied, and the second beast, America, will then speak "as a dragon."

The Final Powers Identified

We are now ready to identify the two warring powers of the final conflict. The king of the South, which began as atheism in France, has now passed to the communist countries of Asia. Many believed that Russia would be the power to represent the king of the South in the final conflict, for atheism became fully developed there; however, with the collapse of communism in Russia, it does not meet the identification of the prophecy as we shall see. Rather, the socialism and communism that now flourishes in China more closely fulfills the atheist power in the last conflict. As with Marx and Engels, Mao Zedong accepted the evolutionary teachings of Darwin, as they were presented through a translation of Thomas Huxley's *Principles of Evolution* by Yen Fu. These principles worked out in the lives of Mao's followers led to the slaughter of millions in China. The following reveals the easy entrance of communism into China:

> "Many writers have noted that the relatively easy entrance of Marxism and communism into Chinese thought and life was greatly facilitated by the prior entrance of Darwinism, which in turn had been smoothed by the long compatibility of the Chinese religions with evolutionary ways of thinking." Morris, *The Long War Against God*, pp. 221-222.

The pagan philosophies of Greece and Rome, which are closely united to modern evolutionism and atheism, went underground during the long ages of papal dominion, were renewed in the Renaissance, ascended to power in atheist France, were expanded in England through Darwin, and are fully embraced by the socialist and communist countries of today. When atheism first reigned in France it was given the designation: "the beast that ascendeth out of the bottomless pit." Revelation 11:7 (See the section: The Atheist Beast). Although France is no longer an atheist nation the beast still survives in China, which is now the greatest atheist kingdom on the earth. Therefore the reigning power of the king of the South, spiritual Egypt, now represents China in the vision by the Tigris.

Likewise, the identification of the king of the North, spiritual Babylon, is clearly described in scripture. It is a conglomerate kingdom made up of three parts: the Dragon, the Beast, and the False Prophet. (See Revelation 16:13, 19.)

We have already seen that the Dragon is Satan working through the various nations of Europe. These nations have united and will yet give their "power," their "seat" of government, and "great authority" to the Papacy to form the European Beast. (See Revelation 13:2.) The False Prophet, or Image to the European Beast, is formed when the Protestants of the United States unite with the government in America. This False Prophet repudiates its constitution by enforcing the papal Sunday institution, "and causes the earth and them which dwell therein to worship the first beast, whose deadly wound was healed." Revelation 13:12. The legislation of Sunday then closely unites Europe and America fully bonding mystical or spiritual Babylon. When these things take place it is then that the kings of the North and the South will enter into the last great conflict described in the vision by the Tigris River.

We are now considering the second phrase of verse 40 where the king of the North, antitypical Babylon, attacks the king of the South, spiritual Egypt: "and the king of the north shall come against him like a whirlwind." Some believe that the collapse of Communism in Russia early in the 1990s was the fulfillment of this passage, but this is not possible for two reasons. (1) The king of the North is not fully developed as yet but will be when the Dragon brings forth the Beast in Europe and the False Prophet in America, and the False Prophet then legislates the Sunday institution. Antitypical, spiritual Babylon, the king of the North, will then be fully formed. (2) No war took place to bring about the fall of Russian Communism. Every time war is mentioned in the prophecy it is speaking of literal war, even between spiritual powers. The wars of Constantine against the king of the south, pagan Rome, revealed in chapter four, are clearly fought between spiritual powers, but they are literal wars. Therefore, when "the king of the north shall come against him like a whirlwind, with chariots, and with horsemen, and with many ships," it is talking of literal war between spiritual powers. Here is where interpreting the prophecy from the beginning becomes important. Those who begin in verse 40 would obviously overlook these two points. Nevertheless, Russia will be included in the last conflict (most likely on the side of spiritual Babylon).

Some may doubt that the United States and its allies could ever make war with China, but any doubt of this is based upon lack of information. The popular, liberal media is lax in presenting the antagonism that is now gaining momentum. For years the Chinese have been helping rogue states and terrorist organizations acquire weapons of mass destruction. They have been selling everything imaginable to anyone. Arms such as surface-to-air missiles, missile and cruise missile components, sophisticated radar and missile defense systems and electronics, numerous conventional weapons and explosives, components for chemical and biological weapons, and technical expertise and documentation for nuclear devices are delivered to its clients. Customers of the Chinese government-ran arms producers have included nations such as Iraq, Iran, North Korea, Pakistan, Syria, Libya, and Cuba. Even Bin Laden made three trips to Beijing and arranged defense contracts for the Taliban prior to the September 11 terror attacks on the United States. Hence, "China is today one of the most dangerous suppliers of advanced conventional arms, dual-use products, and materials for weapons of mass destruction." Gertz, *Treachery*, p. 115. Can anyone doubt that this proliferation will eventually incite war with China?

While actively strengthening America's foes the Chinese Communist Party (CCP) is working intently to develop a strong national sentiment among the Chinese people, which is increasingly becoming hostile. This aggressive nature may soon be displayed over territorial issues. The following from Maria Hsia Chang is insightful: "To secure popular support, the Communist Party might find itself increasingly pressured to take military action against its neighbors over contested territories…and may lead China to military conflict — and possible defeat — against its neighbors and the United States." *Chang, Return of the Dragon*, p. 243.

It is unknown at this time what will spark the conflict. It could be a confrontation over Taiwan's independence, which is a daily issue between China and the United States. The U.S. has pledged its support for Taiwan, and would certainly be drawn into any conflict between them. Nevertheless, as soon as Beijing feels that it has enough power to restrain the U.S. it will act, and that action may include nuclear or other weapons of mass destruction. China has been trying to catch up with the United States in military capability for many years, but through stealing and purchasing of technology it is now capable of threatening America with the most sophisticated nuclear weapons ever created. The following sums up the threat that China poses to the United States:

> "The People's Republic of China is the most serious national security threat the United States faces at present… This grave strategic threat includes the disruption of vital U.S. interests in the Pacific region and even the possibility of a nuclear war that could cost millions of American lives." Gertz, *The China Threat*, p. 199.

Men are oblivious to the events that are now gaining momentum. The world is marching toward the final crisis, and the description of it as given in the prophecy is clear that it will be of short duration: "and the king of the north shall come against him like a whirlwind, with chariots, and with horsemen, and with many ships; and he shall enter into the countries, and shall overflow and pass over." Beijing will have miscalculated the resolve of the European and the American people.

Before the final war against atheism commences some event will stimulate the union of church and state in Europe and America. Major natural disasters, terrorist attacks, or any combination of them could cause the conservative Christian base to rise to the forefront and demand religious control. General Tommy Franks, former commander of the U.S. military's Central Command, declared in an interview with the magazine *Cigar Aficionado*, December 2003, that, if there was ever another terrorist attack with a weapon of mass destruction upon the United States or one of its allies, it would "unravel the fabric of our Constitution." The final crisis could therefore be precipitated by a major terrorist attack in Europe or the simultaneous explosion of nuclear weapons in American cities by al Qaeda sleeper cells, as we have been clearly warned could happen. (See Williams, *Osama's Revenge*.) The event that precipitates the last crisis, whatever it is, will be of great magnitude and bring persecution upon the Church.

Babylon Attacks the Church

It is Satan's purpose to keep men so busy that they will neglect eternal realities. Men are active getting possessions and enjoying worldly entertainment, and when the last crisis breaks they will not have the foundation needed to make the proper decisions. Those who have failed to surrender themselves to the Lord, have neglected Bible study, and have not learned the truth of the prophecies will place themselves upon the wrong side in the spiritual issues then to face the world. Satan so intends to hide the issues from men, by inducing them to selfish gratification, that when the final crisis comes they will be taken unaware. (See 2 Timothy 3:1-7.) They will quickly place themselves upon the easy, popular side in the conflict. Most professed Christians have been deceived and "made drunk with the wine" of spiritual Babylon. Revelation 17:1-2. They have come to trust their teachers and pastors, and they are completely steeped in tradition. They do not know the plan of God!

As the conflict approaches the Spirit of God is gradually being withdrawn from the earth. Disasters of every kind are even now in the land, and they will increase both in number and intensity. (See Matthew 24:6-8.) Evil men will bring devastation in the cities, and Satan will manipulate the elements of nature as he did in the days of Job. (See Job 1:12-19.) The destruction of the world trade center and the ruin of populace cities by hurricanes, floods, tornadoes, and earthquakes are portentous of greater calamities. Men will see the incredible magnitude of events upon the earth; terror will grip the people, and the popular ministry will cry for unity among the churches.

Members of all of the various sects will be admonished to come together in prayer. Appeals will be made to the churches to put aside their distinctive doctrines that have served to separate them from each other, and, no matter how important they may be from a biblical standpoint, these doctrines will be looked upon as the reason for the great disunity and corruption in the land. Even now these appeals are being advocated, and all who conscientiously refuse to join the Ecumenical movement are regarded as stubborn and rebellious. The cry will at length be made that the reason for the loss of divine favor is because of the violation of Sunday. It will be declared that Sunday enforcement will expose the Islamic terrorists, restore divine favor, stop the disasters, and bring security to the world. Hence, a law will be enacted for Sunday exaltation. Religious intolerance of dissenters will again rule; persecution will be called forth upon those who conscientiously refuse to obey Sunday, as happened throughout the Christian dispensation. The popular ministry will point to God's children and declare that the problems and disasters are because of them, and in so doing they will bring a crisis to the Church of God as is next brought out in the vision:

"He shall enter also into the glorious land, and many countries shall be overthrown: but these shall escape out of his hand, even Edom, and Moab, and the chief of the children of Ammon." Daniel 11:41.

The present passage happens more or less simultaneously with the last phrase of verse 40. Palestinian terminology is often used to represent the Church of God in the scriptures. The "holy city," "mount Sion," the "new Jerusalem," "an holy nation," and "the city of the living God, the heavenly Jerusalem" are all typical of God's Church. (See Revelation 11:2; 14:1; 21:2; 1 Peter 2:9; Hebrews 12:22-23.) The "glorious land" in the passage under consideration is also representative of the Church of God at the time of the end. Verse 16 is the type and here we have the antitype. The word "countries" is supplied by the translators, and is not in the original language. The first phrase clearly reads: "He shall enter also into the glorious land, and many shall be overthrown." This is an obvious reference then to an attack upon the Church, "the glorious land," by the king of the North, spiritual Babylon.

As in the Dark Ages the Papacy persecuted God's true children, so again persecution will reign supreme, but this time the persecutors will include the Protestant daughters of the Harlot. At first Sunday will be forced upon God's people in addition to their observance to the Sabbath, but they cannot conscientiously keep Sunday and remain obedient to God; thus they will refuse. As the disasters and the threat of war intensify Sabbath keepers will be singled out. As the great whore rides the beast she makes "war with the saints." Revelation 13:7. Those who refuse to receive the mark of papal authority, enforced by the False Prophet, will be greatly oppressed; they will lose their jobs and fines will be imposed for disobedience. This pressure put on the Church will cause many to yield their faith and join the Sunday movement, and these same ones will form great opposition to God's children.

In Matthew 24 Jesus mingles descriptions of two periods: the destruction of Jerusalem and those events associated with His return. (See Matthew 24:3.) He speaks of the rise of false prophets and counterfeit Christs; He foresees wars and rumors of wars; He describes famines, pestilences, and earthquakes; and He warns of hatred, betrayal, and persecution against His people. In verse 15 He gives the event signaling when the great Roman apostasy is about to come upon His people: "When ye therefore shall see the abomination of desolation, spoken of by Daniel the prophet, stand in the holy place..." Matthew 24:15. The primary application of this passage is to the destruction of Jerusalem in A.D. 70 (see Daniel 9:26-27), but since Jesus was answering two questions the passage has a secondary application as well. He is using phrases that are found in Daniel 11 (i.e. "abomination of desolation" and to "stand"). For over 1800 years God's people sent their faith up to Jesus where He had been ministering in the "holy place" of the heavenly sanctuary. Jesus' words direct us to a time when papal Rome, "the abomination of desolation," will "stand," or rise to power over the Protestants who continue to worship toward the "holy place" in heaven. They have continued to look to Jesus where he was, and Satan, having impersonated the work of Jesus, has led them to give their support to the Papacy, to honor her institutions, and the Papacy will be exalted. Therefore, when the Protestants of America make a law for the enforcement of the papal Sunday, Rome will then "stand in the holy place." ("Whoso readeth, let him understand!" Matthew 24:15.) When this law goes forth it is the signal for God's people to flee the major cities:

> "Then let them which be in Judaea flee into the mountains: Let him which is on the housetop not come down to take any thing out of his house: Neither let him which is in the field return back to take his clothes. And woe unto them that are with child, and to them that give suck in those days!" *Matthew 24:16-19.*

This passage is meant for Christians in our day, and is a warning to us. The cities will be filled with confusion and violence, and persecution will reign supreme, so the Lord calls His people out of them. To the above Jesus adds the following: "But pray ye that your flight be not in the winter, neither on the sabbath day." Matthew 24:20. Obviously God has a people upon this earth that are obeying the Sabbath commandment. These are the ones that receive the persecution called forth in the vision by the Tigris, and "many shall be overthrown."

Through the long years since 1844 God's Church has become filled with the unconverted. Its members have become "wretched, and miserable, and poor, and blind, and naked." Revelation 3:17. Many are longing for salvation, but have not made Jesus their refuge and hold to a legalistic religion, and they will be swept away in the coming storm. However, even though many leave the Church, and it is severely shaken, it will remain while the unconverted are being sifted out. The Church must go through this sifting experience, so that "those things which cannot be shaken may remain." Hebrews 12:27. The trial is given to purify the Church. (See Matthew 13:37-43, 47-50; 22:11-14; Revelation 12:4.)

"But these shall escape out of his hand, even Edom, and Moab, and the chief of the children of Ammon." Edom was Esau, the brother of Jacob, and Moab and Ammon were the two illegitimate sons of Lot that were conceived when he fled Sodom. (See Genesis 19:36-38; 25:24-34.) These represent the spiritual relatives of God's children. Those people from various faiths who have heard the warning but have not accepted the full truth. They will at this time see the truth for what it is. Thus when the final conflict begins many of God's scattered people will come out of the fallen churches and escape the apostasy of Babylon:

> "And it shall come to pass in that day, that the Lord shall set his hand again the second time to recover the remnant of his people, which shall be left... And he shall set up an ensign for the nations, and shall assemble the outcasts of Israel, and gather together the dispersed of Judah from the four corners of the earth...they shall lay their hand upon Edom and Moab; and the children of Ammon shall obey them." *Isaiah 11:11-14.*

Edom, Moab, and Ammon represent the children of God that have heard the message of the third angel but have not yet come out of Babylon. They will do so when the conflict begins, for they shall see the truth of the binding claims of God's Law, and, despite the persecution, they will raise the standard with their brethren.

Babylon Overthrows Egypt

The scripture is clear that all of the world will wonder after the European

Beast: "And all that dwell upon the earth shall worship him, whose names are not written in the book of life of the Lamb slain from the foundation of the world," and "they that dwell on the earth shall wonder..." Revelation 13:8; 17:8. No one will escape except those that have their names "written in the book of life," and it's only through the blood of the slain Lamb, Jesus, that our names can be within that book. Only Jesus can give victory over sin, and lead His people onward to salvation. Nevertheless, the Beast intends that the world shall obey it, and in the last conflict China and its allies, spiritual Egypt, will completely fall to mystical Babylon. It is to this that the prophecy next turns:

> **"He shall stretch forth his hand also upon the countries: and the land of Egypt shall not escape. But he shall have power over the treasures of gold and of silver, and over all the precious things of Egypt: and the Libyans and the Ethiopians shall be at his steps."** Daniel 11:42-43.

As the attack upon God's Church continues the conquest of the kingdom of the South, spiritual Egypt and its allies, is here brought to a completion. The word "power" in the present passage means to rule, govern, or have dominion. Thus great Babylon will have dominion over all of the land and wealth of the nations. Especially is China symbolized here as "the land of Egypt." Whether it is silver, gold, land, oil, or people everything will then be in the control of great spiritual Babylon. Their control of the wealth of the nations must of a necessity take place and will give them the authority to take the next step in tyranny. A decree will go forth at that time that anyone who refuses to yield to the Sunday institution will not be able to "buy or sell." Revelation 13:17. Their assets will be frozen and their property will be confiscated. No country upon the earth will be safe for God's children; all earthly support will be removed, and they will have to entirely rely upon the Lord.

The phrase "and the Libyans and the Ethiopians shall be at his steps" means that they follow along with, and are allies of, the king of the South. (See Exodus 11:8, margin; Judges 4:10; Judges 8:5; 1 Kings 20:10, margin; 2 Kings 3:9, margin.) These represent all of the different nations that join themselves together against the Beast and the False Prophet, but they will be overthrown. The great atheistic powers will collapse. Just as ancient Babylon overthrew Egypt, so type shall meet antitype as great mystical Babylon overthrows spiritual Egypt:

> "And the sword shall come upon Egypt, and great pain shall be in Ethiopia, when the slain shall fall in Egypt, and they shall take away

her multitude, and her foundations shall be broken down. Ethiopia, and Libya, and Lydia, and all the mingled people, and Chub, and the men of the land that is in league, shall fall with them by the sword." *Ezekiel 30:4-5.*

No longer will great Babylon have the threat of nuclear war, the fear of weapons of mass destruction, or the horror of terrorism. Being led by the false teachings of Futurism, which profess a war between the nations of the East and the West, many will claim that the battle of "Armageddon" is over. Revelation 16:12-16. They will declare that the "kings of the east" represented China and its allies, which have been overthrown, and they shall cry "peace and safety." 1 Thessalonians 5:3. All nations will then "have drunk of the wine of the wrath of her fornication." Revelation 14:8; 17:2; 18:3. The Papacy will declare: "I sit a queen, and am no widow, and shall see no sorrow." Revelation 18:7. She will proclaim: "I shall be a lady for ever... I am, and none else beside me; I shall not sit as a widow, neither shall I know the loss of children." Isaiah 47:7-8. All of her Protestant "children" will be with her and will support her. All of the world will then be wondering after the European Beast with the exception of the Remnant.

The Sealed Remnant

In the ancient typical system the work of the final atonement, the cleansing of the sanctuary on earth, was a solemn experience in which the people were to afflict their souls before God while the high priest ministered in the sanctuary. All business was laid aside, and the whole congregation of Israel spent the day in solemn humiliation with prayer, fasting, and deep searching of heart. Those who refused to do this work were cut off from among the people. (See Leviticus 16:29-30; 23:26-32.)

The antitype of the Day of Atonement is a work of judgment, and is of a most glorious nature. (See the section: The Judgment and the Woman.) The judgment, which began in 1844 with those that have died in Christ, will soon pass upon the living saints. (See Ecclesiastes 12:13-14; Romans 14:10; 2 Corinthians 5:10.) The last generation will be judged while alive, for when Jesus appears the second time He declares: "...my reward is with me, to give every man according as his work shall be." Revelation 22:12. He must judge His people before He comes, and therefore He admonishes them to present themselves to the judgment: "...let us judge together: number yourself, that you may be justified." Isaiah 43:26, a literal translation. He warns His people to gather to the heavenly judgment around the antitypical, heavenly sanctuary so that they are not cut off:

> "Gather yourselves together, yea, gather together, O nation not desired; Before the decree bring forth, before the day pass as the chaff, before the fierce anger of the LORD come upon you, before the day of the LORD'S anger come upon you. Seek ye the LORD, all ye meek of the earth, which have wrought his judgment; seek righteousness, seek meekness: it may be ye shall be hid in the day of the LORD'S anger." *Zephaniah 2:1-3.*

> "Blow the trumpet in Zion, sanctify a fast, call a solemn assembly: Gather the people, sanctify the congregation, assemble the elders, gather the children, and those that suck the breasts: let the bridegroom go forth of his chamber, and the bride out of her closet." *Joel 2:15-16.*

As they gather in faith about the heavenly sanctuary Daniel describes Jesus as He comes before the Father to stand as advocate in defense of His people: "I saw in the night visions, and, behold, one like the Son of man came with the clouds of heaven, and came to the Ancient of days, and they brought him near before him." Daniel 7:13. Jesus stands in the Most Holy place in the heavenly sanctuary to apply His blood in behalf of His Church while the Holy Spirit applies the benefits of His atonement to His afflicted people on earth. The prophet Malachi also describes the same event:

> "Behold, I will send my messenger, and he shall prepare the way before me: and the Lord, whom ye seek, shall suddenly come to his temple, even the messenger of the covenant, whom ye delight in: behold, he shall come, saith the LORD of hosts." *Malachi 3:1.*

The people of God, as the judgment proceeds in the Most Holy place in heaven, will be seen gathering together and afflicting their souls. It brings them great distress to see men trampling upon God's Holy Law. In sympathy for Jesus they agonize for the sinners around them. They know that it is transgression that caused Christ's crucifixion; looking up to Jesus, they see His sufferings as a present reality (see John 12:32; Hebrews 2:9; 5:1-5; Revelation 5:6; 14:12), and it leads them into the deepest contrition. They obey the "true witness" and zealously "repent" of their own sins. Revelation 3:14, 19. Being driven from their homes and without food they will then have to depend entirely upon God for help, and they will plead with Him for vindication. "Judge me, O God, and plead my cause against an ungodly nation," will be on the lips of His people. Psalms 43:1. (See also Psalms 26:1-3; 35:1-2, 22-24; Micah 7:7-8.) The Bible relates this experience in many places:

The Final Conflict

> "Arise, O LORD, in thine anger, lift up thyself because of the rage of mine enemies: and awake for me to the judgment that thou hast commanded... The LORD shall judge the people: judge me, O LORD, according to my righteousness, and according to mine integrity that is in me...for the righteous God trieth the hearts and reins." *Psalms 7:6-9.*

> "Save me, O God, by thy name, and judge me by thy strength. Hear my prayer, O God; give ear to the words of my mouth. For strangers are risen up against me, and oppressors seek after my soul: they have not set God before them. Selah." *Psalms 54:1-3.*

> "Let the priests, the ministers of the LORD, weep between the porch and the altar, and let them say, Spare thy people, O LORD, and give not thine heritage to reproach, that the heathen should rule over them: wherefore should they say among the people, Where is their God?" *Joel 2:17.*

Even while the fires of persecution are burning around God's children they will hold on with strong faith to the hope that they have anchored in the sanctuary above. The sins that they have committed, which have caused marks and scars upon their souls, will need to be removed. (See Job 10:14; Jeremiah 2:22; 17:1; Proverbs 8:36.) Jesus will stand to plead the cause of the righteous and will execute judgment for them. (See Daniel 7:22, 26; Micah 7:9; Psalm 72:2, 4, 12; 102:17-21; Zechariah 3:1-4.) The trial of their faith will be intense, but as He applies His blood in their behalf the marks and scars of sin are purged. Just as an imprint in the sand by the seashore is washed away by the ever-ceaseless waves, so every imprint that sin has made upon their characters will be forever washed away into the land of forgetfulness. All of the thoughts and emotions of sin will then be purged from their minds through the ministry of the Holy Spirit in accord with Jesus' work in heaven. The New Covenant promise is then complete: "and their sins and iniquities will I remember [record] no more." Hebrews 10:17. The experiential knowledge of sin is done, their record is clean, and their iniquities are forever "blotted out." Acts 3:19. Other prophets also foretell this experience:

> "But who may abide the day of his coming? and who shall stand when he appeareth? for he is like a refiner's fire, and like fullers' soap: And he shall sit as a refiner and purifier of silver: and he shall purify the sons of Levi, and purge them as gold and silver, that they may offer unto the LORD an offering in righteousness." *Malachi 3:2-3.*

"In that day shall the branch of the LORD be beautiful and glorious, and the fruit of the earth shall be excellent and comely for them that are escaped of Israel. And it shall come to pass, that he that is left in Zion, and he that remaineth in Jerusalem, shall be called holy, even every one that is written among the living in Jerusalem: When the Lord shall have washed away the filth of the daughters of Zion, and shall have purged the blood of Jerusalem from the midst thereof by the spirit of judgment, and by the spirit of burning." *Isaiah 4:2-4.*

"The remnant of Israel shall not do iniquity, nor speak lies; neither shall a deceitful tongue be found in their mouth: for they shall feed and lie down, and none shall make them afraid." *Zephaniah 3:13.*

"And I looked, and, lo, a Lamb stood on the mount Sion, and with him an hundred forty and four thousand… These are they which were not defiled with women; for they are virgins. These are they which follow the Lamb whithersoever he goeth. These were redeemed from among men, being the firstfruits unto God and to the Lamb. And in their mouth was found no guile: for they are without fault before the throne of God." *Revelation 14:1-5.*

The prophecy in Daniel 8:14, "then shall the sanctuary be cleansed," refers not only to the cleansing of the heavenly sanctuary, but to the purification of the people as well. The purging of ancient Israel on the Day of Atonement, "For on that day shall the priest make an atonement for you, to cleanse you, that ye may be clean from all your sins before the LORD," will be fulfilled to God's antitypical Israel. Leviticus 16:29-30. The Church will be pure and will refuse to obey the traditions of men that are in opposition to the Commandments of God. Though Sunday, the mark of the beast, the sign of eternal rebellion, will be forced upon them they will remain steadfast in their faith and will receive God's seal (see Revelation 7:1-8), the mark of His approval:

"And I saw another angel ascending from the east, having the seal of the living God: and he cried with a loud voice to the four angels, to whom it was given to hurt the earth and the sea, Saying, Hurt not the earth, neither the sea, nor the trees, till we have sealed the servants of our God in their foreheads." *Revelation 7:2-3.*

"And the LORD said unto him, Go through the midst of the city, through the midst of Jerusalem, and set a mark upon the foreheads of the men that sigh and that cry for all the abominations that be done in the midst thereof." *Ezekiel 9:4.*

They will be forever sealed with the "Father's name written in their foreheads." Revelation 14:1. This seal is not a mark that can be seen, but it is a token of God's approval when they refuse to yield truth. The Sabbath, given after the work of creation was finished, will then become the outward sign of the finished work of God's creation within them. (See Exodus 31:17; Ezekiel 20:12, 20.) It is a "sign," "a seal of the righteousness of the faith" that they have when apostasy is forced upon them. Romans 4:11. God then numbers His people:

> "And I heard the number of them which were sealed: and there were sealed an hundred and forty and four thousand of all the tribes of the children of Israel." *Revelation 7:4.*

The scriptures will clearly point to this enduring people as "they that keep the commandments of God, and the faith of Jesus." Revelation 14:12. They have chosen to present themselves to the judgment, and, as Jesus ministers in their behalf in the sanctuary above, the Holy Spirit works out the benefits of His atonement within them. The Church of God will appear "fair as the moon, clear as the sun, and terrible as an army with banners?" Song of Solomon 6:10. The Law, the transcript of God's character, will be fully developed within them. They will be called: "The repairer of the breach," because they will have mended the gaping hole in God's Law made by the Sunday institution. Isaiah 58:12. "The Revelation of Jesus Christ," His holy character, will finally be displayed through them to a dying world. Revelation 1:1. These selfless, holy people will then be trusted by God with His divine power; they will receive the latter rain of the Holy Spirit, and will give the Loud Cry to the inhabitants of the earth.

The Loud Cry

The Remnant people, whose names are in the book of life, are the only opposition that the Papacy will then have to its supremacy, and without divine power God's children could do nothing to stop the apostasy. All would be lost, and the cause of God in the earth would cease. The Bible continually admonishes God's people not to trust to men: "Blessed is that man that maketh the LORD his trust, and respecteth not the proud, nor such as turn aside to lies." "In God have I put my trust: I will not be afraid what man can do unto me." "Put not your trust in princes, nor in the son of man, in whom there is no help." "Blessed is the man that trusteth in the LORD, and whose hope the LORD is." Psalms 40:4; 56:11; 146:3; Jeremiah 17:7. As the people of God afflict their souls before Him, and cast themselves entirely upon Him, He blots out their sins and seals them, and then He pours out His Spirit upon them in latter rain power:

> "Then will the LORD be jealous for his land, and pity his people. Yea, the LORD will answer and say unto his people, Behold, I will send you corn, and wine, and oil, and ye shall be satisfied therewith: and I will no more make you a reproach among the heathen: But I will remove far off from you the northern army [great spiritual Babylon]… Be glad then, ye children of Zion, and rejoice in the LORD your God: for he hath given you the former rain moderately, and he will cause to come down for you the rain, the former rain, and the latter rain in the first month." *Joel 2:18-23*.

> "Be patient therefore, brethren, unto the coming of the Lord. Behold, the husbandman waiteth for the precious fruit of the earth, and hath long patience for it, until he receive the early and latter rain." *James 5:7*.

The children of God have always had His Spirit, but it is the special outpouring of the Spirit at this time that is needed to finish the work of God in the earth. Just as the disciples needed the early rain to establish the Church on the day of Pentecost, so God's children at the end need this special outpouring of divine power. (See Joel 2:28; Acts 2:1-21.) This outpouring will greatly exceed the power of Pentecost. They will receive visions and dreams, and signs and miracles will follow them: "…your sons and your daughters shall prophesy, your old men shall dream dreams, your young men shall see visions: And also upon the servants and upon the handmaids in those days will I pour out my spirit. And I will shew wonders in the heavens and in the earth, blood, and fire, and pillars of smoke." Joel 2:28-30. This is the power that the people of God, through the trial of their faith and long days of affliction, have patiently waited for. When they receive it they will be empowered to speak the truth with boldness to the world:

> **"But tidings out of the east and out of the north shall trouble him: therefore he shall go forth with great fury to destroy, and utterly to make away many. And he shall plant the tabernacles of his palace between the seas in the glorious holy mountain; yet he shall come to his end, and none shall help him."** *Daniel 11:44-45*.

At the time when the war against spiritual Egypt is coming to a completion and the sealing of the 144,000 is concluding a message is given by them that enrages great spiritual Babylon: "tidings out of the east and out of the north shall trouble him." Anciently Cyrus the Great led the Medes from the North and the Persians of the East against Babylon. (See Isaiah 45:1-5; Jeremiah 50:1-3; 51:27-28; 36-39; Daniel 5:25-31.) Before its destruction God proclaimed with His own finger, and through the interpretation of the prophet Daniel, the end of the nation:

> "Then was the part of the hand sent from him; and this writing was written. And this is the writing that was written, MENE, MENE, TEKEL, UPHARSIN. This is the interpretation of the thing: MENE; God hath numbered thy kingdom, and finished it. TEKEL; Thou art weighed in the balances, and art found wanting. PERES; Thy kingdom is divided, and given to the Medes and Persians." *Daniel 5:24-28.*

In the antitype Jesus will lead the armies of heaven against great spiritual Babylon from the North and the East. (See Psalm 48:1-2; Ezekiel 1:4; 43:1-2; Matthew 24:27; Revelation 19:11-21.) But before the apostate churches are destroyed God sends a message through His people to them. They obey His call to "Arise, shine." Isaiah 60:1. The message obviously proclaims Babylon's end and the coming of Christ, the antitypical Cyrus, the second time to the earth in power and great glory. Additionally, the message calls the remainder of God's children out of the apostate system (those people that have not until that time heard the message of the fall of great spiritual Babylon). This proclamation is declared in detail in the book of Revelation as coming from angels and it is given with a loud cry. The three angel's messages of Revelation 14, which have been proclaimed since the 1840s, will at this time be given in their fullness, and they will be attended by another mighty angel:

> "And after these things I saw another angel come down from heaven, having great power; and the earth was lightened with his glory. And he cried mightily with a strong voice, saying, Babylon the great is fallen, is fallen, and is become the habitation of devils, and the hold of every foul spirit, and a cage of every unclean and hateful bird. For all nations have drunk of the wine of the wrath of her fornication, and the kings of the earth have committed fornication with her, and the merchants of the earth are waxed rich through the abundance of her delicacies. And I heard another voice from heaven, saying, Come out of her, my people, that ye be not partakers of her sins, and that ye receive not of her plagues. For her sins have reached unto heaven, and God hath remembered her iniquities." *Revelation 18:1-5.*

The message is so powerful that the Bible says: "the earth was lightened with his glory." The entire world receives the message; many learn for the first time what the mark of the Beast is, and those whose hearts are right with God will "come out of her." God's children are hurried out of Babylon just as Lot was hurried out of Sodom before its destruction; they go through the same experience that the 144,000 had already been through, and they will then receive the seal of God also. The message infuriates the Papacy and the apostate churches that have united with her, and they "shall go forth with great fury to destroy, and utterly to make away many." God's people, who have been purified and are described as keeping "the commandments of God" (Revelation 14:12), are at this time faced with total annihilation. Satan working primarily through the power of the American Beast will secure a worldwide decree for the destruction of the Remnant:

> "And he had power to give life unto the image of the beast, that the image of the beast should both speak, and cause that as many as would not worship the image of the beast should be killed." *Revelation 13:15*.

Many of God's children shall lose their lives: "And I heard a voice from heaven saying unto me, Write, Blessed are the dead which die in the Lord from henceforth." Revelation 14:13. Great Babylon is "drunken with the blood of the saints, and with the blood of the martyrs of Jesus." Revelation 17:6. The years that Satan has been preparing for his last deception have come to a climax. If he can eliminate this small remnant his triumph will be complete. The whole world will then be confirmed in rebellion against God, but His people, though greatly troubled, will not give in to Satan to save their own lives: "And they overcame him by the blood of the Lamb, and by the word of their testimony; and they loved not their lives unto the death." Revelation 12:11. The truth has become more important to them then life, and they proclaim the message everywhere.

"And he shall plant the tents of his palace between the seas and the glorious holy mountain…" Daniel 11:45, NKJV. The seas, as we have seen, are "peoples, and multitudes, and nations, and tongues." Revelation 17:15. These multitudes of people incorporate the entire earth over which Babylon will then reign, and the "glorious holy mountain" is the Church. (See Daniel 2:34-35, 44-45; 9:16; Isaiah 2:2-3.) Satan working through the apostate system tries to stop the message from going to the world. How he does this is not entirely clear since it is still future. Nevertheless, the Gospel will go to the entire world: "And this gospel of the kingdom shall be preached in all the world for a witness unto all nations." Matthew 24:14. And, "lo, a great multitude, which no man could number, of all nations, and kindreds, and people, and tongues" (Revelation 7:9) are brought into the Church. Then the Time of Trouble will begin and destroy great spiritual Babylon; the king of the North "shall come to his end, and none shall help him."

Summary of Chapter Six

Although the Moslems are spoken of in the prophecies, the present problems with them will be eclipsed by a greater crisis that will confront the world. With the Renaissance came a revival of the paganism of Greece and Rome, and Evolutionary and Atheistic ideas were reintroduced. This rebaptism of pagan thought in France was the resurrection of the king of the South (the spiritual Egypt of Daniel's vision), and the beginning of verse 40 was fulfilled when France attacked the Papacy in A.D. 1798. Since then these atheist ideas have found their way into Russia, China, and other countries of the world where communism and socialism became established. The next phrase of the verse is yet future, and the king of the South today represents China.

When the Papacy lost its political power to France in A.D. 1798 it was believed that it could never regain the prestige that it once had, but the prophecies declare differently. Papal Rome, "THE MOTHER OF HARLOTS AND ABOMINATIONS OF THE EARTH" (Revelation 17:5), will again ascend to power when the nations of the European Union "give their kingdom unto the beast." Revelation 17:17. This time the papal church-state system will rule the world: "…and they that dwell on the earth shall wonder, whose names were not written in the book of life from the foundation of the world, when they behold the beast that was, and is not, and yet is." Revelation 17:8.

Protestant America is the False Prophet that will cause "the earth and them which dwell therein to worship the first beast, whose deadly wound was healed." Revelation 13:12. This will take place when the United States institutes the "mark of the beast" by the enforcement of the papal Sunday tradition. This event unites spiritual Babylon and is the resurrection of the king of the North. Jesus identifies this event when He declares: "When ye therefore shall see the abomination of desolation, spoken of by Daniel the prophet, stand in the holy place, (whoso readeth, let him understand.)" Matthew 24:15. He then admonishes his people to leave the major cities of the earth.

We must ever remember that it is the dragon that is attempting to bring about the union of church and state in America. Because of the gross wickedness of the people the Spirit of God is being withdrawn. Satan is gaining control of corrupt humanity and the elements of nature, and he will bring about disaster and destruction. The devastation of the World Trade Center on September 11, 2001 is an indication of the magnitude of the destruction that will soon follow. Demons are controlling men, and as terrorism and disasters become more frequent and violent America will set aside its freedom and rights. This will happen under the guise of security and morality, and America will then speak as a dragon.

The final conflict begins when the United States and its allies make war with China. China, the king of the South, and its allies will then be completely overthrown and the king of the North will reign supreme. The Church will at this time see persecution and will be mightily shaken, but many that have once heard the message will then accept the truth and join with God's people. These people will be totally committed to the Lord, they will trust Him implicitly, and He will seal them. The latter rain will then be poured out upon them, and they will go into the world and "a great multitude, which no man could number, of all nations, and kindreds, and people, and tongues" will be converted, turn and obey the Commandments of God, and receive His seal. However, those that reject the message and continue to keep Sunday will receive the "mark of the beast." Satan, working through the governments of the earth, will be furious and very active and try to stop the message from going to the world, but he will ultimately fail and Babylon will be destroyed in the Time of Trouble.

Chapter 7: Babylon's Destruction

In this chapter Babylon receives the seven last plagues while the Lord protects His people. Jesus then returns to take His children to the heavenly kingdom for 1000 years of judgment. After that, sin and sinners are destroyed and the earth made new, and the redeemed shall dwell in eternal peace with the Lord.

The Time of Trouble

At the close of the typical service on the ancient Day of Atonement the priest called for the live goat (also called the scapegoat), laid both his hands upon its head, and confessed upon it all of the people's sins. Their sins, accumulating in the Holy place of the earthly sanctuary throughout the year by the blood of animal sacrifices, were removed by the priest and transferred to the scapegoat. The scapegoat was then led away into an uninhabited wilderness by the hand of a fit man. Consequently, those who refused to afflict their souls, and take part in the service, had to bear their own guilt and were "cut off" from among the congregation. (See Leviticus 16:8, 10, 20-22; 23:29.) The only role of the scapegoat was to bear away from Israel all of their sins into the wilderness, or "land of separation." Leviticus 16:22, margin. The priest, the people, and the sanctuary were thus cleansed.

The antitype of the work of our great high priest in the sanctuary above, concluding the Day of Atonement, returns the guilt of sin back to its originator. The sins that God's people have committed, and that have been confessed, repented of, and transferred by Jesus to the heavenly sanctuary, will finally be placed back upon the head of Satan. Jesus will put His hands upon the head of the antitypical scapegoat and confess over him the sins of His people. Their guilt will be returned to him. All those who failed to enter into the work of cleansing by afflicting their souls before God will receive back the guilt of their own sins; they will suffer the seven last plagues, and will finally be forever "cut off." The period when the seven last plagues are falling is often called the "time of trouble." It is during this time that Satan is given the opportunity to try the remnant just as Job was tested of old. The remnant, symbolized in the type by the "fit man," will then lead Satan, as a stubborn goat, out of the congregation of God's people. By their refusal to return to the paths of sin the remnant will vindicate, before the unfallen universe, the justice of God in the great controversy, and Satan will be eternally overthrown. Thus we see, through the types, that sin and sinners will be eliminated.

The elimination of sin, the destruction of Babylon, and the setting up of God's kingdom on earth are also foretold throughout the prophecies of the Bible. The dream of Daniel chapter two climaxes with the smashing of the Roman power by the "stone" kingdom: "And in the days of these kings shall the God of heaven set up a kingdom, which shall never be destroyed...it shall break in pieces and consume all these kingdoms, and it shall stand for ever." Daniel 2:44. Human works and traditions do not establish this stone kingdom of God, because it is "cut out of the mountain without hands." Daniel 2:45. (See Ephesians 2:11; Colossians 2:11.) The prophecy of Daniel seven likewise ends with the destruction of the Roman beast and the establishment of the Lord's kingdom:

> "I beheld even till the beast was slain, and his body destroyed, and given to the burning flame...and behold, one like the Son of man came with the clouds of heaven... And there was given him dominion, and glory, and a kingdom, that all people, nations, and languages, should serve him: his dominion is an everlasting dominion, which shall not pass away, and his kingdom that which shall not be destroyed." *Daniel 7:11-14.*

The vision of Daniel eight concludes with the destruction of Rome as in chapter two: "but he shall be broken without hand," that is, without human intervention. Daniel 8:25. The vision by the Tigris has also many times forecast the overthrow of Rome: "but they shall fall;" "yet he shall come to his end, and none shall help him." Daniel 11:14, 45. It is during the time of trouble that the papal abomination is finally destroyed, God's people delivered, and His kingdom established:

> **"And at that time shall Michael stand up, the great prince which standeth for the children of thy people: and there shall be a time of trouble, such as never was since there was a nation even to that same time: and at that time thy people shall be delivered, every one that shall be found written in the book."** Daniel 12:1.

A specific time is spoken of in this verse. The closing events of the last chapter are here brought to view. The king of the North makes his last attempt to destroy the Church of God by the establishment of a world wide death decree, and "at that time shall Michael stand up." The time for the development of the great apostasy has come to its climax, and its adherents are fully deceived and have received the mark of eternal apostasy. God's children are likewise fully surrendered to Him; they have cast off all sin, and are sealed with His holy character in their foreheads. The last warning has been given, and all that have desired truth have accepted it. Neither group will return from their selected course, and the scripture speaks of them in the following language:

> "He that is unjust, let him be unjust still: and he which is filthy, let him be filthy still: and he that is righteous, let him be righteous still: and he that is holy, let him be holy still." *Revelation 22:11.*

The destiny of all will be forever decided when Jesus comes forth from the heavenly sanctuary riding on a "white cloud." Revelation 14:14. Jesus work in the sanctuary will be finished. (See Revelation 15:8.) There will then be "no more sacrifice for sins." Hebrews 10:26. The popular belief that men will have a second chance after the rapture will be found to be one of Satan's greatest deceptions, and multitudes will be forever lost.

What does it mean for Michael to stand? We have seen throughout the previous chapters that the word "stand" means to take or rule the kingdom. (See Daniel 11:2-4, 6-7, 14-17, 20-21, 25.) The conflict, which began in heaven with Lucifer, came to this earth through Adam and Eve. It is a struggle for the control of the universe; Satan plans to overthrow God. (See Isaiah 14:12-14.) This war, which has continued for 6000 years, will sweep God's people into the midst of it in the near future. The Protestants of the United States will unite with the corrupt Roman system, and they will use their power to bring the world into harmony with her and to worship her. This action will finally call forth the wrath of God upon men and Satan. Michael will stand to fight for the deliverance of his people, and Satan will have "great wrath, because he knoweth that he hath but a short time." Revelation 12:12-13. Ultimately, Michael shall prevail, and "the kingdoms of this world" will become "the kingdoms of our Lord, and of his Christ." Revelation 11:15.

Those who worship the beast and its image, who receive its mark, and who cry "peace and safety" will experience "sudden destruction." 1 Thessalonians 5:3. They will feel the "wrath" of an offended God. Revelation 11:18. The four angels that are now "holding the four winds of the earth, that the wind should not blow on the earth, nor on the sea, nor on any tree" are then loosed. Revelation 7:1. The plagues described in Revelation 16, as "vials full of the wrath of God," are at that time poured out upon the earth:

> "And I saw another sign in heaven, great and marvellous, seven angels having the seven last plagues; for in them is filled up the

wrath of God... And the seven angels came out of the temple, having the seven plagues, clothed in pure and white linen, and having their breasts girded with golden girdles. And one of the four beasts gave unto the seven angels seven golden vials full of the wrath of God, who liveth for ever and ever. And the temple was filled with smoke from the glory of God, and from his power; and no man was able to enter into the temple, till the seven plagues of the seven angels were fulfilled. And I heard a great voice out of the temple saying to the seven angels, Go your ways, and pour out the vials of the wrath of God upon the earth." *Revelation 15:1; 15:6-16:1.*

These plagues are meant to wholly break the power of Babylon, and are of a most terrible nature. When the plagues begin, the heavenly temple will be closed and Jesus' ministry complete. No more will God deal with sin in His universe. Those who refuse to take part in Jesus' forgiveness and reconciliation now while there is still time will be left without protection when the plagues fall. Many Christians today see no need to obey God, and He will then say to them: "I never knew you: depart from me, ye that work iniquity." Matthew 7:23. They think that simply claiming Jesus' name will save them, but they will be shocked to find that the plagues are called forth upon them! Truly, "there shall be a time of trouble, such as never was since there was a nation even to that same time." And Jesus describes it in the follow words:

> "For then shall be great tribulation, such as was not since the beginning of the world to this time, no, nor ever shall be. And except those days should be shortened, there should no flesh be saved: but for the elect's sake those days shall be shortened." *Matthew 24:21-22.*

Satan will work with great power trying to bring the remnant back into sin. His continued existence depends upon his victory over them, and he will use everything available to accomplish his goal. Jesus warned His children about that time: "Then if any man shall say unto you, Lo, here is Christ, or there; believe it not. For there shall arise false Christs, and false prophets, and shall shew great signs and wonders; insomuch that, if it were possible, they shall deceive the very elect." Matthew 24:23-24. Satan himself will appear as an "angel of light" claiming to be Christ. 2 Corinthians 11:14. God's people, having given the final warning to the world, will flee to desolate and solitary places of the earth where they will be fed by God. (See Isaiah 33:14-16.) And, although tempted and tried during that time, they will be protected from the seven last plagues and will overcome Satan. They will bruise the serpent's head and fulfill the purpose of their creation. (See Genesis 3:15; Galatians 3:16, 29; Luke 10:19; Romans 16:20.)

The Plagues Fall on Babylon

The seven last plagues do not fall indiscriminately upon the entire earth; otherwise it would be destroyed in one quick stroke. The first plague is poured out "upon the men which had the mark of the beast, and upon them which worshipped his image." The "image" is the church-state union in America, and those with the "mark" are the ones that obey the Sunday institution that is enforced upon the world as we have already seen. This plague is obviously poured out upon them; it is sent upon those who have had the greatest light and opportunity, but who have persistently refused to yield to the Lord. They have brought a crisis to God's people and now He brings a crisis to them: "and there fell a noisome and grievous sore" upon them. Revelation 16:2.

The second vial of God's wrath is poured out "upon the sea and it became as the blood of a dead man: and every living soul died in the sea." The third is poured "upon the rivers and fountains of waters; and they became blood." An angel gives the reason why a righteous God will turn water into blood and destroy the apostate Christian world: "For they have shed the blood of saints and prophets, and thou hast given them blood to drink; for they are worthy." Revelation 16:3-6. These plagues obviously last only a limited time as the similar plagues that fell on Egypt (see Exodus 7:14-25).

The plagues follow in rapid succession, and those who survive the first three are subjected to the fourth, which is poured out "upon the sun; and power was given unto him to scorch men with fire. And men were scorched with great heat." This plague reveals the wicked to be just as corrupt and deserving of destruction as Pharaoh was because they "blasphemed the name of God, which hath power over these plagues: and they repented not to give him glory." Revelation 16:8-9. The fifth plague of darkness will be poured "upon the seat of the beast," which is the government of the European Union. It receives this plague because it supports the church-state union with the Papacy and persecutes God's children. The prophecy says that they "gnawed their tongues for pain, and blasphemed the God of heaven because of their pains and their sores;" however, they "repented not of their deeds." Revelation 16:10-11.

The first five plagues will so devastate modern spiritual Babylon that the sixth plague naturally falls in sequence. "And the sixth angel poured out his vial upon the great river Euphrates; and the water thereof was dried up, that the way of the kings of the east might be prepared." In ancient Babylon the water of the river Euphrates, which passed through the city, was diverted so that the armies of Cyrus the Great could enter and overthrow it. Hence, the multitudes supporting modern, antitypical Babylon are symbolically represented by the "great river Euphrates." The sixth plague symbolically dries up the people supporting the apostate system in preparation for the coming of Jesus to make war upon "the kings of the earth and of the whole world." Revelation 16:14.

The "three unclean spirits" are now gathering the wicked "into a place called in the Hebrew tongue Armageddon" in preparation for "the battle of that great day of God Almighty." Revelation 16:12-16. The word Armageddon comes from two Hebrew words: "har" meaning hill or mountain, and "mo'ed" meaning congregation or assembly. The latter is used many times in scripture in reference to an appointed time or place, and is also used in reference to "congregations" and "assemblies" of the people. Psalm 74:4; Ezekiel 44:24. Hence the tent of the earthly sanctuary is called the "tabernacle of the congregation" where the people were to gather for worship. (See Exodus 29:4, 10-11, 30, 32, 42, 44 etc.) Hills and mountains were used as places of worship in scripture as well; both for the worship of God and of idols. (See Leviticus 26:31; Numbers 21:28; 22:41; 1 Samuel 9:12-14.) The city of Jerusalem is often called "mount Zion," and the people were called to worship at the tabernacle in God's "holy hill." (See Psalm 48:1-2; Isaiah 10:12; 24:23; 37:32; Joel 2:32; Psalms 15:1; 43:13; 99:9.) The "mountain of the LORD's house," His sanctuary, is declared to be "in the top of the mountains" in the "last days." Isaiah 2:2. (See also Micah 4:1-7.) And Jesus, the "Lamb," is shown to be standing on "mount Sion" with the 144,000 during the last conflict. Revelation 14:1. (See also 2 Kings 19:30-31.) Consequently, the "three unclean spirits" gather the people in spiritual Babylon into a false form of worship. They gather the deceived to Armageddon, the "mount of the assembly," and Lucifer declared that he would do so:

> "How art thou fallen from heaven, O Lucifer, son of the morning! how art thou cut down to the ground, which didst weaken the nations! For thou hast said in thine heart, I will ascend into heaven, I will exalt my throne above the stars of God: I will sit also upon the mount of the congregation, in the sides of the north: I will ascend above the heights of the clouds; I will be like the most High." *Isaiah 14:12-14.*

God here reveals Satan's strategy for the last conflict. He opens to us his very thoughts. He tells us that Satan will determine to place himself as the leader of the Christian world. The throne of God was at the table of showbread, on the "north side" of the Holy place in the heavenly sanctuary, until 1844 when Jesus entered the second phase of His ministry in the Most Holy place in heaven. (See chapter 4: Types and the Book of Revelation, and chapter 6: The Judgment and the Woman.) Satan then began to carry on the work that Jesus had previously done for over 1800 years from the Holy place in heaven. He has poured out his spirit upon the apostate Christians, and the result has brought them to the plagues. Those organizations that failed to lead their people into the worship of Jesus in the Most Holy place in heaven since 1844 are following Satan and bringing deception upon their people, and it is not until the sixth plague, when it is too late, that their deception is unmasked.

Those who survive the first five plagues will have their deception wiped away at that time. God rebukes the "three unclean spirits" in the sixth plague and they "come out" of spiritual Babylon. The wicked then abandon the apostate system to its destruction. It will be too late when men find that they have been deceived, too late to repent of their sins, too late to acknowledge and proclaim the truth of a Holy God, and too late to be saved. This plague is not one of blood, fire, flood, or other destruction, but a realization of eternal loss. Men will be horrified to find that they have rejected eternal life and they will forsake spiritual Babylon. The people and multitudes of the spiritual Euphrates have dried up.

The wicked will not be converted and turn to the Lord then. When the plagues begin to fall the time of man's probation will be past. Those who have not surrendered themselves to the Lord when probation lingered will not be able to do so during the seven last plagues. Martyrdom had for many centuries served as a means for the conversion of the world, but during the time of trouble there will not be any conversions. Therefore, God will not suffer His children to fall by the hands of their enemies:

> "He that dwelleth in the secret place of the most High shall abide under the shadow of the Almighty. I will say of the LORD, He is my refuge and my fortress: my God; in him will I trust. Surely he shall deliver thee from the snare of the fowler, and from the noisome pestilence. He shall cover thee with his feathers, and under his wings shalt thou trust: his truth shall be thy shield and buckler. Thou shalt not be afraid for the terror by night; nor for the arrow that flieth by day; Nor for the pestilence that walketh in darkness; nor for the destruction that wasteth at noonday. A thousand shall fall at thy side, and ten thousand at thy right hand; but it shall not come nigh thee. Only with thine eyes shalt thou behold and see the reward of the wicked." *Psalms 91:1-8*.

God's people, although protected from the plagues, will be under great pressure to yield their faith: "Ask ye now, and see whether a man doth travail with child? wherefore do I see every man with his hands on his loins, as a woman in travail, and all faces are turned into paleness?" Jeremiah 30:6-7. The pressure is so great that the prophet likens it to "the time of Jacob's trouble," yet, he continues, "he shall be saved out of it." "And at that time thy people shall be delivered, every one that shall be found written in the book." Daniel 12:1. (See also Exodus 32:32; Daniel 7:10; Luke 10:22; Revelation 13:8; 17:8; 20:12, 15; 22:19.) The falling of the first six plagues have broken the power of great spiritual Babylon and have prepared "the way of the kings of the east," the appearance of Christ with the armies of heaven, for the final plague.

The Second Coming

At the Last Supper before Jesus' trial and crucifixion He gave His disciples assurance of His return to this earth to gather His children to Himself. "Let not your heart be troubled," He said, "ye believe in God, believe also in me. In my Father's house are many mansions: if it were not so, I would have told you. I go to prepare a place for you. And if I go and prepare a place for you, I will come again, and receive you unto myself; that where I am, there ye may be also." John 14:1-3. The hope of the Church from the beginning, even from the days of Enoch and Job, has been the Second Coming of Jesus to this earth in power and glory. (See Jude 14-15; Job 19:25-27; Psalms 50:3; Philippians 3:20; Titus 2:13; 2 Peter 1:16.) So strong was the expectation of the coming of the Lord in the days of the apostles that Paul had to warn the believers against false teachers and against their own misguided expectations:

> "Now we beseech you, brethren, by the coming of our Lord Jesus Christ, and by our gathering together unto him, that ye be not soon shaken in mind, or be troubled, neither by spirit, nor by word, nor by letter as from us, as that the day of Christ is at hand. Let no man deceive you by any means: for that day shall not come, except there come a falling away first, and that man of sin be revealed, the son of perdition; Who opposeth and exalteth himself above all that is called God, or that is worshipped; so that he as God sitteth in the temple of God, shewing himself that he is God." *2 Thessalonians 2:1-4.*

The apostle is pointing the believers to study the book of Daniel and to learn and understand about the great apostate church and the papal "man of sin," the "son of perdition," that would rule the world for so many centuries. This admonition still stands today, for the pope will yet rule the world for a short period of time. When this is complete the first six plagues will fall after which Jesus will appear with the armies of heaven:

"And I saw heaven opened, and behold a white horse; and he that sat upon him was called Faithful and True, and in righteousness he doth judge and make war. His eyes were as a flame of fire, and on his head were many crowns; and he had a name written, that no man knew, but he himself. And he was clothed with a vesture dipped in blood: and his name is called The Word of God. And the armies which were in heaven followed him upon white horses, clothed in fine linen, white and clean. And out of his mouth goeth a sharp sword, that with it he should smite the nations: and he shall rule them with a rod of iron: and he treadeth the winepress of the fierceness and wrath of Almighty God. And he hath on his vesture and on his thigh a name written, KING OF KINGS, AND LORD OF LORDS." *Revelation 19:11-16.*

The kings that come form the East, or literally "the kings from the rising of the sun," in the sixth plague cannot be China and its allies as many teach today. The scripture associates the East with the "seal of the living God" (Revelation 7:2) and the Second Coming of Jesus: "For as the lightning cometh out of the east, and shineth even unto the west; so shall also the coming of the Son of man be." Matthew 24:27. Jesus' coming is as the sun rising in the East; He is called "the dayspring from on high," and "the bright and morning star." Luke 1:78; Revelation 22:16. He is "the righteous man from the east," and the "one from the north" who "shall come: from the rising of the sun shall he call upon my name: and he shall come upon princes as upon morter, and as the potter treadeth clay." Isaiah 41:2, 25. Just as the drying up of the Euphrates River prepared the way for the overthrow of ancient Babylon by Cyrus the Great as he came with the Medes from the North and the Persians from the East (Isaiah 44:27-45:4; Jeremiah 50:38; 51:36), so the sixth plague dries up the symbolic Euphrates to prepare the coming of Jesus. The "kings of the earth and of the whole world" have made "war with the Lamb" in the person of His saints, so He now comes forth to make war with them, "and the Lamb shall overcome them: for he is Lord of lords, and King of kings." Revelation 16:14; 17:14.

Not one person alive on the earth at that time will miss His coming: "Behold, he cometh with clouds; and every eye shall see him…" Revelation 1:7. God's children, who fled to the mountains and the solitary places of the earth, will rejoice at His coming, but they will not be alone, for those who have died in Christ will be raise from the dead at that time and triumph in victory over the grave. The vision by the Tigris next points to the resurrections, both of the righteous and the wicked, that are closely connected with the return of Jesus:

"And many of them that sleep in the dust of the earth shall awake, some to everlasting life, and some to shame and everlasting contempt." *Daniel 12:2.*

As the time of trouble and the seven last plagues are coming to a climax the resurrection takes place: "many of them that sleep in the dust of the earth shall awake." The apostle Paul gives us a beautiful description of the event: "For the Lord himself shall descend from heaven with a shout, with the voice of the archangel, and with the trump of God: and the dead in Christ shall rise first." 1 Thessalonians 4:16. Jesus raises His sleeping saints that have fallen into the prison house of the grave, and they shall come forth to glorify Him. He promised His disciple before He left this earth that there would be a resurrection:

"Marvel not at this: for the hour is coming, in the which all that are in the graves shall hear his voice, And shall come forth; they that have done good, unto the resurrection of life; and they that have done evil, unto the resurrection of damnation." *John 5:28-29.*

Along with the saints there will also be resurrected those that were at Christ's trial and those who were at the cross mocking and ridiculing Him. (See Revelation 1:7.) These will be resurrected at this time, according to Jesus, to "see the Son of man sitting on the right hand of power, and coming in the clouds of heaven." Mark 14:62. They had mocked Him in His humility, and they will be utterly fearful of His coming in glory.

For 6000 years the controversy continued upon the earth, and men created every form of abominable religion to cover their lusts and iniquities. These are all unmasked in the sixth plague and the false systems of man, the institutions that were used to deceive the inhabitants of the earth, will then collapse, and God will utterly destroy them in the seventh and final plague:

"And the seventh angel poured out his vial into the air; and there came a great voice out of the temple of heaven, from the throne, saying, It is done. And there were voices, and thunders, and lightnings; and there was a great earthquake, such as was not since men were upon the earth, so mighty an earthquake, and so great. And the great city was divided into three parts, and the cities of the nations fell: and great Babylon came in remembrance before God, to give unto her the cup of the wine of the fierceness of his wrath. And every island fled away, and the mountains were not found. And there fell upon men a great hail out of heaven, every stone about the weight of a talent: and men blasphemed God because of the plague of the hail; for the plague thereof was exceeding great." *Revelation 16:17-21*.

"And the beast was taken, and with him the false prophet that wrought miracles before him, with which he deceived them that had received the mark of the beast, and them that worshipped his image. These both were cast alive into a lake of fire burning with brimstone." *Revelation 19:20*.

Spiritual Babylon will be destroyed just as ancient Babylon was destroyed. Type will meet antitype in its destruction: "As Babylon hath caused the slain of Israel to fall, so at Babylon shall fall the slain of all the earth." Jeremiah 51:49. "And the kings of the earth, who have committed fornication and lived deliciously with her, shall bewail her, and lament for her, when they shall see the smoke of her burning, Standing afar off for the fear of her torment, saying, Alas, alas, that great city Babylon, that mighty city! for in one hour is thy judgment come." "And a mighty angel took up a stone like a great millstone, and cast it into the sea, saying, Thus with violence shall that great city Babylon be thrown down, and shall be found no more at all." Revelation 18: 9-10, 21.

The ministers of that corrupt system will feel the wrath of God. He warned them saying: "Woe be unto the pastors that destroy and scatter the sheep of my pasture... Ye have scattered my flock, and driven them away, and have not visited them: behold, I will visit upon you the evil of your doings." Jeremiah 23:1-2. These ministers are now working to hide the truth from multitudes in order to sustain their authority, and the remaining priests and people will together suffer the punishment of God. The hail will destroy the houses and possessions of the rich as well as the poor, and those who have defrauded others to enrich themselves will then "cast their silver in the streets, and their gold shall be removed: their silver and their gold shall not be able to deliver them in the day of the wrath of the LORD." Ezekiel 7:19. They will seek refuge from the anger of the Lord in the mountains and desolate places of the earth:

> "And they shall go into the holes of the rocks, and into the caves of the earth, for fear of the LORD, and for the glory of his majesty, when he ariseth to shake terribly the earth. In that day a man shall cast his idols of silver, and his idols of gold, which they made each one for himself to worship, to the moles and to the bats; To go into the clefts of the rocks, and into the tops of the ragged rocks, for fear of the LORD, and for the glory of his majesty, when he ariseth to shake terribly the earth." *Isaiah 2:19-21*.

Although men may hide and say "…to the mountains and rocks, Fall on us, and hide us from the face of him that sitteth on the throne, and from the wrath of the Lamb" (Revelation 6:16), they will not then escape the fury of God. All of the wicked that have survived the first six plagues will then die. "For, behold, the LORD cometh out of his place to punish the inhabitants of the earth for their iniquity…" Isaiah 26:21. "And the remnant were slain with the sword of him that sat upon the horse, which sword proceeded out of his mouth: and all the fowls were filled with their flesh." Revelation 19:21. The wicked who were specially resurrected to see Jesus come in His glory will then also experience death a second time. Conversely, Christ, our great High Priest, after the close of His work in the Most Holy place of the heavenly sanctuary, will return "without sin unto salvation" to collect his waiting saints. Hebrews 9:28. Along with the resurrected saints, "…we which are alive and remain shall be caught up together with them in the clouds, to meet the Lord in the air: and so shall we ever be with the Lord." 1 Thessalonians 4:17. The righteous will be taken by Jesus to the heavenly kingdom to live and reign with Him for 1000 years.

The Millennium

In the ancient typical system, five days after the Day of Atonement, the "fifteenth day" of the "seventh month," the "feast of tabernacles" began, and lasted a total of eight days. The first and the last days of the feast were special Sabbath days in which the people were not to work. They gathered into a special place that the Lord chose, and dwelt in booths throughout the course of their stay. Because the Lord was to bless the people with a bountiful harvest the feast was therefore a time of rejoicing. All who were "Israelites born," and who were obviously not separated from the camp on the Day of Atonement, kept the feast. (See Leviticus 23:34-36, 39-43; Deuteronomy 16:13-15.) This feast ended the round of ceremonies for the year.

The antitype of the Feast of Tabernacles will commence at the completion of the time of trouble. Jesus will return and take His people with Him to heaven to live with Him for a period of 1000 years. The word millennium is never used in the Bible, but comes from two Latin words: "milli" meaning 1000 and "annum" meaning years. Thus the term is commonly used today in reference to the 1000-year period found in the Revelation:

> "And I saw an angel come down from heaven, having the key of the bottomless pit and a great chain in his hand. And he laid hold on the dragon, that old serpent, which is the Devil, and Satan, and bound

him a thousand years, And cast him into the bottomless pit, and shut him up, and set a seal upon him, that he should deceive the nations no more, till the thousand years should be fulfilled: and after that he must be loosed a little season." *Revelation 20:1-3.*

We have already seen that at Jesus' Second Coming the saints that had died are raised from the dead, and then they along with the righteous living are caught up together and taken to the heavenly kingdom. The remaining wicked that are then living upon the earth are slain by the brightness of Christ's appearing (see 2 Thessalonians 2:8.) and the earth is desolate. The Bible gives us a vivid picture of the earth at this time:

"Behold, the LORD maketh the earth empty, and maketh it waste, and turneth it upside down, and scattereth abroad the inhabitants thereof... The land shall be utterly emptied, and utterly spoiled: for the LORD hath spoken this word." *Isaiah 24:1-3.*

"I beheld the earth, and, lo, it was without form, and void; and the heavens, and they had no light. I beheld the mountains, and, lo, they trembled, and all the hills moved lightly. I beheld, and, lo, there was no man, and all the birds of the heavens were fled. I beheld, and, lo, the fruitful place was a wilderness, and all the cities thereof were broken down at the presence of the LORD, and by his fierce anger." *Jeremiah 4:23-26.*

"And the slain of the LORD shall be at that day from one end of the earth even unto the other end of the earth: they shall not be lamented, neither gathered, nor buried; they shall be dung upon the ground." *Jeremiah 25:33.*

The earth is totally devastated by the seventh plague of hail at Jesus' coming. The wicked are all dead with none to mourn them, and Satan is "bound" for "a thousand years" by an angel that has a "great chain in his hand." This binding of Satan is not done by a physical chain, but by a chain of circumstances. He has no one that he can tempt since all of the wicked are dead, and he is put out of business for 1000 years. He and the angels that followed him in his rebellion are chained to this earth, delivered "into chains of darkness, to be reserved unto judgment." 2 Peter 2:4. (See also Jude 6.) They will have the entire millennium to reflect upon their course of action in the great controversy, and they will argue and fight among themselves and suffer intensely; with dread they will look to the end of their captivity. The words "bottomless pit" come from the Greek "abusos," and is the same word that the Greek translation of the Old Testament, the Septuagint, uses for the condition of the earth before creation in Genesis 1:2: "And the earth was without form, and void…" Thus the "bottomless pit" to which Satan and his host are "cast" is the devastated earth "that he should deceive the nations no more, till the thousand years should be fulfilled."

As Jesus was preparing His disciples for His departure from this earth He declared: "I go to prepare a place for you." John 14:2. If He has prepared a place for His people, then He is obviously expecting that they will join Him. Finishing His statement He said: "that where I am, there ye may be also." John 14:3. This promise is not only to those who were sitting with Him there, but also to all who would be saved. In the message to His last day Church He declared: "To him that overcometh will I grant to sit with me in my throne, even as I also overcame, and am set down with my Father in his throne." Revelation 3:21. Our passage in Revelation 20 is the fulfillment of this promise:

> "And I saw thrones, and they sat upon them, and judgment was given unto them: and I saw the souls of them that were beheaded for the witness of Jesus, and for the word of God, and which had not worshipped the beast, neither his image, neither had received his mark upon their foreheads, or in their hands; and they lived and reigned with Christ a thousand years." *Revelation 20:4.*

These saints of God will live and reign with Christ for 1000 years, but during this time they will be put to work: "and judgment was given unto them." The saints during the millennium are put to the work of judgment, and according to the apostle Paul they will "judge the world." However, not only are they to judge the world, but he continues and says: "Know ye not that we shall judge angels?" 1 Corinthians 6:1-3. This judgment is not to determine who are saved, since the investigative phase of the judgment is obviously already completed, but this judgment is a review of the records of 6000 years of those who are lost. It is "the time of the dead, that they should be judged." Revelation 11:17. (See also Ephesians 2:1; Colossians 2:13.) The cases of the fallen angels will also be evaluated during that time. The saved shall all have questions about the decisions of God in the great controversy, and He gives them 1000 years to review them so that they will be convinced of His justice and mercy. Perhaps a good friend is not saved that you thought should be, or someone is saved that you believe could not possibly be. Thus, this judgment is for the benefit of the saints. They will examine the actions of God, and He will then be fully vindicated and His decisions will be declared "true and righteous" by all. Revelation 19:2. (See also

Romans 3:4.) They will be satisfied by God's actions and then the antitypical feast of Tabernacles will end.

The End of Sin and Sinners

At the end of the Millennium Christ comes back to the earth a third and final time. When He comes He returns with His saints, and, as unfathomable as it may seem, He transports an entire city from heaven to the earth: "And I John saw the holy city, new Jerusalem, coming down from God out of heaven, prepared as a bride adorned for her husband." Revelation 21:2. This city will be placed where the Mount of Olives now stands, and the mount will be divided and leveled to make room for it. (See Zechariah 14:4.) The 1000 years of Satan's captivity will then be over, and he will "be loosed a little season." Revelation 20:3. This releasing of Satan from the bottomless pit is simultaneous with the resurrection of the wicked: "But the rest of the dead lived not again until the thousand years were finished... And the sea gave up the dead which were in it; and death and hell delivered up the dead which were in them." Revelation 20:5, 13. The wicked come forth to "the resurrection of damnation" (John 5:29), and Satan is then free again to practice his craft of deception upon them. What a spectacle it shall be when everyone that has ever lived will be alive upon the earth at the same time!

This short period of freedom for Satan will give him one more opportunity to prove to the universe that he has not changed:

> "And when the thousand years are expired, Satan shall be loosed out of his prison, And shall go out to deceive the nations which are in the four quarters of the earth, Gog and Magog, to gather them together to battle: the number of whom is as the sand of the sea. And they went up on the breadth of the earth, and compassed the camp of the saints about, and the beloved city..." *Revelation 20:7-9.*

Through persuasion and deception Satan gathers together the vast host of the wicked from the "four quarters of the earth," and they "compassed the camp of the saints about, and the beloved city." He shall attempt to overthrow the New Jerusalem and to set himself up as king on earth, but God Himself will intervene. This last hostility proves to the universe that Satan and his followers have not changed, and God will at this time reveal Himself upon His "great white throne" as He sits to execute judgment upon the wicked: "And I saw the dead, small and great, stand before God." He opens the "books" of record and brings forth the "book of life of the Lamb," and the cross of Calvary is revealed before their eyes. Revelation 13:8; 20:12. Many of the wicked see for the first time that they have totally rejected Jesus and salvation by their own course of action. They are "judged out of those things which were written in the books, according to their works," and the final sentence is handed down for their eternal destruction. Revelation 20:12.

They realize that they cannot possibly take the city, and everyone in that vast company are lead to confess that God has been just; with one accord they bow the knee to Jesus and the divine majesty of the Father. (See Isaiah 45:22-25; Philippians 2:10-11.) "There shall be weeping and gnashing of teeth," when they see "Abraham, and Isaac, and Jacob, and all the prophets, in the kingdom of God," and themselves "thrust out." Luke 13:28. A general slaughter shall breakout among the wicked: "every man's sword shall be against his brother." Ezekiel 38:21. At this the Father executes the final punishment upon them: "…and fire came down from God out of heaven, and devoured them." "And whosoever was not found written in the book of life was cast into the lake of fire." Revelation 20:9, 15. The fire will then do its eternal work of consuming sinners:

> "But the fearful, and unbelieving, and the abominable, and murderers, and whoremongers, and sorcerers, and idolaters, and all liars, shall have their part in the lake which burneth with fire and brimstone: which is the second death." *Revelation 21:8.*

> "For, behold, the day cometh, that shall burn as an oven; and all the proud, yea, and all that do wickedly, shall be stubble: and the day that cometh shall burn them up, saith the LORD of hosts, that it shall leave them neither root nor branch." *Malachi 4:1.*

The wicked do not live on in perpetual agony in the flames of hell. When the fire falls its work will be eternal: "But the wicked shall perish…they shall consume; into smoke shall they consume away." Psalms 37:20. "Let the sinners be consumed out of the earth, and let the wicked be no more." Psalms 104:35. Sinners "…shall be destroyed for ever." Psalms 92:7. They "…shall be punished with everlasting destruction from the presence of the Lord, and from the glory of his power." 2 Thessalonians 1:9. "And these shall go away into everlasting punishment." Matthew 25:46. It is the result of the fire, death, that is the "everlasting punishment" of which the scripture speaks, not continual punishing in the flames of an eternal hell as is often taught today. Hence, "…all the wicked will he destroy." Psalms 145:20. "For the wages of sin is death." Romans 6:23. Thus all of the wicked have met their fate in the lake of fire, which is called the "second death." Revelation 20:14.

Satan and his demons do not escape the final fury of God. The lake of "everlasting fire" was prepared especially for "the devil and his angels" (Matthew 25:41), and it shall at that time consume them also. "And the devil that deceived them was cast into the lake of fire and brimstone, where the beast and the false prophet are, and shall be tormented day and night for ever and ever." Revelation 20:10. (The phrase "for ever" is limited when applied to mortal beings: Samuel was given "for ever" to the service of the Lord by Hannah, which meant "as long as he liveth." 1 Samuel 1:22, 28. Jonah was in the belly of the whale "for ever," which was only "three days and three nights." Jonah 2:6; 1:17. And a slave that loved the service of his master could stay with him "for ever" until his death. Exodus 21:6.) Although this verse sounds as if the fire shall burn Satan to the ceaseless ages of eternity, the fire is not eternal, but it is the consequences of the fire that are eternal. Just as "Sodom and Gomorrha" have suffered "the vengeance of eternal fire" and are not burning today, so the burning of Satan shall be complete. Jude 6-7. (See also 2 Chronicles 36:19; Jeremiah 17:27.) This one time exalted cherub finally comes to his end:

> "Thine heart was lifted up because of thy beauty, thou hast corrupted thy wisdom by reason of thy brightness: I will cast thee to the ground, I will lay thee before kings, that they may behold thee. Thou hast defiled thy sanctuaries by the multitude of thine iniquities, by the iniquity of thy traffick; therefore will I bring forth a fire from the midst of thee, it shall devour thee, and I will bring thee to ashes upon the earth in the sight of all them that behold thee. All they that know thee among the people shall be astonished at thee: thou shalt be a terror, and never shalt thou be any more." *Ezekiel 28:17-19.*

Satan's demise is complete. He will suffer more from the fire than the rest of the lost because of his leadership in rebellion. The followers of his wicked designs, which were raised to "shame and everlasting contempt" at the end of the 1000 years, have also met their fate in the lake of fire. The Lord was forced to commit "his strange work" and brought to pass "his strange act;" He has poured out His "vengeance" upon the wicked in eternal destruction. Isaiah 28:21; 34:8. Sin will at that time be forever at an end, and the earth will be restored to its former beauty.

New Heavens and a New Earth

The 7000 years of the great controversy have finally come to an end. The saints were protected within the walls of that magnificent city, the New Jerusalem, as the evil host met their fate without. Satan and the wicked multitude have been eliminated, and at that time every trace of corruption, which has marred the earth, will be removed:

> "And I saw a new heaven and a new earth: for the first heaven and the first earth were passed away… And I heard a great voice out of heaven saying, Behold, the tabernacle of God is with men, and he will dwell with them, and they shall be his people, and God himself shall be with them, and be their God. And God shall wipe away all tears from their eyes; and there shall be no more death, neither sorrow, nor crying, neither shall there be any more pain: for the former things are passed away. And he that sat upon the throne said, Behold, I make all things new…" *Revelation 21:1-5.*

The surface of the earth as well as the atmosphere that we breathe will be renewed, and shall be more beautiful and glorious than it was in the original creation. (See Isaiah 65:17; 2 Peter 3:13.) God Himself will dwell upon the earth; His throne will be there, and He will brighten the New Jerusalem with His glory: "And the city had no need of the sun, neither of the moon, to shine in it: for the glory of God did lighten it, and the Lamb is the light thereof… And the gates of it shall not be shut at all by day: for there shall be no night there." Revelation 21:23, 25. (See also Revelation 22:5.) The light as it shines forth through the translucent wall of the city causes it to look "like unto a stone most precious, even like a jasper stone, clear as crystal." Revelation 21:11.

The city has "twelve gates" made of "pearls" with "the names of the twelve tribes of the children of Israel" written upon them, and there are "twelve angels" standing at their entrances. Revelation 21:12, 21. The wall of the city has "twelve foundations," which are "garnished with all manner of precious stones," and it stood "an hundred and forty and four cubits," or about 216 feet high. Each foundation is made of its own kind of gem, and upon the foundations are written "the names of the twelve apostles of the Lamb." Revelation 21:14, 17, 19-20. The city itself is made of "pure gold, like unto clear glass" and is "foursquare." Like an immense cube the "length and the breadth and the height of it are equal" being about 375 miles on each side. Revelation 21:16, 18.

The New Jerusalem shall be the center of activity for the universe, and the redeemed of the earth will be seen there: "And the nations of them which are saved shall walk in the light of it… And they shall bring the glory and honour of the nations into it. And there shall in no wise enter into it any thing that defileth, neither whatsoever worketh abomination, or maketh a lie: but they which are written in the Lamb's book of life." Revelation 21:24-27. It is to this time in earth's history that the narrative of Daniel's vision by the Tigris is speaking when it discloses the reward of the righteous:

> **"And they that be wise shall shine as the brightness of the firmament; and they that turn many to righteousness as the stars for ever and ever."** Daniel 12:3.

The redeemed shall brighten the New Jerusalem with their presence: "Then shall the righteous shine forth as the sun in the kingdom of their Father." Matthew 13:43. They will not only reside in the New Jerusalem, for the scripture says "they shall inherit the earth… The righteous shall inherit the land, and dwell therein for ever." Psalms 37:9, 29. "Blessed are the meek," said Jesus, "for they shall inherit the earth." Matthew 5:5. Jesus' promise to prepare a place for His people has finally reached its fulfillment. (See John 14:1-3.) The long awaited home of the redeemed is then complete, for God "hath prepared for them a city," and has given them "new heavens and a new earth, wherein dwelleth righteousness." Hebrews 11:16; 2 Peter 3:13. They will build houses and plant gardens:

> "And they shall build houses, and inhabit them; and they shall plant vineyards, and eat the fruit of them. They shall not build, and another inhabit; they shall not plant, and another eat: for as the days of a tree are the days of my people, and mine elect shall long enjoy the work of their hands." *Isaiah 65:21-22.*

The children of God will have new uncorrupted bodies "fashioned like unto" Jesus' "glorious body." Philippians 3:20-21. These new bodies are not spirits floating about on a cloud, but are as real as the bodies that we now have. Jesus clearly revealed this when He said to Thomas about His resurrected body: "Behold my hands and my feet, that it is I myself: handle me, and see; for a spirit hath not flesh and bones, as ye see me have." Luke 24:39. Our new bodies will not be weak and tired as they are on this earth, but we "shall run, and not be weary," and we "shall walk, and not faint." Isaiah 40:31. The diseases that came because of sin will be forever finished, and all sickness and suffering will cease: "And the inhabitant shall not say, I am sick…" "Then the eyes of the blind shall be opened, and the ears of the deaf shall be unstopped. Then shall the lame man leap as an hart, and the tongue of the dumb sing." Isaiah 33:24; 35:5-6. Thus we can be sure that the new creation is real and will be without disease and pain.

The scripture promises that God's children will "obtain joy and gladness" in their new home, and that all "sorrow and sighing shall flee away." Isaiah 35:10. We shall know our family members and friends from this earth that are saved with us, just as Jesus' disciples new Him after His resurrection. (See John 20:11-29; 21:4-7; Luke 24:30-35; 1 Corinthians 13:9-12.) The "former troubles," as well as the thoughts and feelings of the sins that we committed while on this earth, "shall not be remembered, nor come into mind." Isaiah 65:16-17. The only reminder of sin will be the marks that are "graven," said Jesus, "upon the palms of my hands." Isaiah 49:16. Yet all of these things can only be dimly comprehended now:

> "But as it is written, Eye hath not seen, nor ear heard, neither have entered into the heart of man, the things which God hath prepared for them that love him." *1 Corinthians 2:9.*

The "tree of life" that was taken away from man after sin entered (see Genesis 3:22-24), will be in the New Jerusalem; it will "bare twelve manner of fruit," and its leaves will be "for the healing of the nations." Revelation 22:2. The redeemed will then eat of that tree, and their bodies will be perpetually renewed. "Proceeding out of the throne of God and of the Lamb" in the midst of the New Jerusalem will flow forth the "pure river of water of life, clear as crystal," which shall water the earth. Revelation 22:1. Hence, the "curse" that God pronounces upon the earth because of sin will be removed: "The wilderness and the solitary place shall be glad for them; and the desert shall rejoice, and blossom as the rose." Isaiah 35:1. (See Genesis 3:18-19; Romans 8:21-23; Revelation 22:3.) All of the animals shall also be tame:

> "The wolf also shall dwell with the lamb, and the leopard shall lie down with the kid; and the calf and the young lion and the fatling together; and a little child shall lead them. And the cow and the bear shall feed; their young ones shall lie down together: and the lion shall eat straw like the ox. And the sucking child shall play on the hole of the asp, and the weaned child shall put his hand on the cockatrice' den. They shall not hurt nor destroy in all my holy mountain: for the earth shall be full of the knowledge of the LORD, as the waters cover the sea." *Isaiah 11:6-9.*

The redeemed will worship and serve God, and as ambassadors they will reflect the fullness of His image to the unfallen universe. (See Isaiah 66:22-23; 1 Corinthians 4:9; 2 Corinthians 5:20; Revelation 22:3.) Their testimony will place the universe upon the foundation of eternal security from rebellion.

Thereafter there will be one pulse of harmony throughout God's vast creation, and "affliction shall not rise up the second time." Nahum 1:9. They shall sit with Christ upon His "throne," and "shall reign on the earth" with Him "for ever and ever." Revelation 3:21; 5:10; 22:5. "And they that be wise shall shine as the brightness of the firmament; and they that turn many to righteousness as the stars for ever and ever."

Many Run To and Fro

The angel Gabriel finished his narrative of the prophecy in verse three. We can see that the vision covers the wide scope of history from Daniel's day until the establishment of the kingdom of God upon this earth and the earth is made new. Many throughout history have thought that they knew exactly when the end would be. They had come to various conclusions of the prophecies and expected that their interpretations were correct, but time and again they were disappointed. As we look back in history to the fulfillment of prophecy it is much easier for us to see their errors, and to fit the prophecies properly to the historical events. We certainly cannot condemn them for their faulty conclusions.

The scriptures are broad, and many spiritual truths can be drawn from a few verses. However, when we speak of time prophecy there can be only one possible fulfillment to each. There is only one date to which any time prophecy can reach its completion. Once all of the events and dates are known then the prophecy is considered unsealed. Hence, in Daniel's day the specifics of the prophecy were yet unknown, and the book of Daniel was considered sealed:

> **"But thou, O Daniel, shut up the words, and seal the book, even to the time of the end: many shall run to and fro, and knowledge shall be increased."** Daniel 12:4.

The "words" were to be "shut up" and sealed in a "book," which was then to be unsealed at "the time of the end." These things were then to be clearly understood after the wounding of the beast in A.D. 1798. (See the next section.) The implication is that the understanding of the book of Daniel would be fully opened to men's minds after that time. This increase of knowledge would be accomplished as men began to "run to and fro" in the scriptures. They would be able to view much of the prophecy as history, and all of the principles for their interpretation would then be well understood. However, we must not assume that the prophecies would be immediately unsealed. Searching scripture and history take time, and thus the unsealing of the book is gradual.

In Revelation the tenth chapter the fulfillment of Gabriel's statement is clearly described by an angel with a little book opened in his hand. (See chapter

6: The Second Advent Movement.) The little book opened is that of Daniel and the prophecies it contains. Since the book of Daniel is here mentioned as being closed or sealed until the time of the end, then it logically follows that the opening of the same book would also be mentioned as well. The book of Daniel is the only one in the scripture spoken of as being sealed until a specific time. It follows logically then that the opening of a sealed book in the Revelation be in reference to that of Daniel since nowhere else in the scripture is the book of Daniel mentioned as being opened.

It was the beginning of the unsealing of the book of Daniel that brought the great Second Advent revival early in the 19th century. That movement was based upon the unsealing of the prophecy of Daniel eight and the clarification of the earlier prophecies of the book. Nevertheless, a greater revival is to follow with the unsealing of Daniel's greatest prophecy, the vision by the Tigris River.

The 1260 Years

The "time of the end" commences at a certain period of this earth's history and is not the actual conclusion or end of time. It begins a short period before the Second Coming of Jesus, and the events that surround it are also given throughout the prophecy. It is obvious that Daniel's understanding of the details of the prophecy was at best incomplete. The "time of the end" was not yet clear to him, and one of the heavenly messengers that stood by spoke in Daniel's behalf:

> **"Then I Daniel looked, and, behold, there stood other two, the one on this side of the bank of the river, and the other on that side of the bank of the river. And one said to the man clothed in linen, which was upon the waters of the river, How long shall it be to the end of these wonders? And I heard the man clothed in linen, which was upon the waters of the river, when he held up his right hand and his left hand unto heaven, and sware by him that liveth for ever that it shall be for a time, times, and an half; and when he shall have accomplished to scatter the power of the holy people, all these things shall be finished."** *Daniel 12:5-7.*

Daniel again becomes aware of his present surroundings and mentions "other two" heavenly beings that he saw standing one on each side of the river. Their names are not given. The one "clothed in linen, which was upon the waters of the river," is the Lord Jesus Christ as we have already seen in chapter one. (See also Matthew 14:25.) Nevertheless, the main thrust of the passage before us is not the description of the messengers, but the question of one of these heavenly beings: "How long shall it be to the end of these wonders?" One of the angels here seems to recognize that Daniel wanted a better understanding of "the time of the end." The answer is then given by Jesus: "that it shall be for a time, times, and an half." The end of the first period of Papal rule is at that time reached, and the Papacy having "accomplished to scatter the power of the holy people" then came to its conclusion when it lost its civil power. The end of 1260 years of papal rule is the beginning of "the time of the end."

This 1260-year period of the Roman Abomination is spoken of in seven different places in the Bible: Daniel 7:25; 12:7; Revelation 11:2, 3; 12:6, 14; 13:5. It is referred to in three ways: "forty and two months," a "time, and times, and half a time," and a "thousand two hundred and threescore days." Since there are 30 days to a month in the Bible the 42 months are then equal to 1260 days. (See Genesis 7:11; 8:2-4 where 150 days are equal to five months.) A "time" is a year of 12 months. (See Daniel 11:13, margin. A 13th month was randomly added into the Jewish calendar to correct the yearly shift, but the added month is ignored for prophetic calculations.) Therefore the three and one half times are also equal to 42 months or 1260 days. We have already found that a day is substituted with a year in symbolic time prophecy, thus the 1260 prophetic days are equal to 1260 literal years. This 1260-year period of papal rule reaches from A.D. 538 with the overthrow of the Ostrogoths until A.D. 1798 when the French general Berthier marched into Rome and took Pope Pius VI captive to Valence France and ended the rule of the papal civil power.

The 1260-year period is clearly shown to be the length of time that the Papacy makes war against God's people. The papal little horn is said to "wear out the saints of the most High…until a time and times and the dividing of time." Daniel 7:25. The papal beast with "seven heads and ten horns" in the Revelation also persecuted God's people for 1260 years: "And power was given unto him to continue forty and two months… And it was given unto him to make war with the saints, and to overcome them." Revelation 13:2-7. (See also Daniel 7:3-8.) The Church, represented by a pure "woman clothed with the sun," "fled into the wilderness" to escape the wrath of the "great red dragon." This dragon is "that old serpent, called the Devil, and Satan" working through the civil power of the Roman governments represented by the "seven heads and ten horns." God prepared a place for the woman in the wilderness for "a thousand two hundred and threescore days…where she is nourished for a time, and times, and half a time, from the face of the serpent." Revelation 12:1-6, 9, 14.

The "Gentiles" carried out 1260 years of persecution against "the holy city," the true Church of God. God's people were "tread under foot forty and two months." Revelation 11:2. This aggression was also committed against God's "two witnesses," and they were to "prophesy a thousand two hundred and threescore days, clothed in sackcloth." Revelation 11:3. The two witnesses are "the two olive trees, and the two candlesticks standing before the God of the earth" (Revelation 11:4), and these symbols are said by the prophet Zechariah to be: "the word of the LORD," and "...the two anointed ones, that stand by the Lord of the whole earth." Zechariah 4:6, 14. It was olive oil that was burned in the lamps in the temple of God (see Exodus 27:20), and the Psalmist tells us that God's "word is a lamp...and a light." Psalms 119:105. Thus the "two witnesses" are the Old and New Testaments of the Bible that were greatly despised by the Roman Church, and the scripture makes it clear that the reason for the persecution of God's people was because of the "word of God." Revelation 1:9; 6:9; 20:4. Thus all seven places in the scripture refer to 1260 years of persecution against the people of God and His Word by papal Rome.

The description of the Lord here given as "he held up his right hand and his left hand unto heaven, and sware by him that liveth for ever" is similar to the description of the "mighty angel" revealed in Revelation chapter ten. "And the angel which I saw stand upon the sea and upon the earth lifted up his hand to heaven, And sware by him that liveth for ever and ever, who created heaven, and the things that therein are, and the earth, and the things that therein are, and the sea, and the things which are therein, that there should be time no longer." Revelation 10:1, 5-6. Jesus is often represented as an angel or divine messenger, and this angel in Revelation is also Jesus. (On the discussion of Jesus as an angel see chapter 4: Types and the Book of Revelation.) Nevertheless, the connection between Daniel and the Revelation here is further indication that the book, which the angel holds open in his hand, is that of Daniel, and the times referred to in both books are obviously related. (See Revelation 10:2.) Daniel focuses upon the end of the 1260 years in 1798 and John the revelator upon the conclusion of prophetic time a few years later in 1844. After 1844 we no longer use the "day for a year" principle when calculating time prophecy.

The Wise Understand

One thing that is clear in scripture is that man without the Spirit of God cannot understand spiritual things. Divine truths are nothing but foolishness to those that have not surrendered themselves to Jesus and His Spirit. They do not know Him, and cannot understand the things of the Spirit:

> "For what man knoweth the things of a man, save the spirit of man which is in him? even so the things of God knoweth no man, but the Spirit of God. Now we have received, not the spirit of the

world, but the spirit which is of God; that we might know the things that are freely given to us of God. Which things also we speak, not in the words which man's wisdom teacheth, but which the Holy Ghost teacheth; comparing spiritual things with spiritual. But the natural man receiveth not the things of the Spirit of God: for they are foolishness unto him: neither can he know them, because they are spiritually discerned." *1 Corinthians 2:11-14.*

Many think that they understand the prophecies today, but most have no real concept of what the prophecies are about. They are not subject to man's desires and traditions, but are a reflection of the foreknowledge of a Holy God. All truth emanates from Him, and those that want truth must get it from Him. The angel Gabriel reveals to Daniel this same thought in the vision that he received by the Tigris:

"And I heard, but I understood not: then said I, O my Lord, what shall be the end of these things? And he said, Go thy way, Daniel: for the words are closed up and sealed till the time of the end. Many shall be purified, and made white, and tried; but the wicked shall do wickedly: and none of the wicked shall understand; but the wise shall understand." *Daniel 12:8-10.*

Daniel still did not understand all of the information that the angel related to him, but his persistence reminds us of the words of Jesus: "For verily I say unto you, That many prophets and righteous men have desired to see those things which ye see, and have not seen them; and to hear those things which ye hear, and have not heard them." *Matthew 13:17.* He was particularly interested to know what would be "the end of these things?" However, again the angel tells him that the "words are closed up and sealed till the time of the end," that his people would be "purified, and made white, and tried" as already described in chapter five, and that the wicked would continue in their wickedness and "none of the wicked shall understand." Then comes the guarantee that "the wise shall understand."

Many have never surrendered their lives unto Jesus, and they cannot fully understand or accept the prophecy until they do. They have become playthings in the hands of Satan. He leads them in his interpretation of the Word of God, and the prophecies are twisted to suit their lusts and passions. They are in rebellion and will be "Ever learning, and never able to come to the knowledge of the truth." *2 Timothy 3:7.* They will not learn the truth because they do not love the truth, and shallow surface reading will never get them there. If they would surrender all to Jesus they would receive His spirit, learn to carry the cross as He did, and the truth would become plain.

The 1290 and 1335 Years

Time prophecy has always intrigued God's children, and as we look back upon history it can be placed into its proper context. The 1260-day period has already been explained, but the angel next gives two other time periods that will help solidify our understanding of the prophecy:

> "**And from the time that the daily sacrifice shall be taken away, and the abomination that maketh desolate set up, there shall be a thousand two hundred and ninety days. Blessed is he that waiteth, and cometh to the thousand three hundred and five and thirty days.**" Daniel 12:11-12.

We have seen that the day for a year principle applies to this prophecy as it does to the other prophecies of Daniel. The 1290 days and the 1335 days are to be understood as 1290 and 1335 literal years respectively. The beginning point of these periods is clear from the margin of this verse: "from the time that the daily shall be taken away, to set up the abomination that maketh desolate..." ("Sacrifice" is a supplied word in the verse in question, and should be discarded to understand the text properly.) The "daily" is the pagan Roman power, which fell or was "taken away" in A.D. 508 so that the papal abomination could rise to power. (See chapter 4: The Establishment of the Papacy.) Therefore the 1290 years extend from A.D. 508 and end in the very year that the Papacy lost its political dominion, A.D. 1798. The two prophetic periods, 1260 and 1290 years, end at the same time. The angel is obviously giving us more information that we might be surer of the specifics of the prophecy.

The 1335 years must of necessity begin at the same time that the 1290 years begins, or the passage would not make any sense. The 1335 years extend from A.D. 508 until the year A.D. 1843. (See the timeline on page 210.) What is the blessing that comes upon those of which the prophecy is speaking? The year 1843 was the original date that the advocates of the great Second Advent movement believed would usher in the Judgment and the Second Coming of Jesus Christ. The termination of the 2300-year prophecy of Daniel eight was originally believed to be in 1843 as well. (See chapter 6: The Second Advent Movement.) Nevertheless, both prophetic periods culminated at this time. Prophetic truth, which had accumulated for centuries, climaxed in the 1843-1844 period. Those that went through the experience and the disappointments, both in 1843 and 1844, say that it was the greatest blessing of their lives. Of the disappointment in 1843 we read:

> "Thus we performed in the fear of God what we believed to be our bounden duty; and in the accomplishment of that work we surmounted obstacles, which we could not have hoped to overcome unaided by him who controls the universe. We then believed, and we believe now, that as far as we were faithful in preaching the definite year, we have the approval of God, and have been blessed in our own souls; and that we have been made instrumental of a blessing to others." *The Advent Review*, Special Edition, September 1850, p. 4.

And, from a disappointed believer of the proclamation of the judgment and coming of Christ in the year 1844 we also read:

> "The tenth day of the seventh month of that Jewish year 1844, came and passed, and left impressions upon the minds of believers not easily effaced; and although a quarter of a century has passed since that memorable period, yet that work has not lost its interest and force upon the minds of those who participated in it. Even now, when one who shared in that blessed work, and who feels its hallowed influence rekindling upon his mind…shall speak of that solemn work, of that consecration of all, made in full view of eternal scenes, and of that sweet peace and holy joy which filled the minds of the waiting ones, his words will not fail to touch the feelings of all who shared the blessings of that work and have held fast." White, *Life Incidents*, pp. 180-181.

Those who consecrated themselves so fully could only be blessed by the experience. Whenever the soul turns from sin and surrenders itself to God there is blessing for the Psalmist says: "Blessed is he whose transgression is forgiven, whose sin is covered." Psalms 32:1. The apostle Paul, commenting upon the Psalmist, adds: "Blessed is the man to whom the Lord will not impute sin." Romans 4:8. And Peter also declares: "Unto you first God, having raised up his Son Jesus, sent him to bless you, in turning away every one of you from his iniquities." Acts 3:26. The people that had believed in the judgment message in 1843 and 1844, although disappointed, were greatly blessed

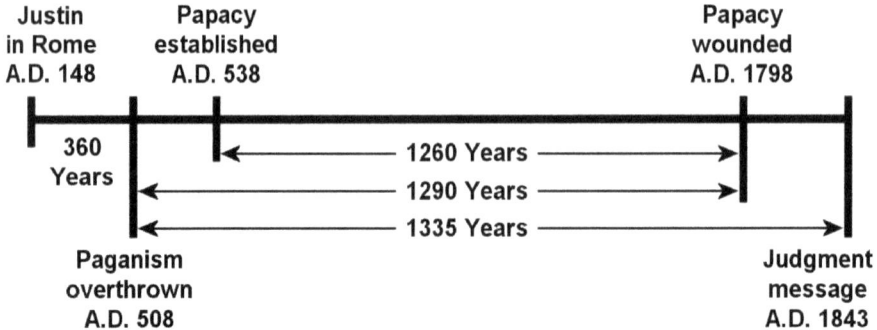

Daniel Rests

The saints that are alive when Jesus comes are among the few who will not have to die. They will experience the judgment while alive, and will be translated into the kingdom of God. The rest of God's children will unfortunately have to experience the sleep of death, for "it is appointed unto men once to die, but after this the judgment." Hebrews 9:27. They will be judged while they sleep. Those that have lived their lives in harmony with heaven will be victorious in the judgment, and will be raised to eternal life. The last words spoken to Daniel by the angel Gabriel were a tremendous promise to him of victory in judgment as well as life everlasting. Nevertheless, he would have to experience death first:

> "But go thou thy way till the end be: for thou shalt rest, and stand in thy lot at the end of the days." *Daniel 12:13.*

The angel here cuts off the conversation with Daniel: "But go thou thy way till the end be." In other words the angel says: "That's it; you have all of the information that you are getting about the prophecy. Go your way." Daniel obviously did not understand everything that he wished to know. Nevertheless, he next receives a few details about his own future: "thou shalt rest." Death is a sleep (see chapter 5: Death and the Immortal Soul), and Daniel would have to take his rest in death for a while.

"And stand in thy lot at the end of the days." The word "lot" here does not refer to "lot of inheritance." This Hebrew word is used 76 times in the Old Testament, and is in connection with the rendering of judgment: "It refers then to some article like a stone which was thrown or allowed to fall in a way to determine a choice." *Theological Wordbook of the Old Testament,* no. 381a. It is first used in Leviticus 16:8 where lots were cast to determine which of the two goats, that were presented before the priest on the Day of Atonement, was to be slain. Lots were cast to determine how the land was to be divided between the different tribes of Israel, they were used to determine who was to bring various offerings, to divide Jesus' garments while He was dying on the cross, and the sailors cast lots to determine that Jonah was the cause of the storm. (See Numbers 26:55-56; Nehemiah 10:34; Psalm 22:18; Jonah 1:7.) Thus, lots were clearly used to determine judgment, and for Daniel to "stand" in his lot is therefore a clear indication to him that when judgment is passed upon him he would be victorious and found to be righteous.

"The end of the days" is not the same as the time of the end that is referred to in other places in Daniel's vision. The end of the days brings the prophecy down to the end of the 1335 years of the previous verse. This is the time when the judgment and the coming of Christ were first proclaimed. Although disappointed, the judgment did begin one year later in A.D. 1844. The connection between Daniel's other prophecies and this one are close and cannot be discarded. Daniel eight gives the exact date when the judgment and the cleansing of the sanctuary actually began. Chapter seven gives the final results of the judgment:

> "But the judgment shall sit, and they shall take away his dominion, to consume and to destroy it unto the end. And the kingdom and dominion, and the greatness of the kingdom under the whole heaven, shall be given to the people of the saints of the most High, whose kingdom is an everlasting kingdom, and all dominions shall serve and obey him." *Daniel 7:26-27*.

It is in the judgment that the final inheritance is determined. The "lots" were cast, and Daniel's inheritance is assured. God's children are to sit with Jesus upon His throne (see Revelation 3:21), and Daniel is just as deserving as any of His followers to receive that position. Jesus has gone to prepare a place for Daniel and for all who overcome as He has, and He says:

> "Let not your heart be troubled: ye believe in God, believe also in me. In my Father's house are many mansions: if it were not so, I would have told you. I go to prepare a place for you. And if I go and prepare a place for you, I will come again, and receive you unto myself; that where I am, there ye may be also." *John 14:1-3*.

You, reader, have a place prepared for you if you are willing to surrender your heart to Jesus as Daniel did. The "lots" are even now being cast in the sanctuary above. The judgment shall soon pass to the cases of the living, and the lots will fall in your favor if you are willing and obedient.

Summary of Chapter Seven

This chapter began with a description of the close of human probation and the beginning of the "time of trouble." At that time all who are just will remain just. They will not return from the direction that they have chosen for their lives no matter how much pressure Satan puts upon them. He will tempt them with every wicked device that he has learned since the beginning of his rebellion, but they will remain steadfast. Those that are wicked will remain wicked still. They will not change their minds to follow truth, and they will receive the seven last plagues. God's children, however, will be protected at that time while the wicked are suffering greatly.

The seventh plague ushers in the resurrection of the righteous, the death of the remaining wicked, and the Second Coming of Christ to this earth in power and glory. Jesus will then take His children to heaven for 1000 years of judgment to evaluate the records of the wicked. At the end of the Millennium the holy city, the New Jerusalem, next comes down from God out of heaven to the earth. The Lord then breaths life into the wicked dead and they are resurrected, and Satan is given one last chance to prove to the universe that he has not changed. He goes out to the host of the wicked and incites them to try to take the holy city. God then reveals Himself and the cross, and the entire host of the wicked will be convinced that the judgments of God are correct and they bow to Him. The wicked then receive their eternal reward — the second death. The earth is next made new, and it becomes the home of the righteous and the throne of God, and health, happiness and unity will finally inhabit the universe to the ceaseless ages of eternity.

The narrative of the prophecy is complete, but the angel Gabriel tells Daniel that it is closed up until the time of the end when God's children will search the scriptures and unseal it. The angel guarantees that the "wise" will understand it, and he then gives Daniel a few specifics about the prophecy. Time periods of 1260, 1290, and 1335 years are introduced, which are given to confirm some of the events of the vision. The angel then closes the dialogue with Daniel by giving him assurance of victory in the judgment and of life everlasting.

Conclusion

The vision that Daniel received beside the Tigris River obviously covers the span of history from his day until the establishment of the kingdom of God upon this earth. It is a concise description of the great controversy. The prophecies are clearly historical in nature, and all of Daniel's prophecies are positively linked and cover the same period of time. They follow the Historicist method of prophetic interpretation. Each prophecy expands upon the previous one. All of the past events of the prophecy can be lined up with the most obvious and well-known events of history. Rome in particular is the empire that establishes the vision, and it lasts until the Lord destroys it at His Second Coming. The rise of the Papacy and its opposition to God's people are clearly included in the description of Rome. Daniel's prophecies begin when he is taken captive to Babylon, and they climax with the destruction of great spiritual Babylon and the deliverance of His people. Thus all of the prophecies fit perfectly into the sweep of history from Daniel's day until the end.

Typology is crucial to the interpretation of the prophecy; Jesus' crucifixion, the establishment of His everlasting covenant, His ministry in heaven, and the founding of His Church upon this earth are key to understanding the typical language. The prophecy transitions from a conflict between two powers that were physically located to the North and South of Jerusalem in the Middle East to a war between two spiritual, ideological powers among which the Church of God is dispersed. The prophecy moves from typical nations before the time of the cross to antitypical powers after the founding of the Church. The conflict transitions from the geographical to the spiritual, yet it is a real conflict fought with real weapons. Thus the kings of the North and South are just as real today as they were in ancient times, and typology is the key to understanding them.

Another lesson from Daniel would be appropriate at this point: An interesting typological relationship can be drawn between the experience of Daniel's three friends, Shadrach, Meshach, and Abednego, and God's people in the last conflict. In Daniel chapter three Nebuchadnezzar, king of Babylon, desiring to establish his kingdom on an eternal basis, setup a giant image made of gold on a plain in Babylon. Then he gathered together "all the rulers of the provinces…unto the dedication of the image." Daniel 3:2. Those present were required to "fall down and worship the golden image." Daniel 3:5. To guarantee obedience to his command those who did not fall down and worship were to be "cast into the midst of a burning fiery furnace." Daniel 3:6. Daniel's friends knew that to worship the image would be detestable to God, and at the peril of their own lives they refused to bow down. They were thrown into the furnace, which was heated "seven times more than it was wont to be heated." Daniel 3:19. In the midst of their trial the "Son of God" appeared and "delivered his servants that trusted in him." Daniel 3:25, 28. The antitype of their experience is obvious: The Second Beast of Revelation 13, the False Prophet, is soon to make an "image" in great spiritual "Babylon" by uniting church and state. All, including God's commandment keeping people, will be required, through various laws, to "worship the image of the beast." Revelation 13:15. As they refuse they will be brought into perilous circumstances that will threaten to consume them; yet in their steadfast obedience to the commandments of God they will find victory, for the Son of God will ultimately appear to deliver them.

The powers of earth are now being gathered for the last great conflict. Futurism has a Satanic hold upon the world. Through the leaders of the religious community the spirits of demons control most of the Christian world in which we live, and these spirits will not let go of their captives without a struggle. That struggle is about to intensify as the Beast arises from the abyss, and the False Prophet develops an image to the Beast. All that are on the Lord's side will feel the ire of the dragon. Every word spoken by them will be scrutinized, every action will be watched, and every motive questioned. Many will be brought before the princes of the earth and courts of justice where they will have to testify for the truth. They will be persecuted, imprisoned, tortured, and some will even be put to death. None know the intensity with which the world will hate the righteous in the last conflict.

When people realize the significance of this prophecy it will bring about an entirely different religious experience. Their minds will engage in spiritual warfare against Satan and the hosts of darkness. The Pope is still the antichrist, but Rome is not spiritual Babylon on its own. The Protestant churches are uniting with her, and the world will soon be brought to obedience to the false doctrines of spiritual Babylon. The issue in the great controversy is the Law of God. Obedience to His Law is not optional or negotiable. His authority is being challenged, and the last conflict revolves around the Sabbath commandment. It is the final test for the inhabitants of this earth. To accept the papal Sunday institution is to deny the authority of the God of heaven, and will result in eternal lose. However, if men yield to Him, and keep His holy day, they will be persecuted for the truth's sake. It's not an easy choice to make, but one that has eternal consequences. Those who through faith obey will be saved, but the rebellious and unbelieving will be lost.

Conclusion

Daniel's greatest prophecy is now unsealed. The hand of God has been lifted, and His plan is revealed. The errors of tradition and speculative theories used to pervert prophetic truth are now exposed. The popular ministry is challenged to prove its worthiness. A revival of primitive godliness is soon to follow among God's people. Time cannot last much longer. The question that confronts us now is: "Where will we stand when the final conflict begins?"

Appendix A

These principles were originally put forth by William Miller in the early 1800s, but are certainly just as valid today. Many of them have been used for centuries, but have never been written as such. It will be worthwhile to spend some time and look up the passages given. The extra passages in parenthesis were added to help clarify the principle.

1. Every word must have its proper bearing on the subject presented in the Bible. Matthew 5:18. (See also Matthew 4:4; Luke 16:17.)
2. All Scripture is necessary, and may be understood by a diligent application and study. 2 Timothy 3:15-17. (See also 2 Peter 1:21; Romans 15:4.)
3. Nothing revealed in the Scriptures can or will be hid from those who ask in faith, not wavering. Deuteronomy 29:29; Matthew 10:26-27; 1 Corinthians 2:10; Philippians 3:15; Isaiah 45:11; Matthew 21:22; John 14:13-14; 15:7; James 1:5-6; 1 John 5:13-15.
4. To understand doctrine, bring all the Scriptures together on the subject you wish to know; then let every word have its proper influence; and if you can form your theory without a contradiction, you cannot be in error. Isaiah 28:7-29; 35:8; Proverbs 19:27; Luke 24:27, 44-45; Romans 16:26; James 5:19; 2 Peter 1:19-20.
5. Scripture must be its own expositor, since it is a rule of itself. If I depend on a teacher to expound to me, and he should guess at its meaning, or desire to have it so on account of his sectarian creed, or to be thought wise, then his guessing, desire, creed, or wisdom, is my rule, and not the Bible. Psalm 19:7-11; 119:97-105; Matthew 23:8-10; 1 Corinthians 2:12-16; Ezekiel 34:18-19; Luke 11:52; Malachi 2:7-8.
6. God has revealed things to come, by visions, in figures and parables; and in this way the same things are oftentime revealed again and again, by different visions, or in different figures and parables. If you wish to understand them, you must combine them all in one. Psalm 89:19; Hosea 12:10; Habakkuk 2:2; Acts 2:17; 1 Corinthians 10:6; Hebrews 9:9, 24; Psalms 78:2; Matthew 13:13, 34; Genesis 41:1-32; Daniel 2, 7, 8-9; Acts 10:9-16, 28.
7. Visions are always mentioned as such. 2 Corinthians 12:1. (See also Ezekiel 1:1; Daniel 7:1; 8:1; Job 4:12-16; Revelation 1:10; 4:1-2.)
8. Figures always have a figurative meaning, and are used much in prophecy to represent future things, times and events — such as mountains, meaning

governments, Daniel 2:35, 44; beasts, meaning kingdoms, Daniel 7:3, 17; waters, meaning people, Revelation 17:1, 15; day, meaning year, Ezekiel 4:6; etc.

9. Parables are used as comparisons, to illustrate subjects, and must be explained in the same way as figures, by the subject and Bible. Mark 4:13.

10. Figures sometimes have two or more different significations, as day is used in a figurative sense to represent three different periods of time, namely: first, indefinite, Ecclesiastes 7:14; second, definite, a day for a year, Ezekiel 4:6; and third, a day for a thousand years, 2 Peter 3:8. The right construction will harmonize with the Bible, and make good sense; other constructions will not.

11. If a word makes good sense as it stands, and does no violence to the simple laws of nature, it is to be understood literally; if not, figuratively. Revelation 12:1-2; 17:3-7. (See also Revelation 6:12-17.)

12. To learn the true meaning of a figure, trace the word through your Bible, and when you find it explained, substitute the explanation for the word used; and if it makes good sense, you need not look further; if not, look again. (See Malachi 4:4, 5; Matthew 17:9-13; Luke 1:13-17.)

13. To know whether we have the true historical event for the fulfillment of prophecy: If you find every word of the prophecy (after the figures are understood) is literally fulfilled, then you may know that your history is the true event; but if one word lacks a fulfillment, then you must look for another event, or wait its future development; for God takes care that history and prophecy shall agree, so that the true believing children of God may never be ashamed. Psalm 22:5; Isaiah 45:17-19; 1 Peter 2:6; Revelation 17:17; Acts 3:18.

14. The most important rule of all is, that you must have faith. It must be a faith that requires a sacrifice, and, if tried, would give up the dearest object on earth, the world and all its desires — character, living, occupation, friends, home, comforts, and worldly honors. If any of these should hinder our believing any part of God's word, it would show our faith to be vain. Nor can we ever believe so long as one of these motives lies lurking in our hearts. We must believe that God will never forfeit his word; and we can have confidence that He who takes notice of the sparrow's fall, and numbers the hairs of our head, will guard the translation of his own word, and throw a barrier around it, and prevent those who sincerely trust in God, and put implicit confidence in his word, from erring far from the truth. (See Romans 10:17; Hebrews 11.)

We invite you to view the complete
selection of titles we publish at:

www.TEACHServices.com

or write or email us your praises,
reactions, or thoughts about this
or any other book we publish at:

TEACH Services, Inc.
P U B L I S H I N G
www.TEACHServices.com
P.O. Box 954
Ringgold, GA 30736

info@TEACHServices.com

Finally, if you are interested in seeing
your own book in print, please contact us at

publishing@teachservices.com.

We would be happy to review your manuscript for free.

www.ingramcontent.com/pod-product-compliance
Lightning Source LLC
Chambersburg PA
CBHW070550160426
43199CB00014B/2439